Irish Pub Favorites Mandolin Tablature Songbook

Ben "Gitty" Baker

Here is a wonderful collection of the best traditional Irish pub songs from Ireland, Scotland and beyond - the sort of songs you'd be likely to hear on St. Patrick's Day in a good Irish pub. All of these timeless songs are arranged for 4-string "GDAE" instruments such as mandolins, Irish tenor banjos and more.

Copyright Notice

TABLE OF CONTENTS

TABLE OF CONTENTS

About This Songbook

This is a collection of traditional Irish, Scottish and related songs and tunes, arranged specifically for playing on mandolins, fiddles, Irish tenor banjos and related four-string instruments tuned to GDAE. These songs are chosen from amongst the older, well-known pieces that are assumed to be in the public domain... in other words, songs that have no active copyright.

For some works where there have been many versions and arrangements over the years, some newer arrangements may still be copyrighted, and in such cases I have made every effort to present the oldest, most traditional and un-copyrighted form.

Celtic music has held a very special place in my heart, from the time I first heard some of the old songs being played. I had stopped by my favorite pub, The Whig and Courier, while living in Bangor, Maine. It was St. Patrick's Day and a band called The Napper Tandies was on stage playing and singing Irish pub favorites. The Jug of Punch, Rare Old Mountain Dew, The Wild Rover... the songs seemed to shoot right through me to something I didn't even know about deep inside.

From that beginning I went on to discover The Clancy Brothers with Tommy Makem, The Dubliners and other Irish bands and performers, and that music changed my life. Just a few years later I would find myself going to Irish music sessions and even joining an Irish band called Bradigan with some amazing musicians, several of whom are related to Tommy Makem.

From the rebel songs to the drinking songs, love songs and laments, sea shanties and instrumental tunes, this music is charged with so much passion and feeling that it cannot help but stir the spirit and soul. I am proud to be able to present this collection of the best traditional Irish pub favorites to the world in easy-to-follow tablature, with full lyrics and chords, to help make sure this amazing music lives on.

I am indebted to my good friends in New Hampshire, from whom I have learned so much about traditional Irish tunes and songs: Patrick Boyle, Charlie Boyle, Tyler Foss, Kim Starling, Patricia O'Brien, Shane and Conor Makem, Frank Landford, Jack Krumm, Mark "Rocky" Rockwell, Dennis Duffy, Kevin McEneaney, Mike Mone and others have all helped expand my repertoire and appreciation of this music - thank you all!

Ben "Gitty" Baker
March 17, 2020

Keys and Arrangements

Almost all of the songs in this book are arranged in the keys of C and G. These are the two most common keys for popular music, and also the easiest to play on the mandolin and other GDAE-tuned instruments.

For all of these songs multiple versions are presented, and you may wonder why this is. There are several reasons: vocal ranges, ease of playing, and playing skill practice.

Vocal Ranges

Different people are able to hit different ranges of notes when singing. A soprano can hit the highest notes, a bass singer can hit the low notes, and most of the rest of us fall somewhere in between. I have arranged the songs in this book in two keys (C and G) because depending on the singer, one key may be easier than the other.

Ease of Playing

You may find as you play your instrument more, that fingering the notes in one key is easier for you than in another. In this case, having the same song tabbed out in multiple keys is handy, since you can pick the one that feels best to you.

Playing Skill Practice

Playing the same song in multiple keys is good practice to help you become more familiar with your instrument. This is true both for picking out the notes that make up the melody of a song, and for strumming the chords. In time, you might begin to notice patterns.

For example, if you look at a song tabbed out in both the key of C and the key of G, you will notice that every C chord in the former is replaced by a G chord in the latter. Likewise, every F is replaced by a C, every G is replaced by a D. This is not coincidence, and you'll see it hold true every time. The specific notes that make up the song also change following the same pattern. In the case of the keys of C and G, you may notice that for many songs the basic melody just moves up or down one string, but the fretting pattern remains the same.

This changing of a song from one key to another is called transposing, and follows specific rules. How to transpose songs from one key to another could be the subject of a separate book. The more you play and practice and study, the more you may begin to get a feel for it.

How to Read & Play Tablature

Tablature (tab) is a visual method for showing you how to play songs on a stringed instrument. It is made up of horizontal lines, which represent the strings on the instrument you're playing. On these lines are placed numbers, which tell you what string to pluck, and which fret to push down on with your finger, to sound a particular note. When played in order with the right cadence and rhythm, these notes make up a song.

Tab also often includes letters to represent chords for rhythm playing, and words of the song as well. See the sample line of tab below.

Tablature is very powerful in this way, as it allows pretty much anyone to easily play the notes of a song. There is one thing though—you have to know in general "how the song goes" beforehand, to get the cadence and rhythm right. You can't really learn a new song entirely from tablature, since the tab doesn't tell you anything about rhythm or how long to hold each note. But if you already know the song well enough to hum along with it, you should be good to go!

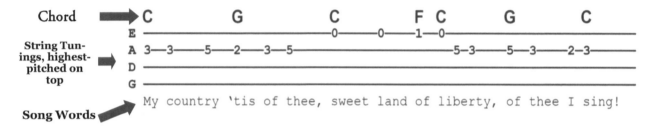

Take a look at the sample line of tab above. It is the first line from the old American patriotic song "My Country 'Tis of Thee".

The letters above the lines are chords that a rhythm player can strum along with the song. Underneath the lines are the lyrics/words of the song.

The four horizontal lines represent the strings of a 4-string GDAE-tuned instrument. The bold capital letters to the left of the lines show which string is which, and help you know what tuning the tablature is intended for.

It is important to realize that the top "E" line is the highest-pitched string on the instrument, which is actually on the bottom when you hold it in playing position. Why is this? Well, the quick answer is that it's just how tab (and standard musical notation) has always been done. Higher pitch means higher up on the lines. Conventional 6-string guitar tab is the same way. It can seem confusing, but it's just something you have to get used to. Also, note that high E is usually referred to as the first string, then A as the second string, etc.

So to walk our way through playing the first few notes from the line of tab above, you would do the following:

1) Pluck the second string (A), using your middle or ring finger to fret it on the third fret, for the note corresponding to the word "My". You would use your middle fin-

ger on shorter-scale instruments like mandolins, and your ring finger for longer-scale instruments like tenor banjos and tenor guitars.

2) Pluck the same note again for the first syllable of the word "country". You are playing a "C" note, and your hand should resemble the image to the right.

3) Now use your ring or pinky finger to fret the same string (A) on the fifth fret for the second syllable of the word "country".

4) Use your index/first finger to fret the A string at the second fret for "tis".

5) Proceed in similar fashion until you hit the words "sweet" and "land". These notes requires you to pluck the high E string (the one all the way on the bottom when playing) open, or unfretted.

6) Now fret that high E string on the first fret using your index/pointer finger, for the word "of," as shown in the photo to the right.

You may have noticed that tablature also doesn't tell you what finger to use for fretting. For that matter, regular sheet music notation doesn't either. A general rule of thumb is: use the first (index) finger for frets one and two; the middle finger for fret three; the third (ring) finger for frets four and sometimes five, and the little finger (pinky) for frets five through seven. A lot of this comes down to what feels comfortable to you when playing. The scale length of your instrument also determines what reaches are feasible. This book assumes that you already have a basic knowledge of how to play your chosen instrument,

Some songs require you to move on up the neck a bit to hit the notes—almost always this is on the high E string. You can decide which fingers to use for these high notes based on whatever feels best to you, though usually the pinky is used. Very few of the arrangements in this book go beyond the fifth fret, and only a couple go to the seventh.

The more advanced "Melody & Chords" tablature arrangements will show multiple strings being plucked/fretted at the same time. These require you to use multiple fingers at a time to hit the notes, and often using one finger to fret more than one string (known as barreing). Some of these arrangements require a good amount of skill and practice to master, but don't feel bad if you can't hit every note. The top note is almost always the melody line, and you can leave out one or more of the additional notes indicated beneath it as your playing level allows.

It will be up to you to figure out which fingers to use for fretting each string, but there are some general guidelines for how to make it easier:

1) Remember that any time you are strumming more than one string, you are actually playing a chord. For all of the Melody & Chords arrangements in this book, the additional notes I've added are based on the indicated chord for that portion of the song (or

in some cases based on the next chord to come, as part of a transition). The chord forms included with each song will help give you an idea of what fingers to use.

2) In general, try to move your fingers as little as possible. Many times you can make a finger go from fretting one string at a particular location to fretting two (as a barre), without having to bring in another finger. This can be a big help in more complex arrangements.

3) Try to figure out ways to keep from moving your hand further up the neck when possible. Practice stretching that pinky out to hit higher notes on the high E string instead of moving your whole hand up.

4) There may be times when it makes sense to use a finger you wouldn't normally use to fret a particular string, based on the fingering that comes immediately after. Focus on figuring out what will allow the easiest and fastest transition between fingerings.

5) The numbers on the chord forms suggest what finger to use. 1 = Index, 2 = Middle, 3 = Ring, 4 = Pinky. A line connecting two circles with the same number indicates a barre.

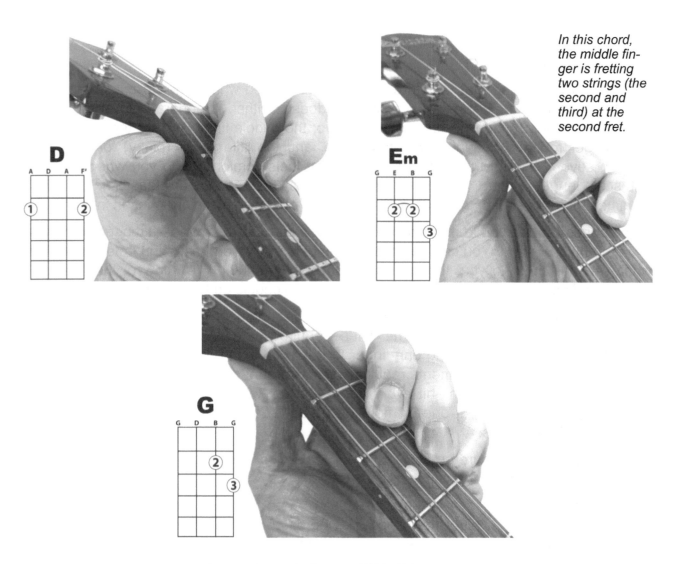

In this chord, the middle finger is fretting two strings (the second and third) at the second fret.

How to Play These Songs

Now that you have an idea of how to make sense of the tablature and chord forms, I want to talk a little bit about how to play the songs in this book.

First, as mentioned above, the tablature doesn't tell you anything about how the song is "supposed to go" - in other words, it doesn't tell you anything about the rhythm. For that, you have to either already know the song, or find somewhere to listen to it. Fortunately this is easier than it's ever been, if you have any sort of Internet access... YouTube should have multiple versions, historic and modern, of pretty much every song in this book.

So that brings us to my first piece of advice for playing these songs: listen to a version or two on YouTube first. Try to find the more traditional/older versions if you can, rather than more modern remakes. For most of these songs, I recommend finding a either a version recorded by the Clancy Brothers with Tommy Makem, Makem and Clancy or the Dubliners, if you can.

Once you have a good idea of how the song is supposed to go, then it's time to start playing it. There are three basic ways these songs can be played: pick the basic melody, strum the chords, or a combination of picking and strumming.

- **Picking the Melody** - this involves plucking the individual notes that make up the melody of the song, one at a time and in the right order, with the timing/rhythm that you have in your head based on how the song is supposed to go. This is the most basic and straightforward way to play a song, and is a good way to start when learning a new tune.

- **Strumming the Chords** - a lot of guitar players don't really worry too much about picking the melody itself, and instead focus on strumming the chord accompaniment. If you ever go to a jam session or campfire singalong, you are unlikely to see any players plucking out the notes of the melody while people sing. Rather, you'll see and hear them strumming the chords. This is sometimes called "playing rhythm", and covering how to do it could be the topic of at least a chapter if not an entire book. Getting the hang of "strumming along" to a song is a great skill to have.

- **Combination of Picking and Strumming** - the "Melody & Chords" arrangements in this book are an attempt to get you started with this method. If you look closely at songs where I give both "Basic Melody" and "Melody & Chords" arrangements, you will notice the latter ones usually just have one to three extra strings/notes added under the basic melody line. Plucking these extra strings helps "fill out" the sound and makes for a more complete performance. This form of playing can be further expanded as you progress rhythmically, to create a sort of hybrid strum/note-picking method. *One thing to be aware of is that hitting every one of these notes perfectly can be tricky, especially on a mandolin where the frets and strings are so close together. Don't get frustrated if you can't play them exactly as shown - just use them as a suggestion of how you can strum some additional strings when playing to fill out the sound.*

There is one important thing to remember as you dive into this: if you're having fun, you are doing it right. Getting good at playing takes time and practice, and you have to be patient with yourself. It doesn't have to be perfect... you don't have to sound like Tommy Makem or The Clancy Brothers or The Chieftains - you just need to sound like you. So take it easy, relax and have fun. Play the songs you know and like, and ignore the ones you don't. The only rules are the ones you set for yourself!

Mandolin / GDAE Chords

The following chord forms are some of the most commonly used for the GDAE tuning found on mandolins, Irish tenor banjos and other related instruments. Multiple versions of some of the chords are given—when playing a song, some fingerings of chords just seem to fit better sound-wise than others. Also, a chord that is easily playable on a short-scale mandolin might be too hard to reach on a long-scale tenor guitar... and a chord that is comfortable on a longer-scale instrument might be too "tight" to be effective on a mandolin.

You are free to use whatever versions you want, based on what sounds best to you -- and what your fingers can reach. If you are having trouble making a transition between two chords, practice making the change over and over. You don't have to even strum, just practice getting your fingers to move back and forth between the two forms. This develops "muscle memory" and will make it much easier to learn and play songs. Feel free to substitute one chord form for another in any song, if it is easier for you to play.

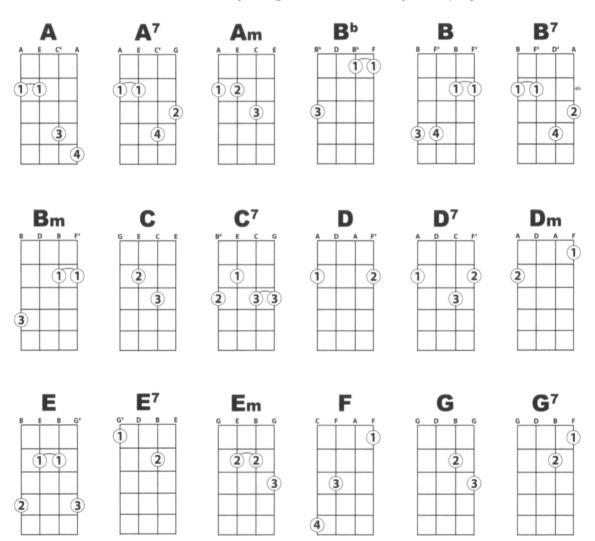

A Jug Of This

Basic Melody
Key of Am

This is an old English folk song, thought to have come down from the oral tradition and first collected in 1907. Its alternate title is "Ye Mourners All" and has also been known by "Ye Mariners All". It is not often heard, but was recorded by The Clancy Brothers and Tommy Makem in 1962. There have been many variations to the lyrics over the years.

Words and Music
Traditional

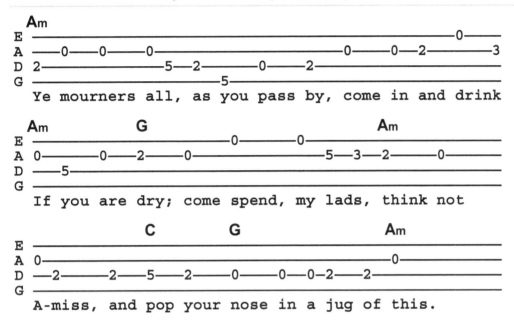

Ye mourners all, as you pass by, come in and drink

If you are dry; come spend, my lads, think not

A-miss, and pop your nose in a jug of this.

Additional Verses

Oh mourners all, if you've half a crown,
You're welcome all for to sit down.
Come spend, my lads, your money brisk,
And pop your nose in a jug of this.

Oh tipplers all, as you pass by,
Come in and drink if you are dry.
Call in and drink, think not amiss,
And pop your nose in a jug of this.

Oh now I'm old and can scarcely crawl,
I've an old grey beard and a head that's bald.
Crown my desire and fulfil my bliss,
A pretty young girl and a jug of this.

Oh when I'm in my grave and dead,
And all my sorrows are past and fled,
Transform me then into a fish,
And let me swim in a jug of this.

Chord Forms

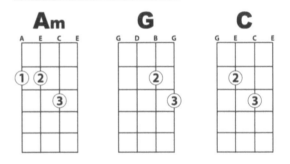

Playing Notes

For such a short and seemingly simple song, figuring out how to play this one can be rather tricky. That may explain why there are so few recordings of it.

The chords indicated above are my best approximation of what Liam Clancy was playing on the 1962 recording. I recommend listening carefully to that recording on YouTube to get an idea of their interpretation of how this song goes, where the chord changes are, etc.

A Jug Of This (continued)

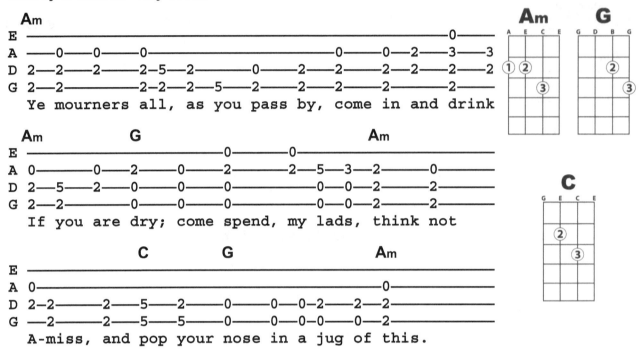

Melody & Chords - Key of Am

```
     Am
E ─────────────────────────────────────────────────0─────
A ─────0─────0─────0───────────────────0─────0──2──3───3
D 2──2─────2─────2─5──2───────0─────2──2─────2──2──2───2
G 2──2──────────2─2──2──5───2─────2──2─────2───────2
     Ye mourners all,  as you pass by,  come in and drink

     Am            G                        Am
E ───────────────────────0─────0──────────────────────
A 0─────0──2─────0──2─────2──5──3──2─────0───────
D 2──5──2─────0─────0──────0──0──2─────2────────
G 2──2──────0─────0──────0──0──2─────2──────────
     If you are dry;  come spend,  my lads,  think not

              C         G            Am
E ──────────────────────────────────────────
A 0─────────────────────────────0────────
D 2─2─────2───5───2─────0────0─0─2───2─2
G ──2─────2───5───5─────0────0─0─0───0─2
     A-miss,  and pop your nose in a jug of this.
```

Basic Melody - Key of Dm

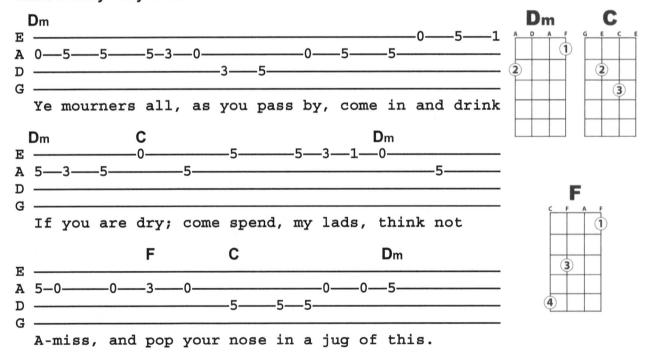

```
     Dm
E ─────────────────────────────────────────0──5───1
A 0──5─────5─────5─3──0───────────0──5─────5
D ──────────────────3──5──────────────────
G ──────────────────────────────────────────
     Ye mourners all,  as you pass by,  come in and drink

     Dm            C                     Dm
E ─────────────0────────5─────5─3──1──0──────────
A 5──3─────5─────────5──────────────────5
D ──────────────────────────────────────────
G ──────────────────────────────────────────
     If you are dry;  come spend,  my lads,  think not

              F         C            Dm
E ──────────────────────────────────────────
A 5─0─────0───3───0─────────0──0──5
D ─────────────────5───5──5────────
G ──────────────────────────────────
     A-miss,  and pop your nose in a jug of this.
```

A Jug Of This (continued)

Melody & Chords
Key of Dm

```
    Dm
E ─────────────────────────────────────────────0──5──1
A 0──5────5────5─3──0────────────0──5────5──5────0──0
D 0──0────0────0─0──0─3────5──────0──0────0──────0
G 2──2─────────2──────2──5────2──2
```
Ye mourners all, as you pass by, come in and drink

```
    Dm           C                              Dm
E ────────────────0───────5────────5─3──1──0
A 5─3────5──3────5────3────3─3─3──0──────5
D 0──0────0──2────2────2──────────0────0
G 0──────0──0────────────────2────2
```
If you are dry; come spend, my lads, think not

```
                F        C              Dm
E ──────────────────────────────────────
A 5─0────0──3──0──────────0──0─5
D 0─0────0──3──3──5────5─5─2──2─0
G ──2────2──────5────5─5─5────2
```
A-miss, and pop your nose in a jug of this.

Chord Forms

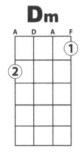

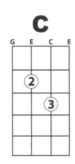

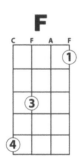

All For Me Grog

Basic Melody
Key of C (Low)

This rollicking old drinking song tells the tale of a sailor who has sold all his possessions to buy booze. It has been recorded by most of the well-known Irish bands and singers over the years, including The Dubliners and The Clancy Brothers & Tommy Makem.

Words and Music
Traditional

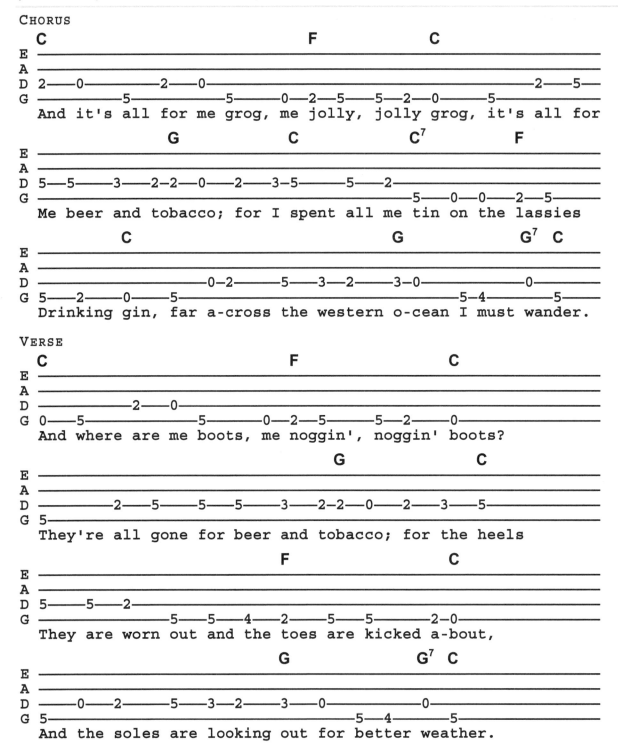

See Chord Forms and Additional Verses on Next Page

All For Me Grog
(continued)

Chord Forms

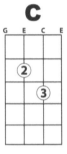
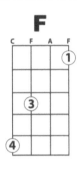
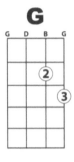
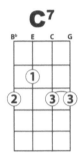
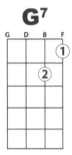

Additional Verses

Where is me shirt, me noggin', noggin' shirt?
It's all gone for beer and tobacco,
For the collar is all worn, and the sleeves they are all torn,
And the tails are looking out for better weather.

Now where is me bed, me noggin', noggin bed?
It's all sold for beer and tobacco,
For the sheets they were all worn,
And the mattress got all torn,
And the springs they're lookin' out for better weather!

I'm sick in the head and I haven't been to bed,
Since I came ashore with me plunder.
I've seen centipedes and snakes,
And I'm full of pains and aches,
And I think I'll make a path for way out yonder.

> *"My mother was from Scotland and my father was from Ireland. So I was born with the curse of the drink, but I'm too cheap to pay for it."*
>
> **Patrick Boyle**

All For Me Grog
(continued)

Basic Melody

Key of C (High)

CHORUS

```
      C                          F            C
E  0-----------0---------------------------------------------------0----3----
A  ----5----3------5---3-------0---3----3---0---------3----
D  ------------------------5-------------------5---------------
G  ---------------------------------------------------------
```
And it's all for me grog, me jolly, jolly grog, it's all for

```
              G          C          C⁷         F
E  3---3--------1--0-0------0---1-3------3----0----------------
A  ------------------5----------------------3---------0---3---
D  ------------------------------------5---5-------------------
G  ------------------------------------------------------------
```
Me beer and tobacco; for I spent all me tin on the lassies

```
         C                              G            G⁷ C
E  ----------------------0------3---1---0------1---------------
A  3---0------------3---5-----------------5---3-2----5---3---
D  --------5---------------------------------------------------
G  ------------------------------------------------------------
```
Drinking gin, far a-cross the western o-cean I must wander.

VERSE

```
      C                     F            C
E  ----------0---------------------------------------------
A  ----3-------5---3-------0---3----3---0-------------------
D  5-------------------5-------------------5---------------
G  --------------------------------------------------------
```
And where are me boots, me noggin', noggin' boots?

```
                              G          C
E  --------0---3---3---3---1--0-0------0---1---3-----------
A  3-----------------------------5------------------------
D  --------------------------------------------------------
G  --------------------------------------------------------
```
They're all gone for beer and tobacco; for the heels

```
                    F            C
E  3-----3---0--------------------------------------------
A  ------------3---3---2---0---3---3--------0-------------
D  -----------------------------------------5-------------
G  --------------------------------------------------------
```
They are worn out and the toes are kicked a-bout,

```
              G          G⁷ C
E  --------0---3---1---0------1------------------------
A  3---5--------------------5---3-2----5---3----------
D  ----------------------------------------------------
G  ----------------------------------------------------
```
And the soles are looking out for better weather.

C

F

G

C⁷

G⁷

15

All For Me Grog
(continued)

Melody & Chords

Key of C (High)

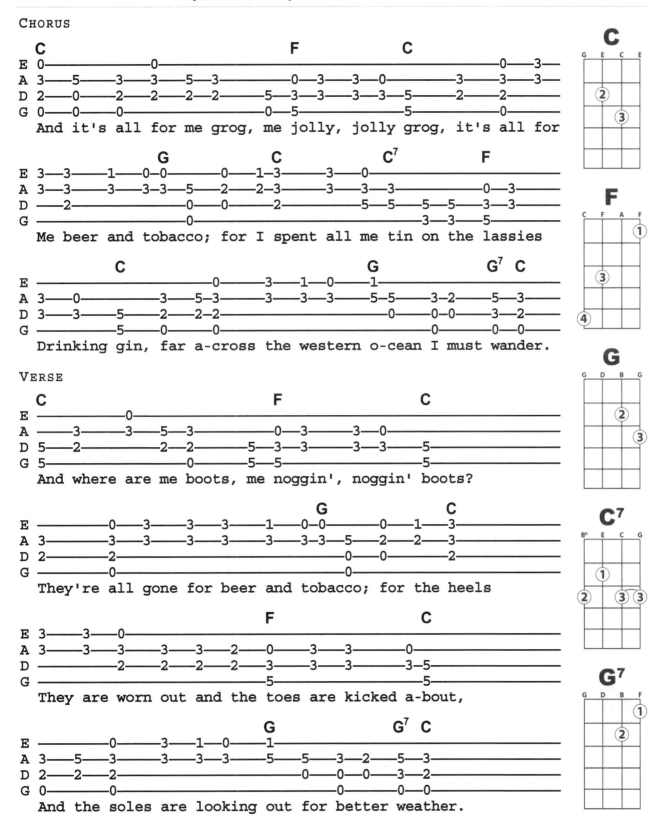

CHORUS

```
   C                          F           C
E  0——————————0—————————————————————————————————0——3——
A  3—5——3——3—5—3————0—3——3—0————3——3—3——
D  2—0——2——2——2—2————5—3—3——3—3—5——2——2——
G  0——0——0—————————0—5————5—————0——
```
And it's all for me grog, me jolly, jolly grog, it's all for

```
      G        C        C⁷      F
E  3—3——1—0-0———0—1-3——3—0—————————
A  3—3——3—3-3—5——2——2-3——3——3—3————0—3——
D  —2———————0——0——2———5—5——5—5—3—3——
G  ——————————0————————3—3—5——
```
Me beer and tobacco; for I spent all me tin on the lassies

```
      C                        G         G⁷ C
E  —————————————0——3——1-0——1———
A  3——0—————3—5-3——3—3-3—5-5—3-2——5—3——
D  3—3——5——2——2-2—————0——0-0—3—2——
G  —————5—0——0—————————0—0-0——
```
Drinking gin, far a-cross the western o-cean I must wander.

VERSE

```
   C                          F           C
E  ————0————————————————————————————
A  —3——3—5—3————0—3——3—0—————————
D  5—2————2—2——5—3—3——3—3——5——
G  5——————0——5—5—————5——
```
And where are me boots, me noggin', noggin' boots?

```
                           G        C
E  —0——3——3—3——1—0-0———0—1——3——
A  3——3—3——3—3——3—3-3—5—2——2——3——
D  2——2————————0—0——2——
G  ——0——————————0————
```
They're all gone for beer and tobacco; for the heels

```
                 F           C
E  3——3——0————————————————
A  3——3—3——3—3—2——0—3——3——0————
D  —2——2—2—2—3——3—3——3—5——
G  —————5——————5——
```
They are worn out and the toes are kicked a-bout,

```
                 G        G⁷ C
E  ——0——3——1-0——1————
A  3—5—3——3—3-3——5-5—3-2——5—3——
D  2—2——2——————0—0-0—3—2——
G  0——0——————————0—0-0——
```
And the soles are looking out for better weather.

16

All For Me Grog
(continued)

Basic Melody

Key of G

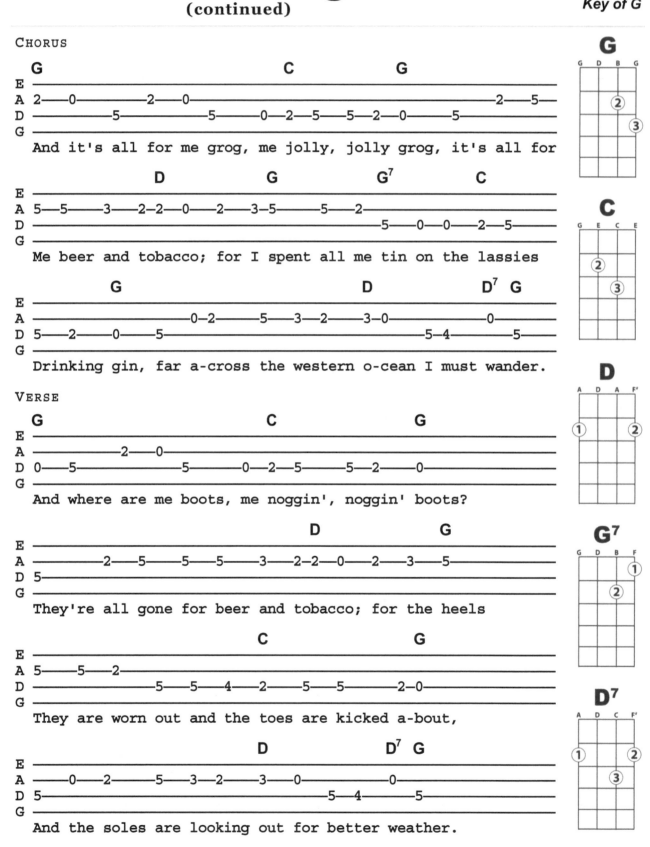

CHORUS

G   **C**   **G**
```
E ————————————————————————————————————————————————————————————————
A 2———0—————————2———0——————————————————————————————————2———5———
D —————————5——————————5————————0—2—5———5—2—0———5————————————
G ————————————————————————————————————————————————————————————————
```
And it's all for me grog, me jolly, jolly grog, it's all for

        D   **G**   **G⁷**   **C**
```
E ————————————————————————————————————————————————————————————————
A 5——5————3——2—2——0——2——3—5———5—2————————————————————
D ——————————————————————————————————5———0——0——2—5———
G ————————————————————————————————————————————————————————————————
```
Me beer and tobacco; for I spent all me tin on the lassies

    G   **D**   **D⁷ G**
```
E ————————————————————————————————————————————————————————————————
A —————————————0—2———5—3—2——3—0—————————0————————
D 5——2——0——5———————————————————————5—4———5———
G ————————————————————————————————————————————————————————————————
```
Drinking gin, far a-cross the western o-cean I must wander.

VERSE

    G   **C**   **G**
```
E ————————————————————————————————————————————————————————————————
A —————————2———0—————————————————————————————————————————
D 0——5————————————5————0—2—5———5—2——0————————————
G ————————————————————————————————————————————————————————————————
```
And where are me boots, me noggin', noggin' boots?

                          D   **G**
```
E ————————————————————————————————————————————————————————————————
A ———2——5———5—5———3——2—2——0——2——3———5————————
D 5————————————————————————————————————————————————
G ————————————————————————————————————————————————————————————————
```
They're all gone for beer and tobacco; for the heels

                          C   **G**
```
E ————————————————————————————————————————————————————————————————
A 5——5——2——————————————————————————————————————————
D ————————5—5——4——2——5—5———2—0—————————————
G ————————————————————————————————————————————————————————————————
```
They are worn out and the toes are kicked a-bout,

                  D   **D⁷ G**
```
E ————————————————————————————————————————————————————————————————
A ——0—2———5—3—2——3—0—————————0————————
D 5————————————————————5—4———5———
G ————————————————————————————————————————————————————————————————
```
And the soles are looking out for better weather.

All For Me Grog
(continued)

Melody & Chords

Key of G

G

CHORUS

```
        G                      C            G
E _____
A 2——0————————2——0————————————————————————————2——5——
D 0——0——5————0——0——5————0——2——5——5——2——0————5————0——0——
G 0——0————0——0————————0——5——5——5——5——0————0————0——0——
        And it's all for me grog, me jolly, jolly grog, it's all for
```

C

```
                D          G          G7          C
E _____
A 5——5————3——2——2——0——2——3——5————5——2————————————
D 0——0————0——0——0——0——0——0——0————0——0——5——0——0——2——5——
G ——0————————2——2————0————0————4——4——4——5——5——
        Me beer and tobacco; for I spent all me tin on the lassies
```

D

```
        G                            D          D7  G
E _____
A ————————————0——2————5——3——2————3——0————————0————
D 5——2——0————5——0——0————0——0——0————0——0——5——4————0——5——
G 5——5——0————0————0————————0————2————2——2——5——0——
        Drinking gin, far a-cross the western o-cean I must wander.
```

VERSE

```
        G                      C            G
E _____
A ————————2——0———————————————————————————————————
D 0——5————0——0——5————0——2——5————5——2————0——————————
G 0——0————0————————0——5——5————5——5————0————————————
        And where are me boots, me noggin', noggin' boots?
```

D

D7

```
                              D            G
E _____
A ————2——5——5——5——3——2——2——0——2——3——5————————
D 5————0——0——0——0——0——0——0——0——0——0——0————————
G 0————0——0————0——0——2——2————2——0————————————
        They're all gone for beer and tobacco; for the heels
```

```
                      C            G
E _____
A 5————5——2——————————————————————————————————————
D 0——0——0——5——5——4——2——5——5————2——0————————————
G ——0————0——0——0——5——5——5——5——4————————————
        They are worn out and the toes are kicked a-bout,
```

```
                      D          D7  G
E _____
A ——0——2————5——3——2——3——0————————0————————————
D 5——0——0————0——0——0——0——0——5——4————0——5————————
G 4————0————0——0——2————2——2——5——0————————————
        And the soles are looking out for better weather.
```

Auld Lang Syne

Basic Melody
Key of G

The words of this well-known song were originally written as a poem by Scots poet Robert Burns in 1788. The words were later set to music, and the tune began to be sung at the stroke of midnight on New Years' Eve to bid farewell to the old year.

Words by Robert Burns
Music Traditional

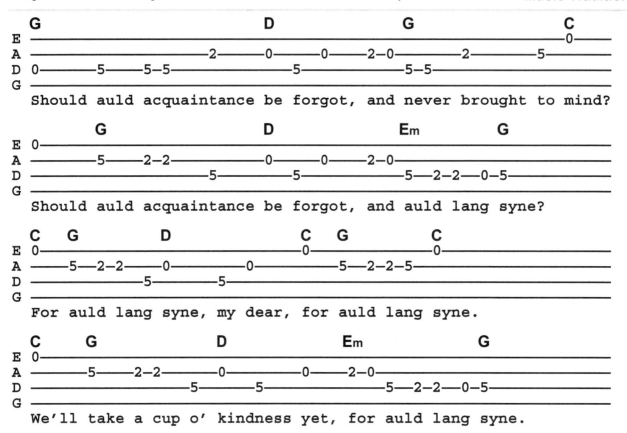

Should auld acquaintance be forgot, and never brought to mind?

Should auld acquaintance be forgot, and auld lang syne?

For auld lang syne, my dear, for auld lang syne.

We'll take a cup o' kindness yet, for auld lang syne.

Chord Forms

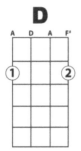

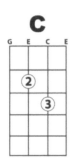

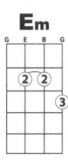

Additional Verses

And surely you'll buy your pint cup,
And surely I'll buy mine!
And we'll take a cup o' kindness yet,
For auld lang syne.

We two have run about the slopes,
And picked the daisies fine;
But we've wandered many a weary foot,
Since auld lang syne.

And there's a hand my trusty friend!
And give me a hand o' thine!
And we'll take a right good-will draught,
For auld lang syne.

19

Auld Lang Syne (continued)

Melody & Chords
Key of G

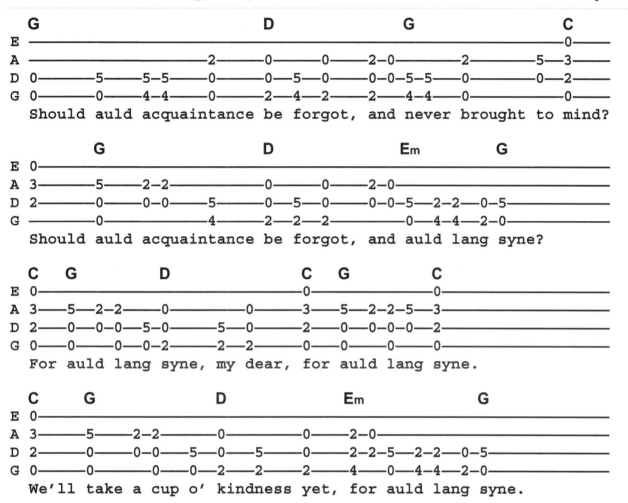

Should auld acquaintance be forgot, and never brought to mind?

Should auld acquaintance be forgot, and auld lang syne?

For auld lang syne, my dear, for auld lang syne.

We'll take a cup o' kindness yet, for auld lang syne.

Chord Forms

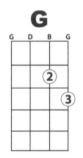
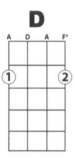
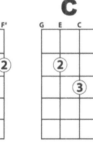
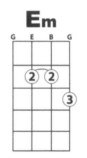

Robert Burns

Auld Lang Syne (continued)

Basic Melody
Key of C

```
     C                              G              C                F
E ------------------------------------------------------------------------------
A ----------------------------------------------------------------------0-------
D -----------------------2------0------0------2-0-------2-------5----------------
G 0-------5------5-5---------------5-----------5-5------------------------------
```
Should auld acquaintance be forgot, and never brought to mind?

```
            C                 G          Am           C
E ------------------------------------------------------------------------------
A 0-----------------------------------------------------------------------------
D -------5-----2-2------------0------0------2-0---------------------------------
G ------------------5------5----------5-2-2---0-5-------------------------------
```
Should auld acquaintance be forgot, and auld lang syne?

```
  F   C        G           F   C        F
E ------------------------------------------------------------------------------
A 0-----------------------0-----------0----------------------------------------
D ----5-2-2------0-----------0------5-2-2-5------------------------------------
G ----------5----------5------------------------------------------------------
```
For auld lang syne, my dear, for auld lang syne.

```
  F   C          G          Am           C
E ------------------------------------------------------------------------------
A 0-----------------------------------------------------------------------------
D -----5----2-2----------0-------0------2-0-----------------------------------
G --------------5------5--------5-2-2---0-5-----------------------------------
```
We'll take a cup o' kindness yet, for auld lang syne.

Chord Forms

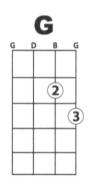
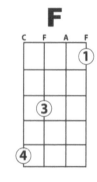
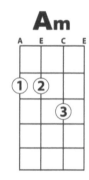

Beer, Beer, Beer (page 1)

Basic Melody
Key of C

This is one of the classic Irish drinking songs, which tells the fictional story of Charlie Mopps, the man who invented beer.

Words and Music
Traditional

INTRO/BRIDGE

```
    C      Em      Am              C      Em      Am
E _____
A 3_____2_____0_____0_2___3_____2_____0_____
D _____5_____
G _____
```
Beer, beer, beer, tid-d-ly beer, beer, beer...

VERSE

```
    C
E _____
A _____
D 5_2_____2_____3_5___5____5____3_2__0_____
G _____5_____
```
A long time a-go, way back in history,

```
    C                              F                  G
E _____
A _____3___3_____3___3_3_____0_____
D 5_____5_____5___3__2____2__0_____
G _____
```
When all there was to drink was nothin' but cups of tea...

```
    C                    F              C
E _____
A __3_____3_____3_3_____0_____3___0_____
D 5_____5__5_____5_____5_____
G _____
```
A-long came a man, by the name of Charlie Mopps,

```
                                             G      C
E _____
A _____
D 2___5_5_5__5___2_5_5_5___5_____2___2_5____0_2_____
G _____4__5_____
```
And he invented a wonderful drink, and he made it out of hops.

Chord Forms

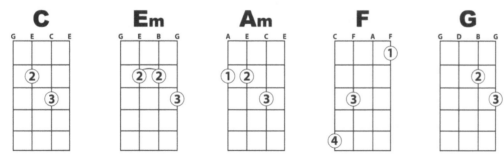

Beer, Beer, Beer (page 2)

Basic Melody
Key of C

CHORUS

```
        C
E  ————————————————————————————————————————————————————————————————————
A  ————————————————————————————————————————————————————————————————————
D  5——5——2————————2——2——0——2-2-2————————0-2——2————0————————————————————
G  ————————————————————————————————————————————————5—0——————————————————
```
Oh he ought to be an emperor, a sultan or a king;

```
        C                       F               G
E  ————————————————————————————————————————————————————————————————————
A  3——3——3——3————————————0———————————————————————————————————————————————
D  ——————————————5————————5————————3-2——0————————————————————————————————
G  ————————————————————————————————————————————————————————————————————
```
And to his praises, we shall always sing.

```
          C                                     F               C
E  ————————————————————————————————————————————————————————————————————
A  ——3——3——3—3——3————————————————————0——————————3—0——————————————————————
D  5————————————————————5——5——5——————————————————5————————————5——————————
G  ————————————————————————————————————————————————————————————————————
```
Oh look what he has done for us, he's filled us up with cheer;

```
                                          G   C
E  ————————————————————————————————————————————————————————————————————
A  ————————————————————————————————————0——2——3——————————————————————————
D  5——5————5——5——5————5——5——5——5————————————————————————————————————————
G  ————————————————————————————————————————————————————————————————————
```
God bless Charlie Mopps, the man who invented beer

```
   Em   Am              C   Em   Am
E  ————————————————————————————————————————————————————————————————————
A  -2————0——————————0-2——3————2————0————————————————————————————————————
D  ——————————5———————————————————————————————————————————————————————————
G  ————————————————————————————————————————————————————————————————————
```
(beer, beer, tid-d-ly beer, beer, beer...)

Additional Verses

The Curtis Bar, the James' Pub, the hole-in-the-wall as well...
One thing ye can be sure of, it's Charlie's beer they sell.
So come on all ye lucky lads, at eleven o'clock we stop;
For five whole seconds, remember Charlie Mopps!
(One... Two... Three... Four... Five...)

A barrel of malt, a bushel of hops, stir it around with a stick,
The kind of lubrication, to make yer engine tick...
Forty pints of wallop a day will keep away the quacks,
It's only eight pence ha'penny, and one and six in tax.

Beer, Beer, Beer (page 1)
(continued)

Melody & Chords

Key of C

INTRO/BRIDGE

```
      C      Em     Am                C      Em     Am
E ────────────────────────────────────────────────────────────────────
A 3──────2──────0──────────0─2──3──────2──────0────────────────────────
D 2──────2──────2──────5──2─2──2──────2──────2────────────────────────
G 0──────────2──────5──────────0──────────2────────────────────────────
```
Beer, beer, beer, tid-d-ly beer, beer, beer...

VERSE

```
      C
E ────────────────────────────────────────────────────────────────────
A ────────────────────────────────────────────────────────────────────
D 5─2──────2──────3─5──────5──────5──────3─2──0────────────────────────
G 5─5──────5──────5─5──────5──────5──────5─5──5─5──────────────────────
```
A long time a-go, way back in history,

```
      C                              F                    G
E ────────────────────────────────────────────────────────────────────
A ──────3──────3──────3──────3─3──────────0────────────────────────────
D 5──────2──────2──────2──────2─2──────5──────3──5──────3──────2──────2─0──────
G 5──────0──────────0──────────0──────5──────5─5──────5──────5──────5─0──────
```
When all there was to drink was nothin' but cups of tea...

```
        C                              F                    C
E ────────────────────────────────────────────────────────────────────
A ──3──────3──────3─3────────────0──────────3──0──────────────────────
D 5─2──────2──────2─2──────5──────5──────3──────5─3──3──────5──────────
G 5─0──────────0──────5──────5──────5──────5──────────5────────────────
```
A-long came a man, by the name of Charlie Mopps,

```
                                                          G      C
E ────────────────────────────────────────────────────────────────────
A ────────────────────────────────────────────────────────────────────
D 2──────5─5─5──────5──────2─5──────5──────5──────5──────2──────2──────5──────0──2──────5──────
G 5──────5─5─5──────5──────5─5──────5──────5──────5──────5──────5──────5─0──4─5──────
```
And he invented a wonderful drink, and he made it out of hops.

Chord Forms

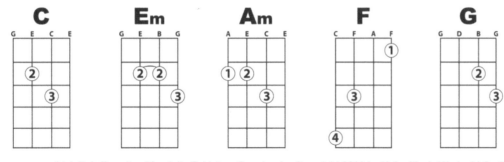

Beer, Beer, Beer (Page 2)
(continued)

Melody & Chords

Key of C

CHORUS

```
     C
E ──────────────────────────────────────────────────────────────────────
A ──────────────────────────────────────────────────────────────────────
D 5──5──2───────2──2──0──2-2-2──────0─2──2────0───────────────────────────
G 5──5──5───────5──5──0──5-5-5──────0─5──5────0──5─0──────────────────────
  Oh he ought to be an emperor, a sultan or a king;
```

```
     C                        F              G
E ──────────────────────────────────────────────────────────────────────
A 3──3──3──3─────────0─────────────────────────────────────────────────────
D 2──2──2──2────5────3──5──────3─2────0────────────────────────────────────
G 0─────────0──5────5──5───────5─5────0────────────────────────────────────
  And to his praises, we shall always sing.
```

```
       C                                    F              C
E ──────────────────────────────────────────────────────────────────────
A ───3────3────3─3──3──────────────────0───────────3──0────────────────────
D 5──2────2────2─2──2────5──5──5────3───────5──3──3────5────────────────────
G 0──0──────────0──5──5──5──5───────2────────────5─────────────────────────
  Oh look what he has done for us, he's filled us up with cheer;
```

```
                                          G     C
E ──────────────────────────────────────────────────────────────────────
A ────────────────────────────────────0──2──3─────────────────────────────
D 5───5───5──5──5──────5──5──5──5─0──0──2──────────────────────────────────
G 5───5───5──5──5──────5──5──5──5─0──────0─────────────────────────────────
  God bless Charlie Mopps, the man who invented beer!
```

```
  Em   Am              C   Em   Am
E ──────────────────────────────────────────────────────────────────────
A ─2──────0──────0─2─3──────2──────0───────────────────────────────────────
D ─2──────2──────5─0-0─2────2──────2───────────────────────────────────────
G ─0──────2──────0─────────0──────2────────────────────────────────────────
  (Beer, beer, tid-d-ly beer, beer, beer...)
```

Beer, Beer, Beer (page 1)
(continued)

Basic Melody

Key of G

INTRO/BRIDGE

```
     G      Bm     Em                G    Bm     Em
E  3———————2——————0————————0—2———3——————2——————0———————————————————
A  ————————————————————5—————————————————————————————————————————
D  ——————————————————————————————————————————————————————————————
G  ——————————————————————————————————————————————————————————————
```
Beer, beer, beer, tid-d-ly beer, beer, beer...

VERSE

```
     G
E  ——————————————————————————————————————————————————————————————
A  5—2———————2——————3—5———5————5————3—2———0————————————————————————
D  ———————————————————————————————————————5————————————————————————
G  ——————————————————————————————————————————————————————————————
```
A long time a-go, way back in history,

```
     G                                    C                D
E  ——————3———3————————3———3—3——————————————0——————————————————————————
A  5——————————————————————————————5———————5——————3——2——————2—0————————
D  ——————————————————————————————————————————————————————————————————
G  ——————————————————————————————————————————————————————————————————
```
When all there was to drink was nothin' but cups of tea...

```
       G                          C                G
E  ———3———3—————3—3——————————————0—————————3———0——————————————————————
A  5——————————————————5———5——————5————————5—————————————————————————
D  ——————————————————————————————————————————————————————————————————
G  ——————————————————————————————————————————————————————————————————
```
A-long came a man, by the name of Charlie Mopps,

```
                                                      D      G
E  ——————————————————————————————————————————————————————————————————
A  2———5—5—5———5————2—5———5—5————5————————2———2—5——————0—2——————————————
D  ——————————————————————————————————————————————————————4—5——————————
G  ——————————————————————————————————————————————————————————————————
```
And he invented a wonderful drink, and he made it out of hops.

Chord Forms

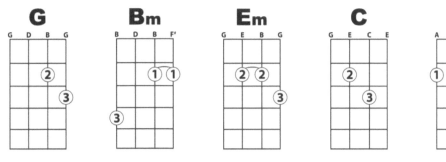

Beer, Beer, Beer (page 2)
(continued)

Basic Melody

Key of G

CHORUS

```
    G
E ——————————————————————————————————————————————————————————
A 5—5—2———2—2—0—2—2—2———0—2—2———0—————————————————————————
D ————————————————————————————————————5—0————————————————————
G ——————————————————————————————————————————————————————————
```
Oh he ought to be an emperor, a sultan or a king;

```
    G                    C              D
E 3——3—3——3————————0—————————————————————————————————————
A ————————————5———————5———3—2———0—————————————————————————
D ——————————————————————————————————————————————————————————
G ——————————————————————————————————————————————————————————
```
And to his praises, we shall always sing.

```
    G                            C            G
E ——3——3——3—3——3————————————————0—————3—0————————————
A 5—————————————————5—5——5————————5————————5——————
D ——————————————————————————————————————————————————————————
G ——————————————————————————————————————————————————————————
```
Oh look what he has done for us, he's filled us up with cheer;

```
                              D   G
E ——————————————————————————0—2——3———————————————————
A 5——5——5—5——5——5—5—5—5—————————————————————————————
D ——————————————————————————————————————————————————————————
G ——————————————————————————————————————————————————————————
```
God bless Charlie Mopps, the man who invented beer!

```
  Bm    Em        G   Bm    Em
E —2————0——————0—2—3——2————0———————————————————————
A ————————5————————————————————————————————————————
D ——————————————————————————————————————————————————————————
G ——————————————————————————————————————————————————————————
```
(Beer, beer, tid-d-ly beer, beer, beer...)

Beer, Beer, Beer (page 1)
(continued)

Melody & Chords

Key of G

INTRO/BRIDGE

```
     G      Bm     Em                     G      Bm     Em
E  3——————2——————0——————————0—2—3——————2——————0———————————
A  2——————2——————2——————5——0—0—2——————2——————2———————————
D  0—————————————2——————0———————0—————————————2———————————
G  0———————————————————————————0———————————————————————————
```
Beer, beer, beer, tid-d-ly beer, beer, beer...

VERSE

```
     G
E  ——————————————————————————————————————————————————————
A  5—2——————2——————3—5——5——5——3—2—0————————————————————————
D  0—0——————0——————0—0——0——0——0—0—0—5——————————————————————
G  0—0——————0——————0——0————————0——0————————————————————————
```
A long time a-go, way back in history,

```
     G                              C              D
E  ——————3——3——————3——3—3——————————0————————————————————————
A  5——————2——2——————2——2—2——————5——3—5——————3——2——————2—0———
D  0——————————0——————————0——————0——2—2——————2——2——————2—0———
G  0——————————0——————————0——————0——————————————————————2————
```
When all there was to drink was nothin' but cups of tea...

```
     G                         C              G
E  ——3——————3——————3—3——————————0————————3——0——————————————
A  5—2——————2——————2—2——————5—5——3——————5—3——2——5——————————
D  0—0——————————————0——————0—0——2——————2——————0————————————
G  0—0——————————————0——————0——————0——————————0————————————
```
A-long came a man, by the name of Charlie Mopps,

```
                                                   D      G
E  ——————————————————————————————————————————————————————————
A  2——5—5—5——5——————2—5——5—5——5——————————2——2——5——0—2————————
D  0——————0—0—0——0——0—0——0—0——0——————0——0—————0——0——0——4—5———
G  0——————0————————————0——————————————0——————0——————2——2—4——
```
And he invented a wonderful drink, and he made it out of hops.

Chord Forms

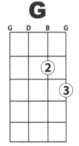

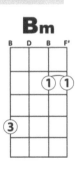

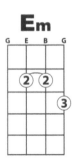

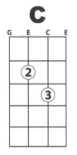

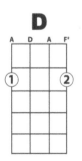

Beer, Beer, Beer (page 2)
(continued)

Melody & Chords

Key of G

CHORUS

```
     G
E ————————————————————————————————————————————————————————————
A 5——5——2————————2——2——0——2-2-2————————0-2——2————0————————————
D 0——0——0————————0——0——0——0-0-0————————0-0————————0——5-0——————
G 0————————0——————————————0—————————————0————————4-0——————————
```
Oh he ought to be an emperor, a sultan or a king;

```
     G                        C              D
E 3——3——3——3——————————0——————————————————————————————————————
A 2——2——2——2——5——3——5————————3-2————0————————————————————————
D 0————————0——0——2-2————————2-2————0————————————————————————
G 0——————0——0——0——————————————————2————————————————————————
```
And to his praises, we shall always sing.

```
       G                                    C              G
E ——3————3————3——3——3————————————————0——————————3——0————————
A 5——2——2——2——2——2——5——5——5——3——————5——3——3————5——————————
D 0——0————————0——————0——0——0——0——2——————2——————————0——————
G 2——0————————0——————0——0——0——0——————————————————0——————————
```
Oh look what he has done for us, he's filled us up with cheer;

```
                                        D    G
E ———————————————————————————————————0——2——3——————————————————
A 5——5——5——5——5——5——5——5——5-0——0——2————————————————————————
D 0——0——0——0——0——0——0——0——0-0——0——0————————————————————————
G 0——0————0————0——————0——0——————2——2——0————————————————————
```
God bless Charlie Mopps, the man who invented beer!

```
  Bm    Em            G    Bm    Em
E —2————0————0——2——3————2————0————————————————————————
A —2————2——5——2-2——2————2————2————————————————————————
D —0————2——0————————0————0————2————————————————————————
G ————————————————————————————————————————————————————
```
(Beer, beer, tid-d-ly beer, beer, beer...)

Black Velvet Band

Basic Melody
Key of C (Low)

Words and Music
Traditional

The earliest known printed broadside versions of this song date from the late 1700's in England. Today it is usually considered to be an Irish song, with a recorded version by the Dubliners in 1967 being possibly the best known.

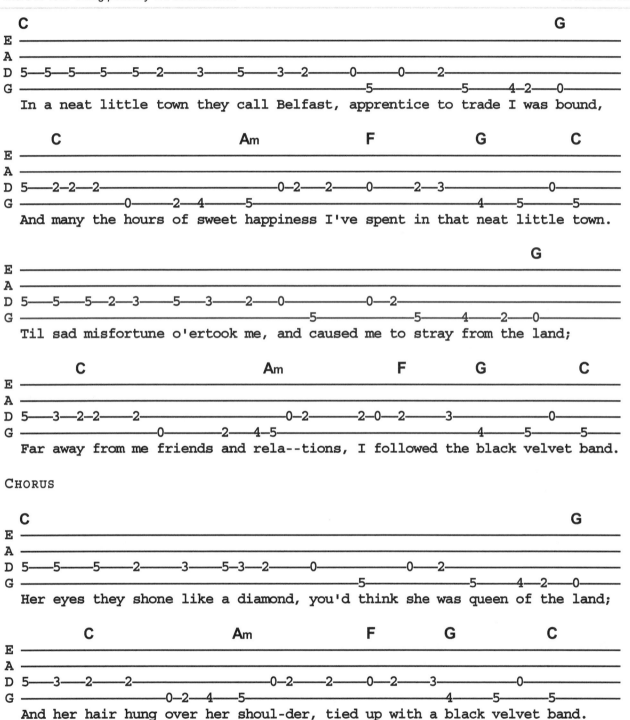

In a neat little town they call Belfast, apprentice to trade I was bound,

And many the hours of sweet happiness I've spent in that neat little town.

Til sad misfortune o'ertook me, and caused me to stray from the land;

Far away from me friends and rela--tions, I followed the black velvet band.

CHORUS

Her eyes they shone like a diamond, you'd think she was queen of the land;

And her hair hung over her shoul-der, tied up with a black velvet band.

See Chord Forms and Additional Verses on Next Page

Black Velvet Band
(continued)

Chord Forms

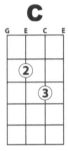
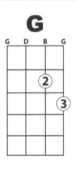
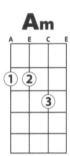
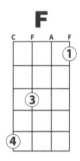

Additional Verses

As I went out strolling one evening,
Not meaning to go very far;
I met with a fickle young damsel,
A-sellin' her trade in the bar.
When a watch she took from a customer,
And slipped it right into my hand;
Then the law came and put me in prison,
Bad luck to her black velvet band!

Next morning before judge and jury,
For trial I had to appear;
Then the judge he says me young fellow,
The case against you is quite clear.
And seven long years is your sentence,
You're goin' to Van Dieman's land...
Far away from your friends and relations,
To follow the black velvet band.

So come all ye jolly young fellows,
I'll have you take warnin' by me;
And when ever you're into the liquor, me lads,
Beware of the pretty colleens.
For they'll fill you with whisky and porter,
'Til you are not able to stand...
And the very next thing that you know, me lads,
You've landed in Van Dieman's land.

Black Velvet Band (continued)

Basic Melody
Key of G

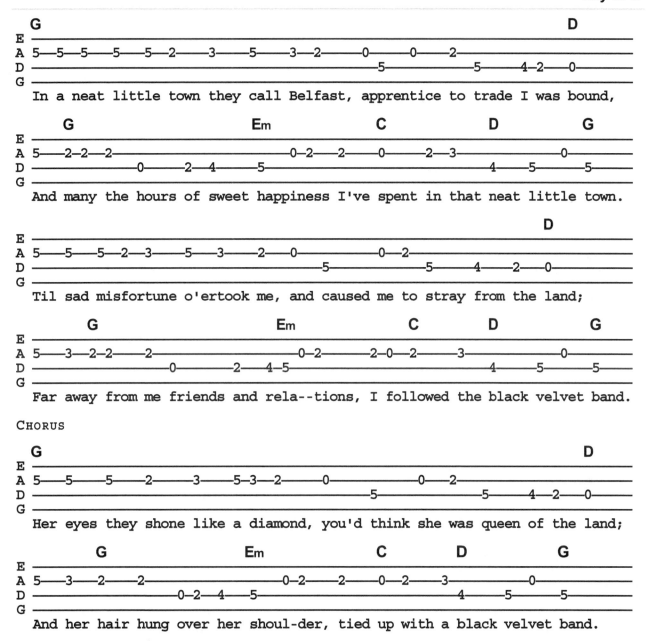

```
            G                                                              D
E --------------------------------------------------------------------------------
A 5--5--5---5---5--2----3----5---3--2-----0-----0--2-----------------------------
D ------------------------------------5--------5----4-2--0-----------------------
G --------------------------------------------------------------------------------
```
In a neat little town they call Belfast, apprentice to trade I was bound,

```
            G               Em            C            D          G
E --------------------------------------------------------------------------------
A 5---2-2--2----------------0-2----2---0---2--3------------0-------------------
D ----------0----2--4-----5-------------------4---5-----5----------------------
G --------------------------------------------------------------------------------
```
And many the hours of sweet happiness I've spent in that neat little town.

```
                                                                  D
E --------------------------------------------------------------------------------
A 5---5---5--2--3----5--3---2--0--------0--2--------------------------------------
D -----------------------5---------------5----4---2--0-------------------------
G --------------------------------------------------------------------------------
```
Til sad misfortune o'ertook me, and caused me to stray from the land;

```
            G               Em            C            D          G
E --------------------------------------------------------------------------------
A 5---3--2-2----2-----------0-2----2-0--2---3-------0---------------------------
D ----------0------2--4-5------------------4---5---5---------------------------
G --------------------------------------------------------------------------------
```
Far away from me friends and rela--tions, I followed the black velvet band.

CHORUS

```
            G                                                              D
E --------------------------------------------------------------------------------
A 5----5---5---2----3----5-3--2------0---------0--2-------------------------------
D -------------------------------5-----------5----4--2--0----------------------
G --------------------------------------------------------------------------------
```
Her eyes they shone like a diamond, you'd think she was queen of the land;

```
            G               Em            C            D          G
E --------------------------------------------------------------------------------
A 5---3--2---2--------------0-2----2---0--2--3-------0----------------------------
D ----------0-2--4--5----------------------4----5----5-------------------------
G --------------------------------------------------------------------------------
```
And her hair hung over her shoul-der, tied up with a black velvet band.

Chord Forms

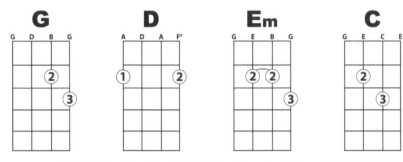

Black Velvet Band (continued)

Melody & Chords
Key of G

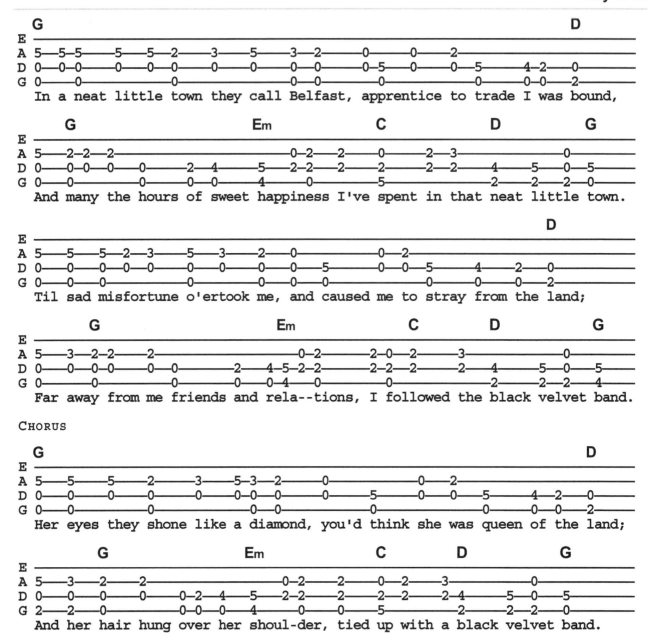

In a neat little town they call Belfast, apprentice to trade I was bound,

And many the hours of sweet happiness I've spent in that neat little town.

Til sad misfortune o'ertook me, and caused me to stray from the land;

Far away from me friends and rela--tions, I followed the black velvet band.

CHORUS

Her eyes they shone like a diamond, you'd think she was queen of the land;

And her hair hung over her shoul-der, tied up with a black velvet band.

Chord Forms

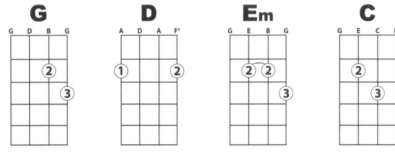

Black Velvet Band (continued)

Basic Melody
Key of C (High)

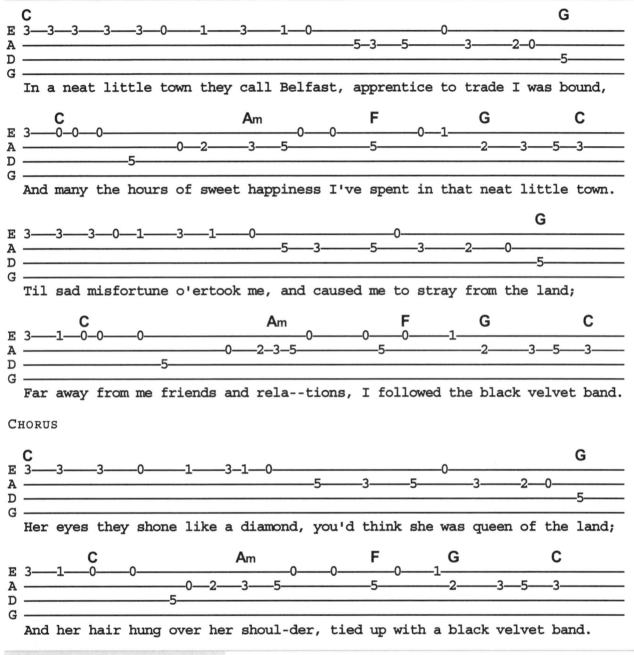

In a neat little town they call Belfast, apprentice to trade I was bound,

And many the hours of sweet happiness I've spent in that neat little town.

Til sad misfortune o'ertook me, and caused me to stray from the land;

Far away from me friends and rela--tions, I followed the black velvet band.

CHORUS

Her eyes they shone like a diamond, you'd think she was queen of the land;

And her hair hung over her shoul-der, tied up with a black velvet band.

Chord Forms

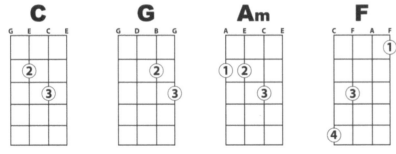

Black Velvet Band (continued)

Melody & Chords
Key of C (High)

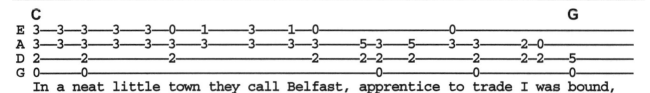

In a neat little town they call Belfast, apprentice to trade I was bound,

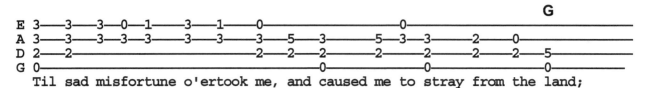

And many the hours of sweet happiness I've spent in that neat little town.

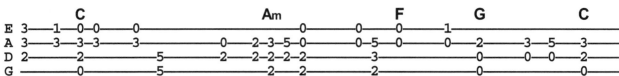

Til sad misfortune o'ertook me, and caused me to stray from the land;

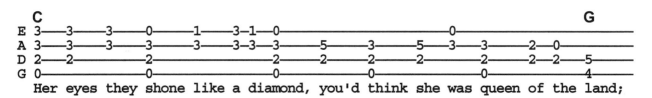

Far away from me friends and rela--tions, I followed the black velvet band.

CHORUS

Her eyes they shone like a diamond, you'd think she was queen of the land;

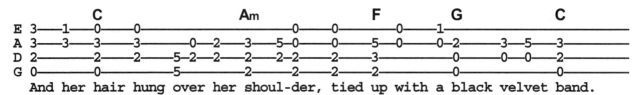

And her hair hung over her shoul-der, tied up with a black velvet band.

Chord Forms

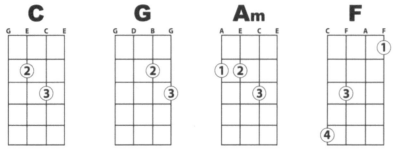

The Bold Thady Quill (page 1)

Basic Melody
Key of C

It is said that this song was written by an Irish farmer, Johnny Tom Gleeson, around 1895 about one of his itinerant laborers. The Clancy Brothers and Tommy Makem helped revive the popularity of this old song.

Words by Johnny Tom Gleeson
Music Traditional

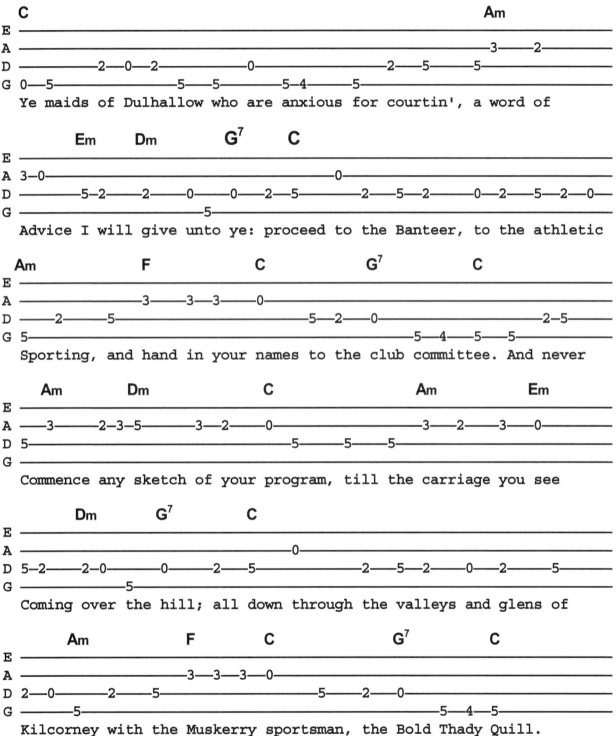

Ye maids of Dulhallow who are anxious for courtin', a word of

Advice I will give unto ye: proceed to the Banteer, to the athletic

Sporting, and hand in your names to the club committee. And never

Commence any sketch of your program, till the carriage you see

Coming over the hill; all down through the valleys and glens of

Kilcorney with the Muskerry sportsman, the Bold Thady Quill.

See Chorus and Chord Forms Next Page

The Bold Thady Quill

Basic Melody

Key of C

(page 2)

CHORUS

```
        C                                                    Am
E ————————————————————————————————————————————————————————————————————
A ——————————————————————————————————————————————————3———2———————————————
D ————————2———0———2—————————0—————————————2———5—————————————————————————
G 0———5—————————————5———5—————————5———4———5—————————————————————————————
```
For ramblin for rovin' for football and sportin', for drinkin'

```
        Em        F         G⁷        C
E ——————————————————————————————————————————————————————————————————————
A 3———————0——————————————————————————————————0—————————————————————————
D ————————————5———2———2——————0————————0———2———5—————————2———5—2———0——————
G ————————————————————————5—————————————————————————————————————————————
```
Black porter as fast as you fill; in all your days rovin' you'll

```
        Am              F         C         G⁷              C
E ——————————————————————————————————————————————————————————————————————
A ——————————————————————3———3———3———0———————————————————————————————————
D 2———5———2———0—————2———5—————————————————5———2———0—————————————————————
G ——————————————5—————————————————————————————————————————5———4———5————
```
Find none so jovial, as the Muskerry sportsman the Bold Thady Quill.

Chord Forms

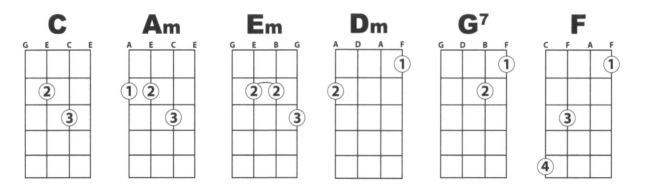

See Additional Verses on Next Page

The Bold Thady Quill
(continued)

Additional Verses

Thady was famous in all sorts of places,
At the athletic meeting held out in Cloghroe;
He won the long jump without throwing off his braces,
Going fifty-four feet from the heel to the toe.
At the put of the shot was a Dublin man foremost,
But Thady out-reached and exceeded him still;
Around the whole field rang the wild ringing chorus,
'Here's luck to our hero, the bold Thady Quill'.

At the great hurling match between Cork and Tipperary,
That was held in the park on the banks of the Lee;
Our own darling boys were afraid of being beaten,
So they sent for Bold Thady in Ballinagree.
Well he hurled the ball left and right in their faces,
He showed those Tipperary boys daring and skill;
If they touched on his lines he would certainly brain them,
And the papers sang praises of the Bold Thady Quill.

The inclusion of this song on the 1959 album "Come Fill Your Glass With Us" by The Clancy Brothers and Tommy Makem helped to re-introduce it to the folk music world.

In the year ninety-one before Parnell was taken,
Thady was outrageously breaking the peace;
He got a light sentence for causing commotion,
And six months hard labour for beatin' police.
But in spite of coercion, he's still agitating,
Each drop of his life's blood, he's willing to spill;
To gain for old Ireland complete liberation,
Till then, there's no rest for the bold Thady Quill.

At the Cork Exhibition there was a fair maiden,
Who's fortune exceeded one million or more;
But a poor constitution had ruined her completely,
And medical treatment had failed o'er and o'er.
Ah mother she says sure I know what will ease me,
And all the diseases most certainly kill;
Give over your potions and medical treatment,
I'd rather one squeeze from the Bold Thady Quill.

The Bold Thady Quill
(continued - page 1)

Basic Melody

Key of G

```
       G                                                      Em
E ——————————————————————————————————————————————————3———2————
A ——————————2—0—2—————————0———————————2—5———5———————————————
D 0—5——————————————5———5———————5—4———5—————————————————————
G ————————————————————————————————————————————————————————
```
Ye maids of Dulhallow who are anxious for courtin', a word of

```
          Bm    Am          D7    G
E 3—0————————————————————————————0—————————————————————————————
A ———————5—2———2———0———0—2—5———2—5—2———0—2—5—2—0——————
D ——————————————5—————————————————————————————————————
G ——————————————————————————————————————————————————
```
Advice I will give unto ye: proceed to the Banteer, to the athletic

```
   Em          C      G         D7        G
E ——————————3———3—3———0————————————————————————————————————
A ———2———5—————————————5—2———0——————————————2—5———————
D 5—————————————————————————————5—4———5———5—————————
G ——————————————————————————————————————————————————
```
Sporting, and hand in your names to the club committee. And never

```
   Em          Am          G           Em          Bm
E ——3———2—3—5———3—2———0—————————————3———2———3——0————
A 5—————————————————5———5———5———————————————————————
D ——————————————————————————————————————————————————
G ——————————————————————————————————————————————————
```
Commence any sketch of your program, till the carriage you see

```
          Am      D7      G
E ——————————————————————0—————————————————————————————————
A 5—2———2—0————0———2—5————————2—5—2———0—2———5——————
D ——————————5———————————————————————————————————————
G ——————————————————————————————————————————————————
```
Coming over the hill; all down through the valleys and glens of

```
          Em          C      G      D7          G
E ——————————————————3—3—3—0————————————————————————————————
A 2—0———2———5—————————————5—2———0——————————————————
D ——————————5————————————————————————5—4—5——————
G ——————————————————————————————————————————————————
```
Kilcorney with the Muskerry sportsman, the Bold Thady Quill.

See Chord Forms on Next Page

The Bold Thady Quill
(continued - page 2)

Basic Melody

Key of G

CHORUS

```
          G                                                    Em
E ──────────────────────────────────────────────────────3───2──────
A ──────────2───0───2───────────0───────────────2───5────────────────
D 0───5─────────────────5───5───────5───4───5────────────────────────
G ───────────────────────────────────────────────────────────────────
```
For ramblin for rovin for football and sportin', for drinkin'

```
      Bm          C           D⁷          G
E 3───────0──────────────────────────────────0───────────────────────
A ─────────────5───2───2───0───────0───2───5────────2───5─2───────0────
D ─────────────────────────5───────────────────────────────────────────
G ───────────────────────────────────────────────────────────────────
```
Black porter as fast as you fill; In all your days rovin' you'll

```
              Em              C       G           D⁷          G
E ─────────────────────────────3───3───3───0──────────────────────────
A 2───5───2───0──────────2───5────────────────────5───2───0───────────
D ──────────────5──────────────────────────────────────────5───4───5──
G ───────────────────────────────────────────────────────────────────
```
Find none so jovial, as the Muskerry sportsman the Bold Thady Quill.

Chord Forms

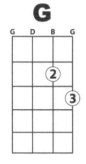
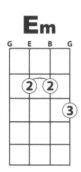
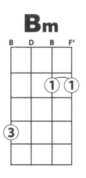

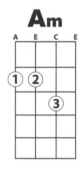
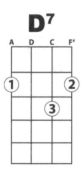
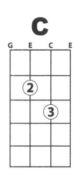

The Bold Thady Quill
(continued)

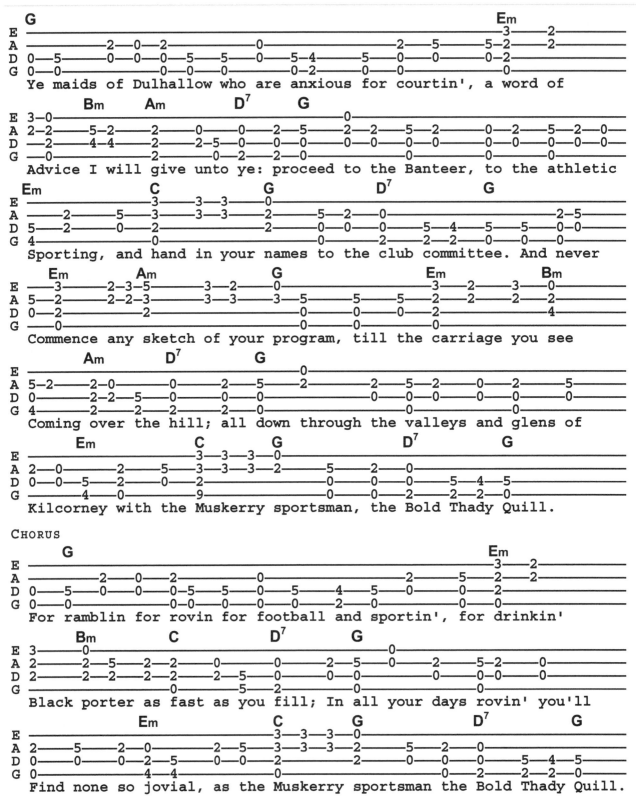

See Chord Forms on Previous Page

The Boys From the County Armagh

Basic Melody

Key of G

This song is the pride of people from the County Armagh in Northern Ireland, including many of those whose ancestors emigrated to the Dover, New Hampshire area to work in the mills in the mid-to-late 1800's. The third verse is a recent addition by the author of this book, who has always felt the song ended too soon.

Words by Thomas Keenan

Music Traditional

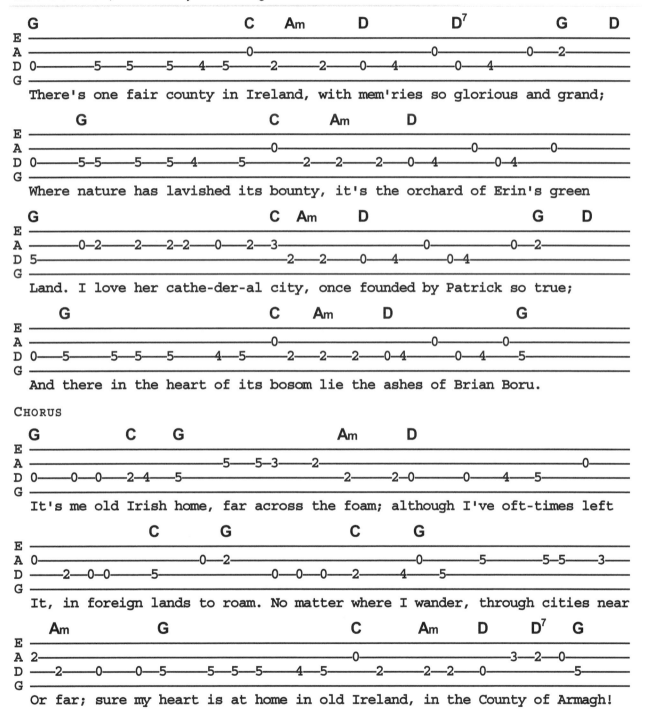

See Chord Forms and Additional Verses on Next Page

The Boys From the County Armagh (continued)

Chord Forms (Key of G)

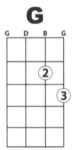
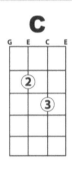
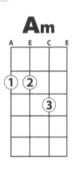
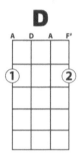
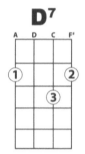

Additional Verses

I've traveled that part of the county,
Through New Town, Fork Hill, Crossmaglen;
Around by the gap of Mountnorris,
And down by Blackwater again.
Where the girls are so hale and so hearty,
None finer in Erin Go Bragh;
But where are the boys that can court them,
Like the boys from the County Armagh?

'Twas me grandparents first left Ireland,
To come to Amerikay.
They settled in Dover, New Hampshire...
And that's where you will find me today.
But my mind oft goes back to old Ireland,
To a place that is fairer by far...
'Tis up in the north you will find it,
And it goes by the name of Armagh!

*A home scene from
County Armagh, Ireland, 1903.*

Chord Forms (Key of C)

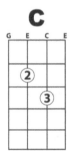
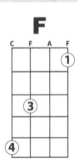
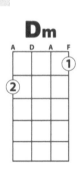
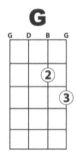
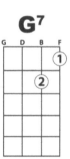

The Boys From the County Armagh (continued)

Melody & Chords

Key of G

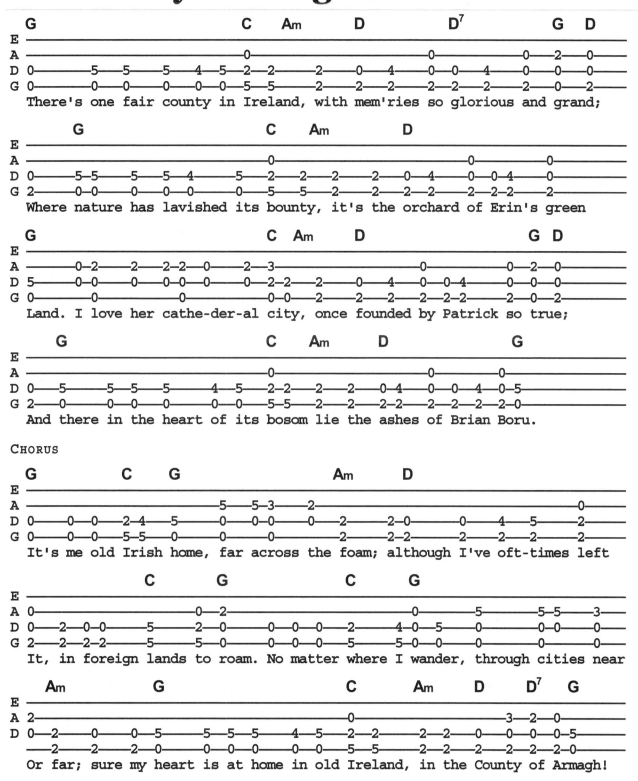

There's one fair county in Ireland, with mem'ries so glorious and grand;

Where nature has lavished its bounty, it's the orchard of Erin's green

Land. I love her cathe-der-al city, once founded by Patrick so true;

And there in the heart of its bosom lie the ashes of Brian Boru.

CHORUS

It's me old Irish home, far across the foam; although I've oft-times left

It, in foreign lands to roam. No matter where I wander, through cities near

Or far; sure my heart is at home in old Ireland, in the County of Armagh!

See Chord Forms and Additional Verses on Previous Page

The Boys From the County Armagh (continued)

Basic Melody

Key of C (Low)

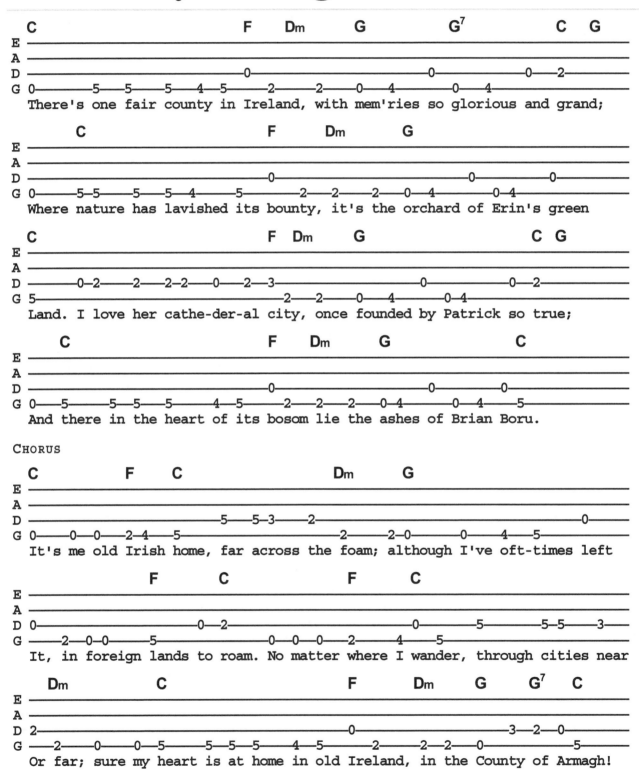

There's one fair county in Ireland, with mem'ries so glorious and grand;

Where nature has lavished its bounty, it's the orchard of Erin's green

Land. I love her cathe-der-al city, once founded by Patrick so true;

And there in the heart of its bosom lie the ashes of Brian Boru.

CHORUS

It's me old Irish home, far across the foam; although I've oft-times left

It, in foreign lands to roam. No matter where I wander, through cities near

Or far; sure my heart is at home in old Ireland, in the County of Armagh!

See Chord Forms and Additional Verses Two Pages Previous

The Boys From the County Armagh (continued)

Basic Melody

Key of C (High)

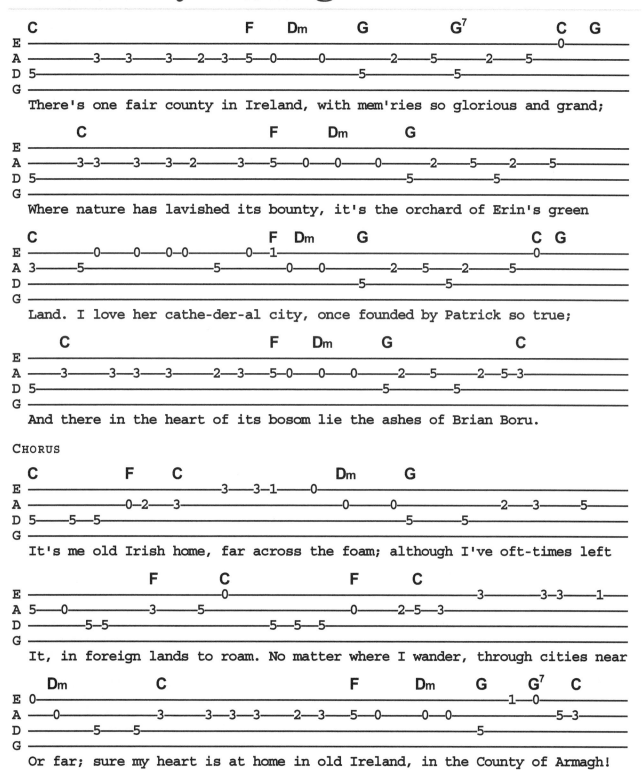

There's one fair county in Ireland, with mem'ries so glorious and grand;

Where nature has lavished its bounty, it's the orchard of Erin's green

Land. I love her cathe-der-al city, once founded by Patrick so true;

And there in the heart of its bosom lie the ashes of Brian Boru.

CHORUS

It's me old Irish home, far across the foam; although I've oft-times left

It, in foreign lands to roam. No matter where I wander, through cities near

Or far; sure my heart is at home in old Ireland, in the County of Armagh!

See Chord Forms and Additional Verses Three Pages Previous

The Boys From the County Armagh (continued)

Melody & Chords

Key of C (High)

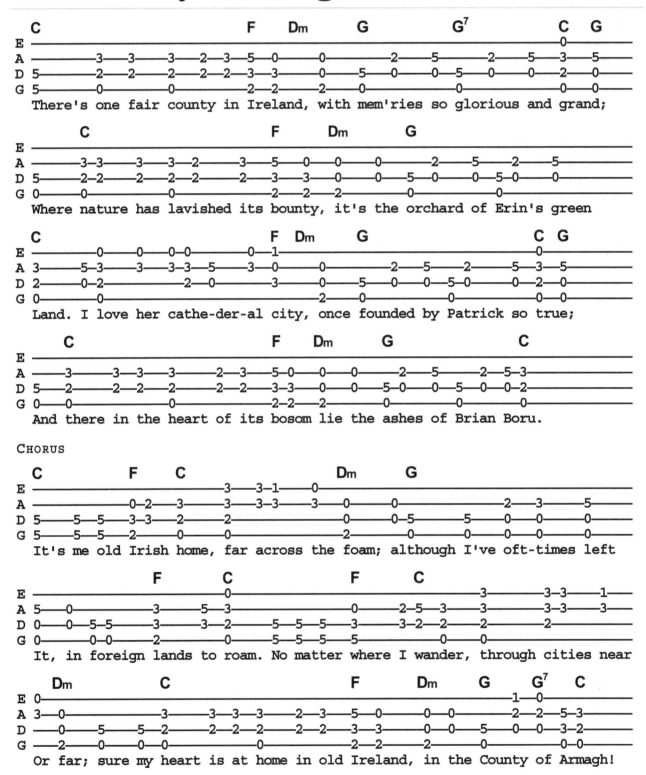

There's one fair county in Ireland, with mem'ries so glorious and grand;

Where nature has lavished its bounty, it's the orchard of Erin's green

Land. I love her cathe-der-al city, once founded by Patrick so true;

And there in the heart of its bosom lie the ashes of Brian Boru.

CHORUS

It's me old Irish home, far across the foam; although I've oft-times left

It, in foreign lands to roam. No matter where I wander, through cities near

Or far; sure my heart is at home in old Ireland, in the County of Armagh!

See Chord Forms and Additional Verses Four Pages Previous

Brennan On the Moor

Basic Melody
Key of G (Low)

This ballad tells the story of the highwayman William "Willy" Brennan, who was caught and hanged in Cork in the early 1800's. This song entered the folk tradition a few years later, and has been an Irish favorite ever since.

Words and Music
Traditional

```
          G                                    C              G
E ————————————————————————————————————————————————————————————————————————
A ————————————————————————————————————————————————————————————————————————
D ————————————————————————————————————0———0————————————————————————————————
G 0——2——————4—4—4————————2————4————————————————4————2—0——0—2——————0—————————
```
Oh it's of a brave young highway man this story I will tell,

```
                              C              G
E ————————————————————————————————————————————————————————————————————————
A ——————————————2———0———————————————————————————————————————————————————————
D 0——5——————5——————————————5———0———0———0—5—5——————5————————0—————————————————
G ————————————————————————————————————————————————————4—————————————————————
```
His name was Willie Brennan and in Ireland he did dwell;

```
                                              C                    G
E ————————————————————————————————————————————————————————————————————————
A ——————————2———0———————————————————————————————————————————————————————————
D 0——0——5——5——————————————5———0————————0———0—5—————————5——5—————0————————————
G ——————————————————————————————————————————————————————————4———————————————
```
It was on the Kilworth Mountains he commenced his wild career,

```
     C                        G                      D
E ————————————————————————————————————————————————————————————————————————
A ————————————————————————————————————————————————————————————————————————
D 0————2—2—2—2————2———2—4—5————2—0——————0———2—————0—————————————————————————
G ————————————————————————————————————————————————4————————————————————————
```
And many a wealthy nobleman before him shook with fear.

CHORUS

```
          G                   Bm
E ————————————————————————————————————————————————————————————————————————
A ————————————————————————————————————————————————————————————————————————
D ——————————————————————————0———0———0———0———0———————————————————————————————
G 4——2———————0———0———0—0———0—————————————————————————————————————————————————
```
And it's Brennan on the moor, Brennan on the moor,

```
     C        G              D               G
E ————————————————————————————————————————————————————————————————————————
A ————————————————————————————————————————————————————————————————————————
D 2——4———5——————5———0—2——————0——————————————————————————————————————————————
G ——————————————————————————4———0—————2———2———0——0———0———————————————————————
```
Bo-ld, brave and undaunted was young Brennan on the moor.

See Chord Forms and Additional Verses on Next Page

Brennan On the Moor
(continued)

Chord Forms and

Additional Verses

Chord Forms

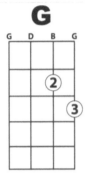
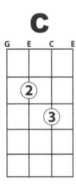
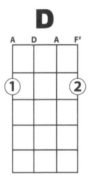
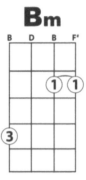

Additional Verses

One day upon the highway as young Willie he went down,
He met the Mayor of Cashel a mile outside the town;
The Mayor he knew his features he said "Young man," said he:
"Your name is Willie Brennan you must come along with me!"

Then Willie's wife went into town provisions for to buy,
And when she saw her Willie she began to weep and cry;
She said, "Hand me that tenpenny!" as soon as Willie spoke,
She handed him a blunderbuss from underneath her cloak.

Now it's of this loaded blunderbuss the truth I will unfold,
He made the mayor to tremble and robbed him of his gold;
A hundred pounds was offered for his apprehension there,
So he with horse and saddle to the mountains did repair.

Now Brennan became an outlaw upon the mountains high,
With cavalry and infantry to take him they did try;
He laughed at them with scorn until at last they say,
By a false hearted woman he was cruelly betrayed.

They hung him at the crossroads, and there he hung and dried,
But some still say that in the night, they still hear Willie ride.
They see him with his blunderbuss, all in the midnight still,
And all along the king's highway... rides Willie Brennan still!

Brennan On the Moor

(continued)

Basic Melody

Key of G (High)

```
      G                                    C           G
E ————————————————————————————————————————————————————————————
A ———0———2—2—2———————0————2———5———5———2———0———————0————————————
D 5——————————————————————————————————————————5—5————5—————————
G —————————————————————————————————————————————————————————————
```
Oh it's of a brave young highway man this story I will tell,

```
                                           C           G
E ———3———3———7———5———3———————————————3———3———3————————————————
A 5——————————————————————5———5———5——————————————2———5—————————
D —————————————————————————————————————————————————————————————
G —————————————————————————————————————————————————————————————
```
His name was Willie Brennan and in Ireland he did dwell;

```
                                              C          G
E —————————3—3———7—5—————3————————————————3———————3———3———————
A 5—5———————————————————————5————5———5—————————————————2—5————
D —————————————————————————————————————————————————————————————
G —————————————————————————————————————————————————————————————
```
It was on the Kilworth Mountains he commenced his wild career,

```
      C                          G              D
E ———0—0———0—0———0———0—2———3———0——————————0——————————————————
A 5——————————————————————————————5———5————————5———2——————————
D —————————————————————————————————————————————————————————————
G —————————————————————————————————————————————————————————————
```
And many a wealthy nobleman before him shook with fear.

Chorus

```
      G                   Bm
E —————————————————————————————————————————————————————————————
A 2———0———————————————————5———5———5———5———5————————————————————
D ————————5———5———5—5———5———————————————————————————————————————
G —————————————————————————————————————————————————————————————
```
And it's Brennan on the moor, Brennan on the moor,

```
      C       G              D           G
E 0———2———3———3———0———————————————————————————————————————————
A ————————————5———5———2———————0———0————————————————————————————
D ————————————————————————5————————————5———4———5——————————————
G —————————————————————————————————————————————————————————————
```
Bo-ld, brave and undaunted was young Brennan on the moor.

See Chord Forms and Additional Verses on Previous Page

Brennan On the Moor
(continued)

Melody & Chords

Key of G (High)

```
      G                                    C              G
E _____
A ___0___2—2—2_____0____2—5—5__2____0_____0_____
D 5—0___0—0—0_____0____0—0__0__0___2—5—5—2____5_____
G 0_____0___0_____0_____5—5—5_____5_____
```
Oh it's of a brave young highway man this story I will tell,

```
      E      3___3__7—5—3_____3—3____3_____
      A 5___5___5__5__5—5__5___5___5—3—3____3—2—5_____
      D 0___0_____0___0__0__0—2____2—3__0_____
      G 0___0_____0—0—0_____0_____
```


```
      E ___3___3__7—5—3_____3—3____3_____
      A 5—5___5__5__5—5—5___5___5—3—3____3—2—5_____
      D 0—0___0_____0___0__0__0—2____2—3__0____
      G 0_____0_____0—0—0_____0__
                          C            G
```
His name was Willie Brennan and in Ireland he did dwell;

```
                                        C            G
E _____3—3__7—5_____3_____3____3—3_____
A 5—5___5__5__5—5____5—5_____5—5—3_____3—3__2—5_____
D 0—0___0_____0___0__0—2_____2____2—0_____
G 0_____0_____0_____0_____
```
It was on the Kilworth Mountains he commenced his wild career,

```
      C                        G                    D
E ___0—0__0—0___0___0—2—3___0_____0_____
A 5—3—3—3—3___3___3—3—3___3—5___5___2____5___2_____
D 0—2_____2_____2___2___0___0—0___0____0_____
G 0—0_____0_____2_____
```
And many a wealthy nobleman before him shook with fear.

CHORUS

```
      G                    Bm
E _____
A 2___0_____5___5___5—5___5_____
D 0—0___5—5__5—5___5_____4___4___4—4_____
G 2—2___0—0__4—4___4_____4_____
```
And it's Brennan on the moor, Brennan on the moor,

```
      C            G                    D              G
E 0—2—3_____3_____0_____
A 2—2—3___3—5—2__5___2_____0—0_____
D _____2_____0—0__0___0—5___0—0___5—4__5_____
G _____0_____0—0____2_____2—2__0_____
```
Bo-ld, brave and undaunted was young Brennan on the moor.

See Chord Forms and Additional Verses Two Pages Previous

Brennan On the Moor
(continued)

Basic Melody

Key of C

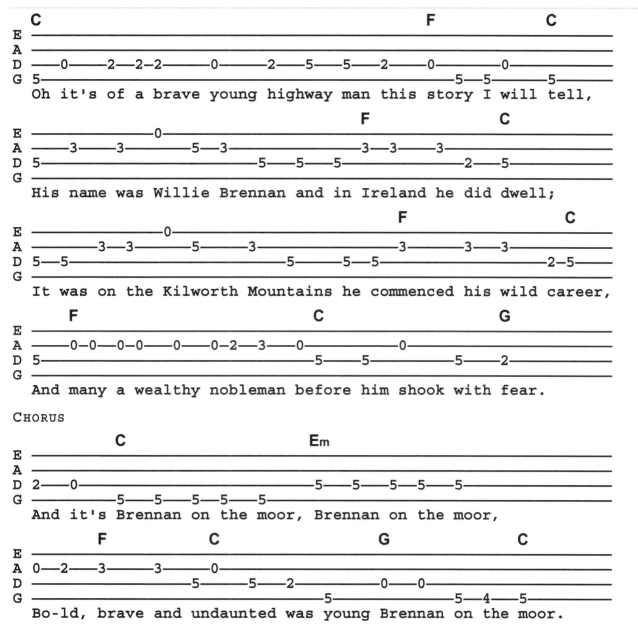

```
        C                                        F           C
E -----------------------------------------------------------------------
A -----------------------------------------------------------------------
D ----0----2--2-2------0----2---5---5---2----0---------0------------------
G 5----------------------------------------------5--5------5--------------
  Oh it's of a brave young highway man this story I will tell,

        C                                        F           C
E --------------------0--------------------------------------------------
A ------3----3------------5---3----------3---3---3------------------------
D 5----------------------------5--5---5-------------2---5----------------
G -----------------------------------------------------------------------
  His name was Willie Brennan and in Ireland he did dwell;

        C                    0                    F           C
E --------------------0--------------------------------------------------
A ------3--3--------5-----3----------------3----3--3--------------------
D 5--5-------------------------5----5--5----------------2-5-------------
G -----------------------------------------------------------------------
  It was on the Kilworth Mountains he commenced his wild career,

        F                    C                    G
E ----------------------------------------------------------------------
A ----0-0---0-0----0---0-2-3----0----------0----------------------------
D 5--------------------------------5----5---------5---2-----------------
G ----------------------------------------------------------------------
  And many a wealthy nobleman before him shook with fear.
```

CHORUS

```
        C                    Em
E ----------------------------------------------------------------------
A ----------------------------------------------------------------------
D 2----0------------------------5---5---5---5---5------------------------
G --------5---5---5--5---5-----------------------------------------------
  And it's Brennan on the moor, Brennan on the moor,

        F           C                    G           C
E ----------------------------------------------------------------------
A 0--2---3----3----0----------------------------------------------------
D ------------5----5---2------------0---0-------------------------------
G -----------------------5-----------------5--4--5--------------------
  Bo-ld, brave and undaunted was young Brennan on the moor.
```

Chord Forms

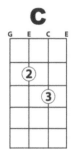
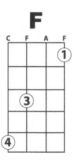
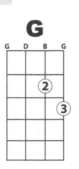
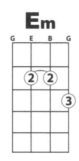

52

Carrickfergus

Carrickfergus is the name of a town in County Antrim in Northern Ireland. This song is based on an old Gaelic song "Do Bhi Bean Uasal", believed to have originated in the southwest of Ireland in County Limerick or County Clare.

Basic Melody
Key of G (Low)

Words and Music
Traditional

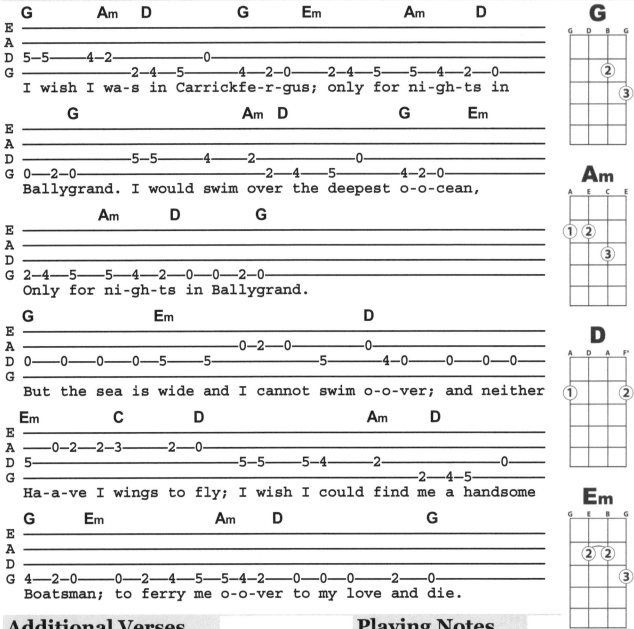

Additional Verses

Now in Kilkenny, it is reported,
They have marble stones there, as black as ink.
With gold and silver, I would support her;
But I'll sing no more now, till I get a drink.
I'm drunk today, and I'm seldom sober.
A handsome rover, from town to town.
Ah but I'm sick now, my days are numbered.
So come all you young men, and lay me down.

Playing Notes

There are several places in the song above where the chord change is indicated in between notes, or at/just past the end of words. This is part of the flowing nature of the song, where the chord change comes during the pause in between words.

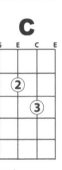

Carrickfergus (continued)

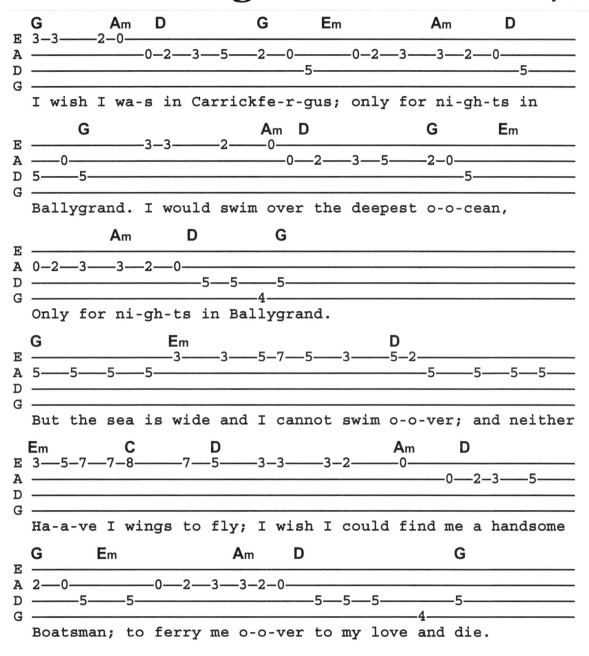

```
       G           Am      D          G          Em              Am          D
E  3—3——————2—0————————————————————————————————————————————————————————————————
A  —————————————————0—2——3—5————2—0————0—2——3———3—2—0————————————————————————————
D  —————————————————————————————5—————————————————————————————5—————
G  ————————————————————————————————————————————————————————————————————
   I wish I wa-s in Carrickfe-r-gus; only for ni-gh-ts in
```

```
                   G                    Am    D          G          Em
E  ———————————————3—3——————2————0————————————————————————————————————————
A  ———0————————————————————————0—2——3—5————2—0————————————————————————————
D  5————5—————————————————————————————————————————5—————————
G  ——————————————————————————————————————————————————————————
   Ballygrand. I would swim over the deepest o-o-cean,
```

```
                Am          D          G
E  ——————————————————————————————————————————————————————————
A  0—2——3———3—2—0——————————————————————————————————————————————
D  ——————————————5——5————5———————————————————————————
G  ——————————————————————4—————————————————————
   Only for ni-gh-ts in Ballygrand.
```

```
   G                   Em                          D
E  ——————————————————3———3——5—7—5——3———5—2———————————————————
A  5———5———5———5————————————————————————5———5——5—5———
D  ——————————————————————————————————————————————————————
G  ——————————————————————————————————————————————————
   But the sea is wide and I cannot swim o-o-ver; and neither
```

```
   Em          C          D                    Am          D
E  3——5—7——7—8————7——5———3—3———3—2——————0————————————————————
A  —————————————————————————————————————0——2—3———5——————
D  ——————————————————————————————————————————————————————
G  ——————————————————————————————————————————————————
   Ha-a-ve I wings to fly; I wish I could find me a handsome
```

```
   G     Em              Am          D                    G
E  ——————————————————————————————————————————————————————————
A  2—0——————————————0—2——3——3—2—0——————————————————————————
D  ——————5————5—————————————————5——5—5————5———————
G  ————————————————————————————————————————4————————
   Boatsman; to ferry me o-o-ver to my love and die.
```

Chord Forms

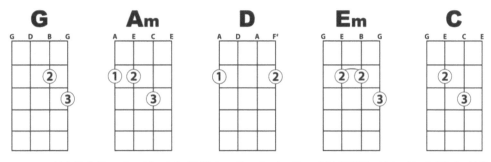

Carrickfergus (continued)

```
      G        Am     D              G        Em            Am          D
E  3—3————————2—0————————————————————————————————————————————————————————————
A  2—2————————2—0———0—2——3——5———2——0—————0—2——3———3—2——0————————————————————
D  0—0——————————2——2—0———0—0————0—0—5———2—2—2———2—2—2——5——————————————————
G  0—0——————————2——2—2————————0——————0———4————————2————————2—2——————————
   I wish I wa-s in Carrickfe-r-gus; only for ni-gh-ts in
```

```
              G                        Am    D              G        Em
E  ————————————————3—3————————2——————0————————————————————————————————————————
A  ———0——————————————2—2————————2————0—0——2———3——5———2—0——————————————————
D  5—0—5——————————0—0————————————————2—2——0———0—0————0—0—5——————————————
G  2—2—0——————————0—0————————————————2—2—2———2————————0——0——————————————
   Ballygrand. I would swim over the deepest o-o-cean,
```

```
              Am          D           G
E  ————————————————————————————————————————————————————————————————————————————
A  0—2——3———3—2——0————————————————————————————————————————————————————————
D  2—2—2———2—2—2—2—5——5—4—5————————————————————————————————————————————————
G  4——————————2——————2—2—2—2—0————————————————————————————————————————————
   Only for ni-gh-ts in Ballygrand.
```

```
      G              Em                          D
E  ——————————————————3———3——5—7—5———3————5—2——————————————————————————————
A  5——5——5——5——2———2——5—5——5———2————0—0—5———5——5—5————————————————————————
D  0——0——0——0—2———2————5——————————0——————0——————0——0—0——————————————————
G  0———————0————————0————————————————————————2————2——2————————————————————
   But the sea is wide and I cannot swim o-o-ver; and neither
```

```
   Em            C          D                      Am         D
E  3—5—7——7—8————————7—5———3—3————3—2————0————————————————————————————————
A  2—5—5——5—7————5—5———5—5————5—0————0———0—2—3———5————————————————————————
D  2————5———7————————0———0—0——————————2————2—0—0——4——————————————————————
G  0————————————————————————————————————2————2—2——————————————————————————
   Ha-a-ve I wings to fly; I wish I could find me a handsome
```

```
   G      Em            Am      D              G
E  —————————————————————————————————————————————————————————————————————————
A  2—0————————————0—2——3——3—2—0——————————————————————————————————————————
D  0—0—5————5—2——2—2——2—2—2—2———5—5—5———4——5——————————————————————————————
G  0———0——4—4————————2—2—2—2—2——————2——0————————————————————————————————
   Boatsman; to ferry me o-o-ver to my love and die.
```

Chord Forms

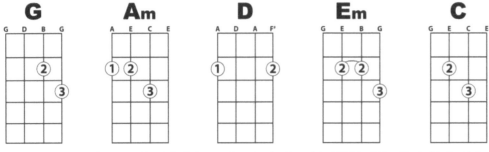

Carrickfergus (continued)

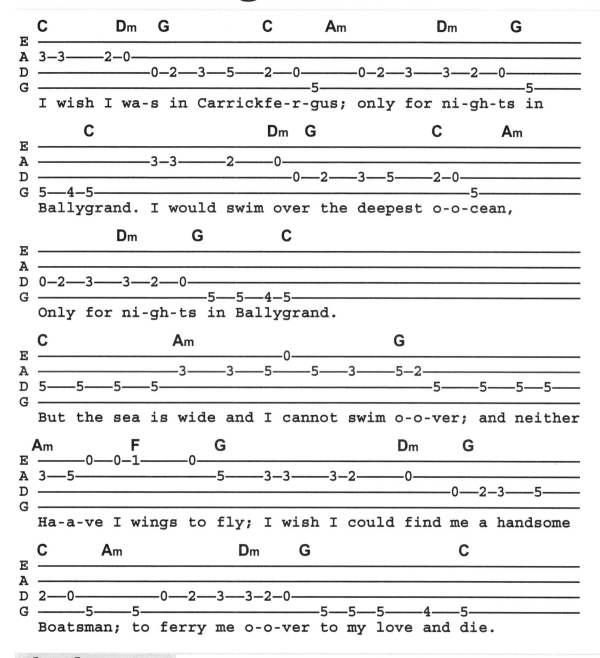

```
      C        Dm   G          C        Am          Dm        G
E ------------------------------------------------------------------------
A 3-3-----2-0------------------------------------------------------------
D --------------0-2---3---5----2---0-----0-2---3---3---2---0---------------
G --------------------------5--------------------------------5-----------
  I wish I wa-s in Carrickfe-r-gus; only for ni-gh-ts in
```

```
          C                    Dm   G          C        Am
E ------------------------------------------------------------------------
A ---------3-3------2------0----------------------------------------------
D ----------------------------0-2---3---5----2-0-------------------------
G 5---4-5-----------------------------------------5----------------------
  Ballygrand. I would swim over the deepest o-o-cean,
```

```
          Dm       G        C
E ------------------------------------------------------------------------
A ------------------------------------------------------------------------
D 0-2---3---3---2---0----------------------------------------------------
G ------------5---5---4-5------------------------------------------------
  Only for ni-gh-ts in Ballygrand.
```

```
  C                Am                     G
E --------------------------------0-------------------------------------
A --------------3-----3---5-----5---3-----5-2----------------------------
D 5----5----5----5----------------------------5----5----5---5-----------
G ----------------------------------------------------------------------
  But the sea is wide and I cannot swim o-o-ver; and neither
```

```
  Am        F        G                Dm       G
E -------0---0-1-----0---------------------------------------------------
A 3---5-----------------5----3-3-----3-2-----0--------------------------
D --------------------------------------------0---2-3----5--------------
G ----------------------------------------------------------------------
  Ha-a-ve I wings to fly; I wish I could find me a handsome
```

```
  C        Am              Dm       G          C
E ----------------------------------------------------------------------
A ----------------------------------------------------------------------
D 2-0-------------0-2---3---3-2-0----------------------------------------
G ----5-----5---------------------5-5-5-----4---5-----------------------
  Boatsman; to ferry me o-o-ver to my love and die.
```

Chord Forms

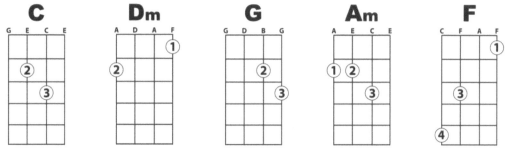

Carrickfergus (continued)

```
      C        Dm   G          C        Am           Dm        G
E ————————————————————————————————————————————————————————————————————
A 3—3———————2—0————————————————————————————————————————————————————————
D 2—2———————2—0———0—2———3———5———2—0—————————0—2———3———3—2—0————————————
G 0—0———————————2—2—0———0—0———5———5—5———2—2—2———2—2—2—2—5——————————————
  I wish I wa-s in Carrickfe-r-gus; only for ni-gh-ts in
```

```
         C                      Dm  G           C        Am
E ——————————————————————————————————————————————————————————————————————
A ——————3———————————3—3———————2———————0—————————————————————————————————
D ——————0—2—————————2—2———————2———————0—0———2———3———5———2—0——————————————
G 5———0—5———————————0—0———————————————2—2———0———0—0———5—5—5——————————————
  Ballygrand. I would swim over the deepest o-o-cean,
```

```
         Dm       G           C
E ——————————————————————————————————————————————————————————————————————
A ————————————————————————————3—————————————————————————————————————————
D 0—2———3———3—2—0——————————0—2——————————————————————————————————————————
G 2—2———2———2—2—2—2—5———5—4—5———————————————————————————————————————————
  Only for ni-gh-ts in Ballygrand.
```

```
  C             Am                        G
E ———————————————————————————0——————————————————————————————————————————
A ——————————————3———————3———5—3———5———3———5—2————————————————————————————
D 5———5———5———5—2———2———2—2—2———2———0—0—5———5———5—5——————————————————————
G 5———5———5———5—2———————————————————————0———0———0———0—0—————————————————
  But the sea is wide and I cannot swim o-o-ver; and neither
```

```
  Am        F         G                    Dm        G
E ————————0—0—1———————0——————————————————————————————————————————————————
A 3—5—0———0—0—————————0—5———3—3———3—2———0———————————————————————————————
D 2—2—2———2—3—————————2—0———0—2———2—2———0———0—2—3———5———————————————————
G 2———————2———————————0———————0———————0———2———2—0—0———0————————————————
  Ha-a-ve I wings to fly; I wish I could find me a handsome
```

```
  C        Am        Dm        G              C
E ——————————————————————————————————————————3—————————————————————————
A ——————————————————————————————————————————3—————————————————————————
D 2—0——————————0—2—3———3—2—0————————0—0——————2—————————————————————————
G 5—5—5————————5—2—2———2—2—2—2———5—4—4———4———5—————————————————————————
  Boatsman; to ferry me o-o-ver to my love and die.
```

Chord Forms

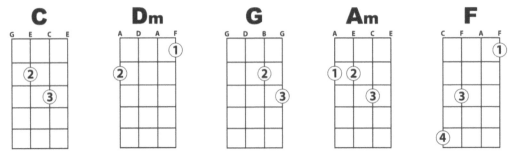

Courtin' In the Kitchen

Basic Melody
Key of C

The Clancy Brothers and Tommy Makem helped revitalize this old song which tells the tale of a love-on-the-sly gone wrong. The would-be beau of the song ends up serving six months in jail over his ill-fated wooing attempts.

Words and Music
Traditional

```
        C                                          G
E  ──────────────────────────────────────────────────────────────
A  ──────────────────────────────────────────────────────────────
D  5──────2──────────────────────────5─2────────────0─────────────
G  ───────────5──5────5──5────────────────5──5──5─4──────────────
   Come single belle and beau, unto me pay attention:
```

```
        C                            F           G
E  ──────────────────────────────────────────────────────────────
A  ──────────────────────────────────────────────────────────────
D  5──────2──────────────0──2──3─2──────0──────────0──────────────
G  ───────────5──5────5──5────────────────────────5─4────────────
   Don't ever fall in love, tis the devil's own invention.
```

```
        C
E  ──────────────────────────────────────────────────────────────
A  ──────────────────────────────────────────────────────────────
D  ──────────2─5────5──5────5────2────2──5──5─2──5─────────────────
G  5──────5───────────────────5───────────────────────────────────
   For once I fell in love, with a maiden so bewitchin',
```

```
        F                    Dm          G
E  ──────────────────────────────────────────────────────────────
A  ────0──0──────────────────────────────────────────────────────
D  5──────────5─2──3──────0──2──3─2──────0──────────0─────────────
G  ───────────────────────────────────────5──────4───────────────
   Miss Henrietta Bell out of Captain Kelly's kitchen.
```

CHORUS

```
        C                                          G
E  ──────────────────────────────────────────────────────────────
A  ──────────────────────────────────────────────────────────────
D  5──────5─2────────────────────5─2─────────────0───────────────
G  ───────────5──5────5──5─────────────5──5──5─4──────────────────
   With me too-ra-loo-ra-lal, me too-ra-loo-ra-laddy,
```

```
        C                    G           C
E  ──────────────────────────────────────────────────────────────
A  ──────────────────────────0────────────────────────────────────
D  5──────5─2────────────────5──────5──3─2────────────────────────
G  ───────────5──5────5──5─────────────────────5──────────────────
   With me too-ra-loo-ra-lal, too-ra-loo-ra-laddy.
```

See Additional Verses on Next Page

Courtin' In the Kitchen

(continued)

Additional Verses

At the age of seventeen,
I was 'prenticed to a grocer,
Not far from Stephen's Green,
Where Miss Henry used to go sir;
Her manners were sublime,
And she set my heart a-twitchin'
And she invited me
To a hoolie in the kitchen.

Next Sunday bein' the day
That we were to have the flare-up,
I dressed myself quite gay,
And I frizzed and oiled me hair up.
The captain had no wife,
And he had gone a-fishin',
And we kicked up high life,
Down below stairs in the kitchen.

With her arms around me waist,
She slyly hinted marriage,
When to the door in dreadful haste,
Came Captain Kelly's carriage.
Her eyes they filled with hate,
And poison she was spittin',
When the captain at the door
Walked straight into the kitchen.

She flew up off me knees
Full five feet up or higher,
And over head and heels
Threw me slap into the fire.
Me brand new peeler's coat,
That I bought from Mr. Mitchell,
With a twenty shilling note,
Went to blazes in the kitchen.

Well I grieved to see me duds
All smeared with soot and ashes,
When a tub of dirty suds
Right in me face she dashes.
As I lay on the floor,
The water she kept pitchin',
The footman broke the door
And walked straight into the kitchen.

When the captain came downstairs,
Though he saw me situation;
In spite of all my prayers,
I was marched off to the station.
For me they'd take no bail,
Though to get home I was itchin',
And I had to tell the tale,
How I came into the kitchen.

I said she did invite me,
But she gave a flat denial.
For assault she did indict me,
And I was sent to trial.
She swore I robbed the house,
In spite of all her screechin',
And I got six months hard,
For me courtin' in the kitchen.

An Irish farmhouse kitchen scene

Courtin' In the Kitchen
(continued)

Basic Melody

Key of G

```
       G                                           D
E  ----------------------------------------------------------------
A  5------2--------------------------5-2----------------0----------
D  ----------5--5------5---5------------------5--5--5-4-------------
G  ----------------------------------------------------------------
```
Come single belle and beau, unto me pay attention:

```
       G                        C              D
E  ----------------------------------------------------------------
A  5------2------------------0--2--3-2------0--------0-------------
D  ----------5--5------5--5------------------------5-4-------------
G  ----------------------------------------------------------------
```
Don't ever fall in love, tis the devil's own invention.

```
       G
E  ----------------------------------------------------------------
A  ----------2-5------5--5------5----2----2--5--5-2--5------------
D  5------5---------------------------5----------------------------
G  ----------------------------------------------------------------
```
For once I fell in love, with a maiden so bewitchin',

```
       C                       Am          D
E  -------0--0-----------------------------------------------------
A  5----------------5-2--3------0--2--3--2------0--------0---------
D  ----------------------------------------5------4----------------
G  ----------------------------------------------------------------
```
Miss Henrietta Bell out of Captain Kelly's kitchen.

CHORUS

```
       G                                           D
E  ----------------------------------------------------------------
A  5------5--2------------------5-2--------------------0----------
D  ----------5--5------5--5------------5--5--5-4--------------------
G  ----------------------------------------------------------------
```
With me too-ra-loo-ra-lal, me too-ra-loo-ra-laddy,

```
       G                        D              G
E  ----------------------------------0----------------------------
A  5------5--2------------------5-------5--3--2-------------------
D  ----------5--5------5--5-----------------------5----------------
G  ----------------------------------------------------------------
```
With me too-ra-loo-ra-lal, too-ra-loo-ra-laddy.
```

G
G D B G
②
③

D
A D A F♯
① ②

C
G E C E
②
③

Am
A E C E
① ②
③

For whenever you're into the liquor, me lads, beware
of the pretty colleens...

*Traditional Irish Song Lyric*

60
```

Courtin' In the Kitchen

(continued)

Melody & Chords

Key of G

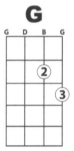

```
      G                                    D
E ─────────────────────────────────────────────────────────
A 5─────2─────────────────────5─2─────────────────0─────────
D 0─────0───5──5─────5───5─────0─0─5──5────5─4──0───────────
G 0─────0───0──0─────0───0─────0─0─0──0────0─2──2───────────
```
Come single belle and beau, unto me pay attention:

```
        G                             C               D
E ─────────────────────────────────────────────────────────
A 5─────2──────────────0────2───3─2────────0──────────0─────
D 0─────0─5──5─────5──5─────0───0──2─2──────2──5─4──0────────
G 2─────0─0──0─────0──0─────0───0──────0────0──5─2──2────────
```
Don't ever fall in love, tis the devil's own invention.

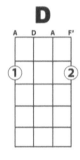

```
        G
E ─────────────────────────────────────────────────────────
A ───────────2─5─────5──5─────5────2────2───5─5─2──5─────────
D 5─────5────0─0─────0──0─────0────0─5──0───0─0─0──0─────────
G 0─────0──────0────────0──────────0──────0──────0──────────
```
For once I fell in love, with a maiden so bewitchin',

```
        C                 Am              D
E ────0──0───────────────────────────────────────────────
A 5─────3──3─5─2──3─────0────2─3──2─────0──────────0───────
D 0─────2────2─2──2─────2────2─2──2─────2──5─────4──0──────
G 0─────0────────0──────2────2─2──────2──2───────2──2──────
```
Miss Henrietta Bell out of Captain Kelly's kitchen.

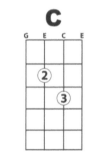

CHORUS

```
        G                                    D
E ─────────────────────────────────────────────────────────
A 5────5───2─────────────────5──2────────────────0──────────
D 0────0───0───5──5─────5──5─────0─0──5──5────5─4──0─────────
G 2────────0───0──0─────0──0─────0─0──0──0────0─2──2─────────
```
With me too-ra-loo-ra-lal, me too-ra-loo-ra-laddy,

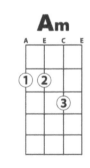

```
        G                 D               G
E ──────────────────────────────0──────────────────────────
A 5────5───2────────────────5───0─5──3──2───────────────────
D 0────0───0───5──5─────5──5─────0──────0──0──0──5───────────
G 2────────0───0──0─────0──0─────2──────2──────2──0──────────
```
With me too-ra-loo-ra-lal, too-ra-loo-ra-laddy.

Courtin' In the Kitchen

Basic Melody

Key of C (High)

(continued)

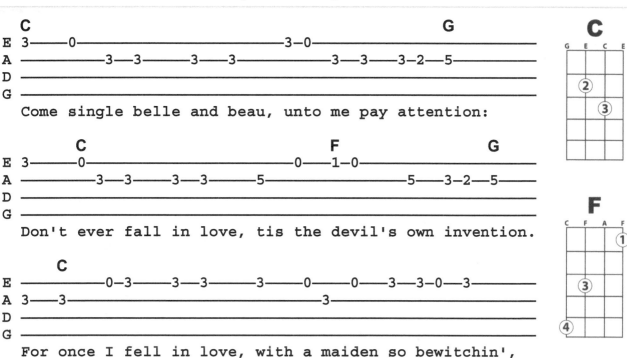

Come single belle and beau, unto me pay attention:

Don't ever fall in love, tis the devil's own invention.

For once I fell in love, with a maiden so bewitchin',

Miss Henrietta Bell out of Captain Kelly's kitchen.

CHORUS

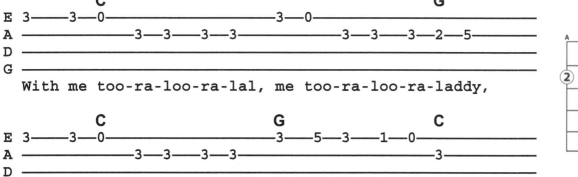

With me too-ra-loo-ra-lal, me too-ra-loo-ra-laddy,

With me too-ra-loo-ra-lal, too-ra-loo-ra-laddy.

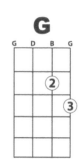
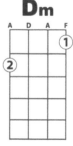

Courtin' In the Kitchen

(continued)

Melody & Chords

Key of C (High)

```
         C                                          G
E  3————0————————————————————————3—0————————————————————
A  3————3———3———3————————3————3————3—3———3———3————3—2—5——
D  2————2———2———2————————2————2————2—2———2———2————2—2—0——
G  0————0———————0————————0——————————0————————0————0—————
```
Come single belle and beau, unto me pay attention:

```
         C                          F              G
E  3————0————————————————————————0————1—0————————————————
A  3————3—3———3————3———3————5————3————3—3————5————3—2—5——
D  2————2—2———2————2———2————3————————3————————3————3—3—0—
G  0————0———0————0————————————————————————————————0—————
```
Don't ever fall in love, tis the devil's own invention.

```
          C
E  ——————————0—3————3—3————————3————0————0————3—3—0——3—
A  3————3————3—3————3—3————————3————3—3———3————3—3—3——3—
D  0————2————2————————2————————————2————————2————2—2——2—
G  0————0————0————————0————————————0—————————————————————
```
For once I fell in love, with a maiden so bewitchin',

```
          F                       Dm             G
E  3————5—5—3—0——1————————————0——1—0————————————————————
A  3————3—3—3—3————3————5————3——3—3————5————3————2—5——————
D  2————3————3————3————3————————0——————3———3————0—0——————
G  ————————————————————————————————————2————————0—0——————
```
Miss Henrietta Bell out of Captain Kelly's kitchen.

CHORUS

```
            C                                         G
E  3————3———0————————————————————3———0————————————————————
A  3————3———3———3———3————3———3————3———3———3———3————3—2—5——
D  2————2———2———2———2————2———2————2———2———2———2————2—0—0——
G  0————————0———————0————————0————0————————————0————0—0——
```
With me too-ra-loo-ra-lal, me too-ra-loo-ra-laddy,

```
            C                     G                 C
E  3————3———0————————————————————3———5—3————1—0——————————
A  2————2———3———3———3————3———3————2———2—2————2—2———3——————
D  0————————2———2———2————2———2————0————————0————————2——————
G  0————————0————————0————————0————0—————————————————————
```
With me too-ra-loo-ra-lal, too-ra-loo-ra-laddy.

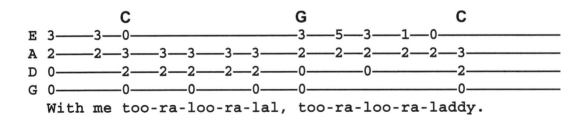

Danny Boy

Basic Melody
Key of C

This is one of the best known of the Irish love ballads, and its melancholy setting and soaring melody is a favorite of both singers and instrumentalists. The words were first published in 1913, and are set to an ancient Irish tune known as the Londonderry Air. This song remains popular with Irish-Americans and Irish-Canadians, and is also one of the unofficial anthems of Northern Ireland.

Words by Frederic Weatherly

Music Traditional

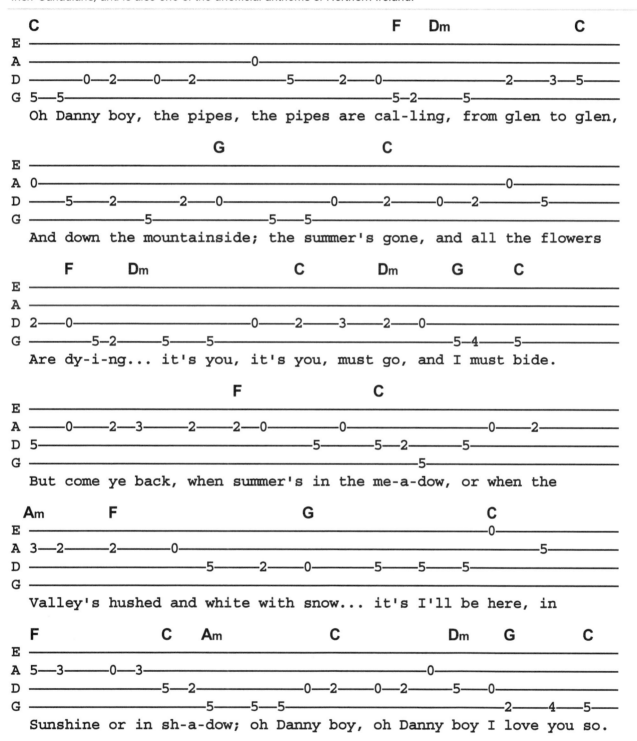

See Chords and Additional Verses on Next Page

Danny Boy (continued)

Additional Verse

And if you come, and all the flowers are dying;
And I am dead, as dead I well may be.
You'll come and find the place where I am lying,
And you will say an Ave there for me.
And I will hear those soft footsteps above me;
And all my grave will warmer, sweeter be...
And then you'll kneel, and tell me that you love me,
And I will sleep in peace until you come to me.

Chord Forms

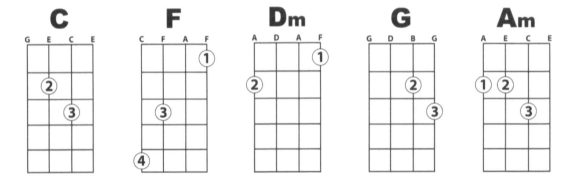

Ross Castle, Killarney, Ireland

Danny Boy (continued)

Melody & Chords

Key of C

```
      C                                    F   Dm              C
E ──────────────────────────────────────────────────────────────────
A ────────────────────────────0───────────────────────────────────────
D ──────0──2────0──2────────2──5────2──0──3──────3────2──3──5──────────
G 5──5──0──5────5──5──────5──5──────5──2-5-2────5────5────5──5────────
  Oh Danny boy, the pipes, the pipes are cal-ling, from glen to glen,

                    G              C
E ──────────────────────────────────────────────────────────────────
A 0──────────────────────────────────────────0──────────────────────
D 2──5────2──────2──0──────────0────2────0──2──2──5────────────────────
G 5──5────5──5──5──0────5──5──0────5────5──5──5──5────────────────────
  And down the mountainside; the summer's gone, and all the flowers

      F   Dm                  C        Dm    G    C
E ──────────────────────────────────────────────────────────────────
A ──────────────────────────────────────3───────────────────────────
D 2──0────3──────────0──2────3──2──0──0-0────2────────────────────────
G 5──2-5-2────5──────5──2──5──5──2──2──5-4────5──────────────────────
  Are dy-i-ng... it's you, it's you, must go, and I must bide.

                    F              C
E ──────────────────────────────────────────────────────────────────
A ──0────2──3────2────2──0────────0────────────0────2────────────────
D 5──2────0──2────2──3──3────5──3──5──2────5──2────2──────────────────
G 5────────────0──────2────2──2──5──5-5──5──5────────────────────────
  But come ye back, when summer's in the me-a-dow, or when the

  Am    F                    G                    C
E ──────────────────────────────────────────────0──────────────────
A 3──2────2────0────────────────────────3────5──────────────────────
D 2──2────3────3──5────2──0────────5──5──5──2────2──────────────────
G 2────────2────5──2──0──────4──0──0-0────────────────────────────
  Valley's hushed and white with snow... it's I'll be here, in

  F          C  Am          C              Dm    G    C
E ──────────────────────────────────────────────────────────────────
A 5──3────0──3────────────────────0──────────────────3──────────────
D 3──3────3──3──5──2──────0──2──0──2──2──5──0-0────0──2──────────────
G 2────────5──2-5──5──5──5──5────5──5──5──2──2-2────4──5────────────
  Sunshine or in sh-a-dow; oh Danny boy, oh Danny boy I love you so.
```

Danny Boy (continued)

Basic Melody
Key of G

```
        G                                           C    Am              G
E ─────────────────────────────────0──────────────────────────────────────────
A ──────0──2────0──2───────5──2──0──────────────────────2──3──5──────────
D 5──5────────────────────────────────5─2──────5──────────────────────────
G ──────────────────────────────────────────────────────────────────────────
```
Oh Danny boy, the pipes, the pipes are cal-ling, from glen to glen,

```
                   D              G
E 0───────────────────────────────────────────0──────────
A ────5──2────2──0──────0──2───0──2────5──────────────────
D ──────────5────────5──5──────────────────────────────────
G ───────────────────────────────────────────────────────
```
And down the mountainside; the summer's gone, and all the flowers

```
    C       Am                    G     Am      D    G
E ─────────────────────────────────────────────────────────
A 2──0────────────────0──2──3──2──0──────────────────────────
D ──────5─2────5────5──────────────────5─4────5──────────────
G ─────────────────────────────────────────────────────────
```
Are dy-i-ng... it's you, it's you, must go, and I must bide.

```
                              C              G
E ──────0──2──3────2────2──0──────0──────────────0──2────────
A 5──────────────────────────5────5─2────5──────────────────
D ──────────────────────────────────────5──────────────────
G ─────────────────────────────────────────────────────────
```
But come ye back, when summer's in the me-a-dow, or when the

```
  Em      C              D              G
E 3─2────2────0──────────────────────────7────5──────────────
A ────────────5──2──0──5────5────5──────────────────────────
D ─────────────────────────────────────────────────────────
G ─────────────────────────────────────────────────────────
```
Valley's hushed and white with snow... it's I'll be here, in

```
  C         G   Em              G         Am    D    G
E 5─3────0──3─────────────────────0──────────────────────────
A ──────────5──2──────0──2──0──2──5──0──────────────────────
D ──────────5────5──5───────────────────2────4──5───────────
G ─────────────────────────────────────────────────────────
```
Sunshine or in sh-a-dow; oh Danny boy, oh Danny boy I love you so.

Chord Forms

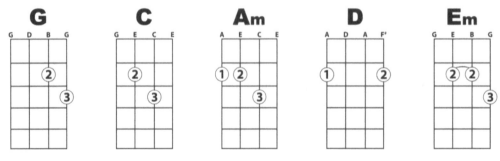

Danny Boy (continued)

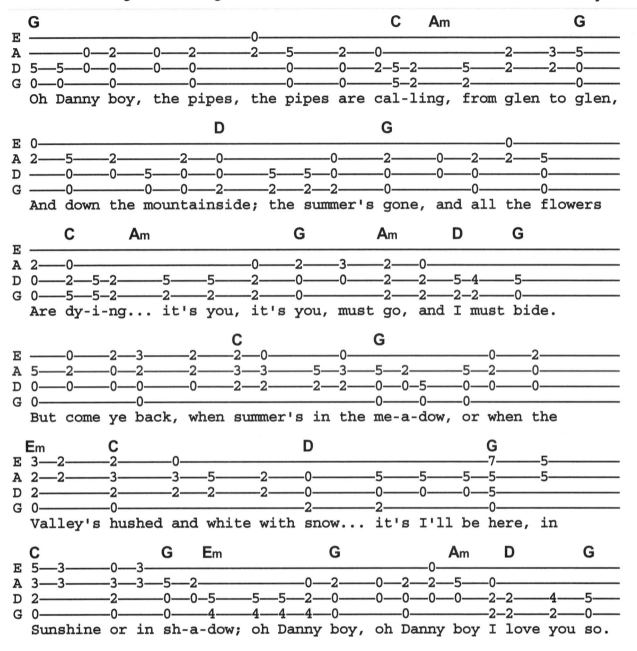

Chord Forms

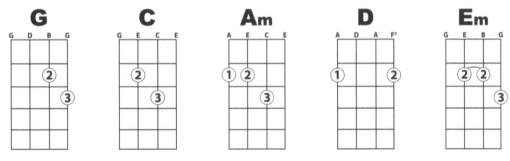

Donkey Riding

Basic Melody
Key of Em

This old work song appeared in the mid 1800's, and is based on the older Scottish song "Bonnie Hieland Laddie." The "donkey" in the song is thought to be an old "steam donkey" steam-powered winch engine used for logging and other hard work, rather than the farm animal. This is a great song for belting out while downing a few pints of beer with friends.

Words and Music

Traditional

```
     Em              C   G                        D
E  ———————————————————————————————————————————————————————————
A  ————————2—2——3—0——2————2——0——————0————————2—0——0———
D  2————5————————————————————————————5——————————————5—
G  ———————————————————————————————————————————————————————————
   Was you ever in Quebec, launching timber on the deck,
```

```
     Em                  C     G   D        Em
E  ———————————————————————————————————————————————————————————
A  ————————2————2——3—0——2————2————0——————————————
D  2———————5———————————————————————5————4—2——2——
G  ———————————————————————————————————————————————————————————
   Where ya break yer bleedin' neck, riding on a donkey.
```

CHORUS

```
   C  G     C     G  Em           D
E  0———————————————————————————————————————————————————————
A  ————5———3—3——5—2——2——0——0————2—0——0———
D  ——————————————————————5——————————5———————
G  ———————————————————————————————————————————————————————
   Way hey a-way we go, donkey riding donkey riding,
```

```
   C  G     C     G  D        Em
E  0———————————————————————————————————————————————————————
A  ————5———3—3——5—2——2————0———————————————
D  ——————————————————5————4—2——2————
G  ———————————————————————————————————————————————————————
   Way hey a-way we go, riding on a donkey.
```

Additional Verses

Was you ever 'round Cape Horn, where the weather's never warm,
Wish to God you'd never been born, riding on a donkey.

Was you ever in Miramichi, where they tie you to a tree,
Have a girl sit on your knee, riding on a donkey.

Was you ever in Fortune Bay, hear the girls all shout hurray,
Here comes Jack with last month's pay, riding on a donkey.

Was you ever in Fredericton, see the king he does come down,
See the king in his golden crown, riding on a donkey.

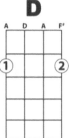

Donkey Riding (continued)

Melody & Chords
Key of Em

```
      Em              C     G                       D
E ————————————————————————————————————————————————————————————————
A ——————————2—2——3—0—2———————2———0————————0————————2—0——0————
D 2————5——2—2——2——2——0————————0———0————————0—5——0——0———0—5——
G 4————4——4———0———————0———————0———————————————0———2————2—2—
      Was  you  ever  in  Quebec,  launching  timber  on  the  deck,
```

```
      Em                      C        G     D           Em
E ————————————————————————————————————————————————————————————————
A ——————————————2——————2——3——0————2———————2—————0———————————
D 2——————5——2———————2——2——2——0————————0—5——————0—4—2——2——
G 4——————4—4————————0————————0————————2—2———2—2—4——4——
      Where  ya  break  yer  bleedin'  neck,  riding  on  a  donkey.
```

CHORUS

```
      C    G      C        G   Em              D
E 0————————————————————————————————————————————————————————————————
A 3————5——3—3————5——2———2——0————0————————2—0——0—————————————
D 2————0——0—2————2——0——2——2————2—5——————2—0——0—5————————
G 0————0————0————————0——4————————4—4————4———————2—2————
      Way  hey  a-way  we  go,  donkey  riding  donkey  riding,
```

```
      C    G      C     G     D           Em
E 0————————————————————————————————————————————————————————————————
A 3————5——3—3————5——2———2——————0——————————————————————————
D 2————0——2—2————2——0——0—5———0—4—2——2————————————————
G 0————0————0————————0——2—2——2—2—4——4————————————————
      Way  hey  a-way  we  go,  riding  on  a  donkey.
```

Chord Forms

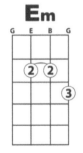
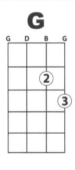
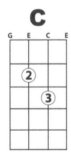
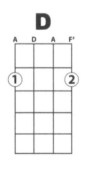

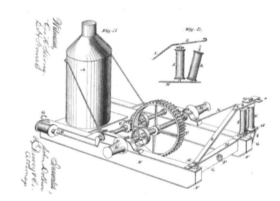

*Diagram from an 1882
steam donkey patent.*

Donkey Riding (continued)

Basic Melody
Key of Am (Low)

```
     Am              F    C                   G
E  ────────────────────────────────────────────────────────
A  ────────────────────────────────────────────────────────
D  ──────────2─2──3──0──2─────2───0──────0───────2──0────0───
G  2────5────────────────────────────────5──────────────5───
   Was you ever in Quebec, launching timber on the deck,
```

```
     Am                      F         C    G         Am
E  ────────────────────────────────────────────────────────
A  ────────────────────────────────────────────────────────
D  ──────────2──────2──3──0─────2─────2──────0───────────────
G  2────5───────────────────────────5──────────4─2──2───────
   Where ya break yer bleedin' neck, riding on a donkey.
```

CHORUS

```
   F  C     F     C  Am            G
E  ────────────────────────────────────────────────────────
A  0───────────────────────────────────────────────────────
D  ──5───3─3──5──2───2──0──0──────2──0────0──────────────────
G  ───────────────────5──────────────5──────────────────────
   Way hey a-way we go, donkey riding donkey riding,
```

```
   F  C     F     C  G       Am
E  ────────────────────────────────────────────────────────
A  0───────────────────────────────────────────────────────
D  ──5───3─3──5──2───2─────0──────────────────────────────────
G  ───────────────5──────4─2──2──────────────────────────────
   Way hey a-way we go, riding on a donkey.
```

Chord Forms

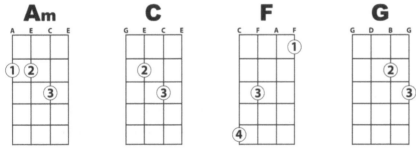

Donkey Riding (continued)

Basic Melody
Key of Am (High)

```
      Am              F      C                    G
E ——————————0—0——1————0————0———————————————0——————————
A 0————3——————————5————————5————5—3————5———5——3—
D ——————————————————————————————————————————————
G ——————————————————————————————————————————————
```
Was you ever in Quebec, launching timber on the deck,

```
      Am                  F      C    G        Am
E ——————————0————0——1————0————0—————————————————
A 0————3——————————————5——————————3————5—2—0——0——
D ——————————————————————————————————————————————
G ——————————————————————————————————————————————
```
Where ya break yer bleedin' neck, riding on a donkey.

CHORUS

```
  F    C    F      C  Am              G
E 5——3——1—1——3—0——0—————————0——————————
A ————————————————5——5—3————5——5—3————
D ——————————————————————————————————————
G ——————————————————————————————————————
```
Way hey a-way we go, donkey riding donkey riding,

```
  F    C    F      C  G        Am
E 5——3——1—1——3—0——0——————————————
A ————————————————3——5—2—0——0——————
D ——————————————————————————————————
G ——————————————————————————————————
```
Way hey a-way we go, riding on a donkey.

Chord Forms

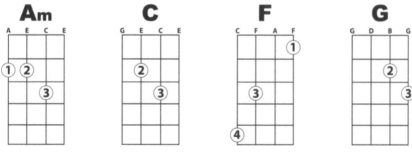

Donkey Riding (continued)

Melody & Chords
Key of Am (High)

```
   Am                    F     C                        G
E ——————————0—0——1————0————0——————————————————0—————————
A 0————3——0—0——0—5—3————3—5——————5—3——2—5——5—3—
D 2——2——2—2—0—3—2————2——2——————2—2——0—0——0—0—
G 2————————2——————0——————————————————0————0——
```
Was you ever in Quebec, launching timber on the deck,

```
   Am                    F        C      G        Am
E ——————————0——————0——1————0————0——————————————
A 0————3——0——————0—0—5————3——2-3——5—2-0—0——
D 2————2—2——————2—3—5————2——0-0——0—0-2—2——
G 2————2——————————5————————0————0——————0—2—2——
```
Where ya break yer bleedin' neck, riding on a donkey.

CHORUS

```
   F   C      F      C  Am                  G
E 5——3——1-1——3—0——0——————————0—————————
A 0——3——0-0——0—3——0—5——5-3——0—5——5-3——
D 3——2——0——————2—2—2——2-2——2—0——0-0——
G ——————————————0—2————2——2————0——
```
Way hey a-way we go, donkey riding donkey riding,

```
   F   C      F      C  G              Am
E 5——3——1-1——3—0——0——————————————————
A 0——3——0-0——0—3——2-3——5—2-0—0——
D 3——2——0——————2—0-0——0—0-2—2——
G ——————————————0—0————0—2—2——
```
Way hey a-way we go, riding on a donkey.

Chord Forms

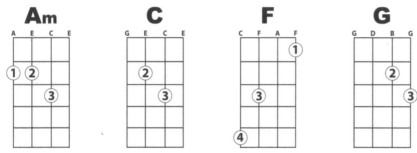

Finnegan's Wake (page 1)

Basic Melody
Key of C

This is one of the quintessential Irish drinking songs, covering most of the favorite Irish topics in one go: living, dying, drinking and fighting. It tells the tale of Tim Finnegan's revival in the middle of his own funeral. The song is said to have been the inspiration for James Joyce's novel of the same name. The version by the Dubliners is perhaps the best-known, and it has been recorded more recently by the Irish-American band Dropkick Murphys.

Words and Music

Traditional

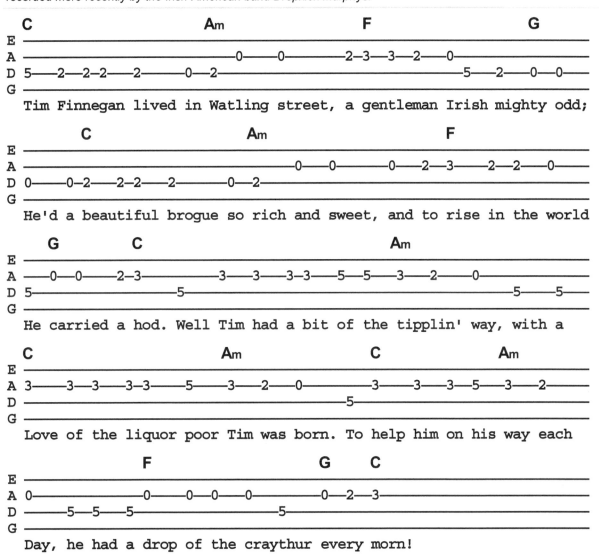

Tim Finnegan lived in Watling street, a gentleman Irish mighty odd;

He'd a beautiful brogue so rich and sweet, and to rise in the world

He carried a hod. Well Tim had a bit of the tipplin' way, with a

Love of the liquor poor Tim was born. To help him on his way each

Day, he had a drop of the craythur every morn!

Chord Forms

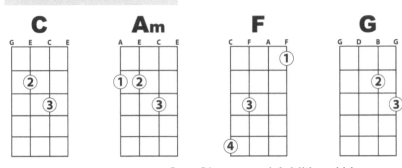

See Chorus and Additional Verses on Next Page

Finnegan's Wake (page 2)

Basic Melody
Key of C

CHORUS

```
         C                           Am
E  ———————————————————————————————————————————————————————
A  ——————————————————————————————0———0——0———2——————————————
D  2———————2——2-2——0———0—2————————————————————————————————
G  ———————————————————————————————————————————————————————
```
Whack-fol-a-dol will ye dance with yer partners,

```
         F              G              C
E  ———————————————————————————————————————————————————————
A  3———————2——0————————————————————————————————————————————
D  —————————————————5——2——0———0————————2——2-2—0—————————————
G  ———————————————————————————————————————————————————————
```
Round the floor yer trotters shake. Wasn't it the

```
   Am              F              G              C
E  ———————————————————————————————————————————————————————
A  ——————0—0————2——3————2—0————————0——0-2———————3——————————
D  2——————————————————————————————5————————————————————————
G  ———————————————————————————————————————————————————————
```
Truth I told ya lots of fun at Finnegan's wake!

Additional Verse

One mornin' Tim felt rather full,
His head felt heavy, which made him shake.
He fell off the ladder and he broke his skull,
And they carried him home his corpse to wake.
They rolled him up in a nice clean sheet,
And laid him out upon the bed,
With a gallon of whiskey at his feet,
And a barrel of porter at his head.

His friends assembled at the wake,
And Mrs. Finnegan called for lunch.
First they brought in tea and cake,
Then pipes, tobacco and whiskey punch.
Biddy O'Brien began to cry,
"Such a nice clean corpse did you ever see?
Tim mavourneen why did you die?"
"Get ahold a your gob" said Biddy McGee.

Then Maggie O'Connor took up the job,
"O Biddy, " says she, "You're wrong I'm sure."
Biddy gave her a belt on the gob,
And left her sprawling on the floor.
Then the war did soon engage,
It was woman to woman and man to man;
Shillelagh law was all the rage,
And a row and a ruction soon began.

Then Mickey Maloney raised his head
When a noggin of whiskey flew at him
It missed and landed on the bed,
And the liquor scattered over Tim;
Well be-God, see how he rises...
Timothy rising from the bed,
Sayin' "Fling your whiskey around like blazes,
Thundering jays, do you think I'm dead?"

Finnegan's Wake
(continued)

Melody & Chords

Key of C

```
     C                    Am                F              G
E ————————————————————————————————————————————————————————————————
A ——————————————————————0———————0———————2—3——3——2————0——————————————
D 5———2——2-2————2——————0—2——2—————2———————2—3——3——3————3-5——2————0——0——
G 5———5——5-5————5——————0—5————————5——————————2————————2——2———0——0——
  Tim Finnegan lived in Watling street, a gentleman Irish mighty odd;
```

```
        C                    Am                 F
E ————————————————————————————————————————————————————————————————
A ——————————————————————————0———0————0——2——3————2—2———0—————————
D 0———0-2———2-2————2———————0—2—————2———2————2——3————3——3———3—————
G 0———0-5———5-5————5———————0—5—————————5—————————2——————————————
  He'd a beautiful brogue so rich and sweet, and to rise in the world
```

```
     G          C                                 Am
E ————————————————————————————————————————————————————————————————
A ———0——0————2-3————————3———3———3-3———5——5———3——2———0——————————————
D 5—0——0—————0-2———5————2———2———2-2———2——2———2——2———2———5————5————
G 0—0———————0—0———5———0———————————0———————2————5——2———2—————————
  He carried a hod. Well Tim had a bit of the tipplin' way, with a
```

```
     C                        Am                C              Am
E ————————————————————————————————————————————————————————————————
A 3———3——3——3-3————5———3———2———0————————3———3———3-5——3——2————————
D 2———2——2——2-2————2———2———2———2————5——2———2———2——2——2——2————————
G 0————————0———————2———5———2—0———————0————0—————2———————————————
  Love of the liquor poor Tim was born. To help him on his way each
```

```
     F                        G      C
E ————————————————————————————————————————————————————————————————
A 0————————————0——————0—0———0————————0——2——3——————————————————————
D 2———5—5———5-3————3——3—3———3——5——0——0——2—————————————————————————
G 5———2—2———2-2————————————2——2———0———0———————————————————————————
  Day, he had a drop of the craythur every morn!
```

CHORUS

```
     C                        Am
E ————————————————————————————————————————————————————————————————
A ———————————————————————————0———0———0——2——————————————————————————
D 2———————2——2-2————0———————0—2———2———2———2————————————————————————
G 5———————5——5-5————0———0—5———————5———————5————————————————————————
  Whack-fol-a-dol will ye dance with yer partners,
```

```
     F              G              C
E ————————————————————————————————————————————————————————————————
A 3————2——0——————————————————————————————————————————————————————
D 3————3——3——————5——2——0———0————2———2-2——0————————————————————————
G 5————————5—————2——0——0———0————5———5-5——0————————————————————————
  Round the floor yer trotters shake. Wasn't it the
```

```
     Am              F              G              C
E ————————————————————————————————————————————————————————————————
A ———————0-0———2——3————2——0————————0——0-2————3————————————————————
D 2———————2-2————2——3———3——3————5——0——0-0————2————————————————————
G 5———————5———————5————————5——0————0————0————0————————————————————
  Truth I told ya lots of fun at Finnegan's wake!
```

See Chord Forms and Additional Verses on Previous Pages

Finnegan's Wake
(continued)

Basic Melody

Key of G (Low)

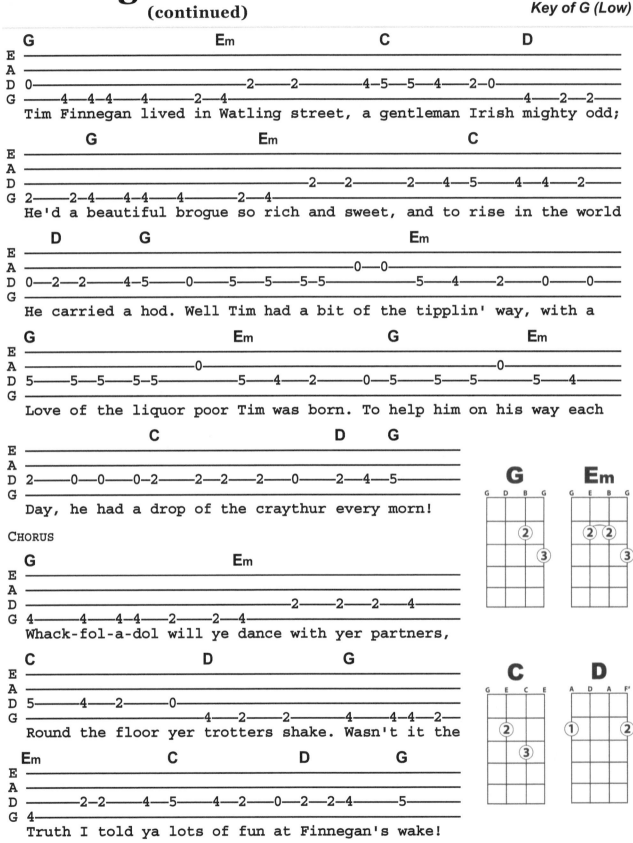

```
     G                    Em                  C            D
E ──────────────────────────────────────────────────────────────────
A ──────────────────────────────────────────────────────────────────
D 0──────────────────────────2────2─────4─5──5──4───2─0───────────────
G ────4──4─4────4──────2──4──────────────────────────────4────2──2────
  Tim Finnegan lived in Watling street, a gentleman Irish mighty odd;
```

```
        G                    Em                    C
E ──────────────────────────────────────────────────────────────────
A ──────────────────────────────────────────────────────────────────
D ──────────────────────────────2────2────────2──4─5───4──4───2───────
G 2─────2─4───4─4────4──────2──4──────────────────────────────────────
  He'd a beautiful brogue so rich and sweet, and to rise in the world
```

```
     D       G                                 Em
E ──────────────────────────────────────────────────────────────────
A ────────────────────────────────────0──0───────────────────────────
D 0──2──2───4─5────0──5────5──5─5──────────5──4───2────0────0──────────
G ──────────────────────────────────────────────────────────────────
  He carried a hod. Well Tim had a bit of the tipplin' way, with a
```

```
  G                    Em                  G              Em
E ──────────────────────────────────────────────────────────────────
A ─────────────────0──────────────────────────────0──────────────────
D 5────5──5───5─5──────5──4──2───0─5───5──5────────────5──4────────────
G ──────────────────────────────────────────────────────────────────
  Love of the liquor poor Tim was born. To help him on his way each
```

```
           C                     D      G
E ──────────────────────────────────────────────────────────────────
A ──────────────────────────────────────────────────────────────────
D 2───0──0───0─2───2─2────2───0───2──4──5─────────────────────────────
G ──────────────────────────────────────────────────────────────────
  Day, he had a drop of the craythur every morn!
```

CHORUS

```
  G                          Em
E ──────────────────────────────────────────────────────────────────
A ──────────────────────────────────────────────────────────────────
D ──────────────────────────2────2──────2───4────────────────────────
G 4─────4────4─4───2─────2──4─────────────────────────────────────────
  Whack-fol-a-dol will ye dance with yer partners,
```

```
  C               D              G
E ──────────────────────────────────────────────────────────────────
A ──────────────────────────────────────────────────────────────────
D 5─────4───2───0─────────────────────────────────────────────────────
G ────────────────4──2───2────4───4─4──2──────────────────────────────
  Round the floor yer trotters shake. Wasn't it the
```

```
  Em              C            D        G
E ──────────────────────────────────────────────────────────────────
A ──────────────────────────────────────────────────────────────────
D ────2─2───4──5────4──2──0─2──2─4───5─────────────────────────────────
G 4───────────────────────────────────────────────────────────────────
  Truth I told ya lots of fun at Finnegan's wake!
```

Finnegan's Wake
(continued)

Basic Melody

Key of G (High)

```
      G                    Em              C           D
E ------------------------------0----0----2-3-3-2--0------------------
A 5--2--2-2----2--------0--2------------------------5--2---0--0-------
D ------------------------------------------------------------------
G ------------------------------------------------------------------
```
Tim Finnegan lived in Watling street, a gentleman Irish mighty odd;

```
        G                    Em              C
E ----------------------------------0----0----0--2-3----2--2---0-----
A 0-----0-2----2-2--2--------0--2------------------------------------
D ------------------------------------------------------------------
G ------------------------------------------------------------------
```
He'd a beautiful brogue so rich and sweet, and to rise in the world

```
      D        G                          Em
E --0--0----2-3------3--3--3-3----5--5---3--2------0-----------------
A 5-----------------5------------------------------------5----5------
D ------------------------------------------------------------------
G ------------------------------------------------------------------
```
He carried a hod. Well Tim had a bit of the tipplin' way, with a

```
    G                Em              G              Em
E 3--3--3----3-3----5--3--2----0----3--3---3-5---3--2---------------
A ------------------------------5-----------------------------------
D ------------------------------------------------------------------
G ------------------------------------------------------------------
```
Love of the liquor poor Tim was born. To help him on his way each

```
          C              D   G
E 0---------0----0--0----0----0--2--3-------------------------------
A ---5-5--5-------------5-------------------------------------------
D ------------------------------------------------------------------
G ------------------------------------------------------------------
```
Day, he had a drop of the craythur every morn!

CHORUS

```
      G                    Em
E ------------------------------0----0---0--2----------------------
A 2----2--2-2--0----0-2--------------------------------------------
D ------------------------------------------------------------------
G ------------------------------------------------------------------
```
Whack-fol-a-dol will ye dance with yer partners,

```
    C           D              G
E 3------2--0----------------------------------------------------
A -----------5--2--0----0----2--2-2--0--------------------------
D ------------------------------------------------------------------
G ------------------------------------------------------------------
```
Round the floor yer trotters shake. Wasn't it the

```
  Em              C           D        G
E ----0-0--2-3----2--0----0--0-2----3---------------------------
A 2-----------------5------------------------------------------
D ------------------------------------------------------------------
G ------------------------------------------------------------------
```
Truth I told ya lots of fun at Finnegan's wake!

Finnegan's Wake
(continued)

Melody & Chords

Key of G (High)

```
    G                        Em              C              D
E ──────────────────────────0────0──────2─3──3──2────0──────────────────
A 5────2──2─2────2──────0──2──2────2─────2─3──3──3────3─5────2────0──0────
D 0────0──0─0────0──────0──2────────5────2────────────2────0────0──0─────
G 0────0─────────0──────4──────────────────0──────────────2─────────2────
```
Tim Finnegan lived in Watling street, a gentleman Irish mighty odd;

```
        G                        Em              C
E ──────────────────────────────0────0────0──2─3────2──2────0──────
A 0────0─2────2─2────2──────0──2──2────2────2──2─3────3─3────3──────
D 0────0─0────0─0────0──────0──5────────5────2──────────2──────────
G 2──────0──────────0──────4──────────────────0──────────0─────────
```
He'd a beautiful brogue so rich and sweet, and to rise in the world

```
    D       G                              Em
E ───0──0────2─3──────3────3──3─3──5──5────3────2────0──────────
A 5──0──0────0─2────5────2──2────2─2────2──2────2────2────5────5──
D 2──0──────0─0────0──────0──────────0────2────5────2────2──────
G ───2──────2─0────0──────0──────────────────────────────0─────
```
He carried a hod. Well Tim had a bit of the tipplin' way, with a

```
    G                                Em           G                 Em
E 3────3──3────3─3──────5────3────2────0──────3────3──3──5────3────2──────
A 2────2──2────2─2──────2────2────2────2──────5─2──2────2─2────2────2──────
D 0──────0──────────────2────2────2──0──────0──────0──────2──────────
G 0────────────────────0────0────0──────────0──────────0───────────
```
Love of the liquor poor Tim was born. To help him on his way each

```
        C                    D       G
E 0──────────────0────0──0────0──────0─2──3──────
A 2────5─5────5─3────3─3────3──5──────0──0──2──────
D 2────2─0────0─2──────────2────2────0──0──────────
G 0──────────0──────────────────2────0─────────────
```
Day, he had a drop of the craythur every morn!

CHORUS

```
    G                        Em
E ──────────────────────────────0──────0────0──2────
A 2────2──2─2────0──────0──2────2────2────2──2────
D 0────0──0─0────0──────0──2────2────2──────────
G 0──────0──0────0──────0──────────────────────
```
Whack-fol-a-dol will ye dance with yer partners,

```
    C                    D              G
E 3──────2────0──────────────────────────────────
A 3────2──3────5──2────0────0────2────2─2──0──────
D 2────────2────2──0────0────0────0────0─0──0──────
G 0──────────────2────────2──────0──────0─────────
```
Round the floor yer trotters shake. Wasn't it the

```
    Em            C              D            G
E ──────0─0────2─3────2──0──────0──0─2────3──────
A 2────2─2────2─3────2─3────5──0──0─0────2──────
D 2──────2──────2──────2──────2────0──0────0──────
G 4──────────0────────────────2────2──────0──────
```
Truth I told ya lots of fun at Finnegan's wake!

The Holy Ground

Basic Melody
Key of C

Words and Music
Traditional

This is one of those Irish songs that is perfect for shouting out while drinking some Guinness. In fact the "FINE GIRL YOU ARE" lines in the chorus are literally meant to be shouted out rather than sung. The definitive recorded version of this song by The Clancy Brothers and Tommy Makem is highly recommended.

```
      C                 G           C               G           C
E  ————————————————————————————————————————————————————————————————————
A  ————————————————————————————————————————————————————————————————————
D  ———————0———2———5——5——3—2—0————————0—2———5———5———2———————————
G  5———————————————————————————5———5———————————————————5——————
   Fare thee well my lo-ve-l-y Dinah, a thousand times a-dieu,
```

```
                        Am          F   G               C
E  ————————————————————————————————————————————————————————————————————
A  ———————————————————0———2———2———3—3—2———————0———0——————————
D  2———2———5——5———5————————————————————————————————5————————
G  ————————————————————————————————————————————————————————————————————
   For we're sailing a-way from the Holy Ground, and the girls
```

```
            G           C       G       C
E  ————————————————————————————————————————————————————————————————————
A  ————————————————————————————————————————————————————————————————————
D  2———————2———0————————0———2———5——5—3—2—0—————2——5——————
G  ——5———————————————5————————————————————5—5——————————
   We all loved true. We will sail the salt sea o-ver, and we'll
```

```
   Am      F  G       C   Am          F           C
E  —0———2——3—2————————3——2—0—————————————————————————
A  5———————————————5———————————5———————5—2——————0————
D  ————————————————————————————————————————————5—————————
G  ————————————————————————————————————————————————————————————————————
   Return for shore, to see a-gain the girls we love, and the
```

```
       G           C
E  ————————————————————————————————————————————————————————————————————
A  ————————————————————————————————————————————————————————————————————
D  2—5——5———3———2—0—————————————————————————————————————————
G  ——————————————5————————————————————————————————————————————
   Holy Ground once more... FINE GIRL YOU ARE!
```

CHORUS

```
   C             Am   F  G       C       Am      F           C
E  ————————————————————————————————————————————————————————————————————
A  ——————————————0—2—3—2————3——2—0————————0—————————————
D  5———————5——5———5——————————5——————————————5———5—2——
G  ————————————————————————————————————————————————————————————————————
   You're the girl I do a-dore, and still I live in hopes to see,
```

```
       G           C
E  ————————————————————————————————————————————————————————————————————
A  ————————————————————————————————————————————————————————————————————
D  ——2—5——5———3—2—0—————————————————————————————————————————
G  5————————————5———————————————————————————————————————————
   The Holy Ground once more... FINE GIRL YOU ARE!
```

See Chords and Additional Verses on Next Page

The Holy Ground
(continued)

Additional Verses

And now the storm is raging,
And we are far from shore;
And the good old ship is tossing about,
And the rigging is all torn.
And the secrets of my life, my love,
You're the girl I do adore!
And still I live in hopes to see
The Holy Ground once more...
FINE GIRL YOU ARE!

And now the storm is over,
And we are safe and well.
We will go into a public house,
And we'll sit and drink black ale!
We will drink strong ale and porter,
And we'll make the rafters roar,
And when our money is all spent
We'll go to sea once more...
FINE GIRL YOU ARE!

Chord Forms

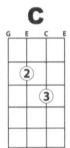
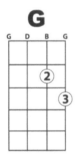
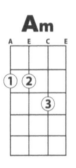
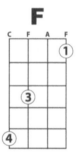

The Holy Ground
(continued)

Melody & Chords

Key of C

```
      C              G            C              G        C
E  _____
A  _____
D  _____0_____2_____5—5—3—2—0_____0—2——5_____5_____2_____
G  5_____0_____5____5—0—0—0—0—5——5—0—5—5_____0_____0—5_____
   Fare thee well my lo-ve-l-y Dinah, a thousand times a-dieu,
```

```
                    Am           F   G              C
E  _____
A  _____0_____2____2—3-3—2_____0____0_____
D  2____2_____5—5____5-2__2____2—3-3—0_____0__0__5_____
G  0____0_____5—5____5-5__5_____5____0_____0____5_____
   For we're sailing a-way from the Holy Ground, and the girls
```

```
           G           C     G       C
E  _____
A  _____
D  2_____2____0_____0__2____5__5-3—2-0_____2__5_____
G  0—5__0____0____5—0__5____5__0-0—0-0-5-5____5__5_____
   We all loved true. We will sail the salt sea o-ver, and we'll
```

```
   Am   F  G    C   Am     F        C
E  _____
A  —0____2—3—2_____3—2-0_____0_____
D  5-2__2—3—0__5—2__2-2____5__3____5—2_____0_____
G  5-5__5—5—0—0—0_____5__0__5____5-5____5—0_____
   Return for shore, to see a-gain the girls we love, and the
```

```
        G        C
E  _____
A  _____3_____
D  2—5—5—3—2-0—5_____
G  5-5—0—0——0-0—5_____
   Holy Ground once more... FINE GIRL YOU ARE!
```

CHORUS

```
   C              Am  F  G      C      Am      F         C
E  _____
A  _____0—2-3—2_____3____2-0_____0_____
D  5_____5__5__5-2—2-3—0—5__2____2-2__5—3____5—2_____
G  5_____5__5__5-5—5-5—0—0__0____2__0-5____5-5_____
   You're the girl I do a-dore, and still I live in hopes to see,
```

```
        G         C
E  _____
A  _____3_____
D  ___2—5—5—3—2-5—2_____
G  5——5-5—0——0-0-0—0_____
   The Holy Ground once more... FINE GIRL YOU ARE!
```

The Holy Ground
(continued)

Basic Melody

Key of G

```
        G                   D         G               D         G                  G
E ------------------------------------------------------------------------------    G D B G
A ------0-----2-----5---5---3--2-0----------0-2---5-------5-------2-------------      
D 5--------------------------------5---5----------------------------5--------        ②
G --------------------------------------------------------------------------        ③

Fare thee well my lo-ve-l-y Dinah, a thousand times a-dieu,
```

```
                      Em          C   D              G
E ------------------0-----2-----2---3--3---2--------0---0----------       D
A 2-----2-----5---5-----5------------------------------------5----      A D A F'
D ---------------------------------------------------------------       ① ②
G ---------------------------------------------------------------        

For we're sailing a-way from the Holy Ground, and the girls
```

```
              D               G         D         G
E -----------------------------------------------------------
A 2--------2-----0--------0-----2-----5---5--3--2-0-------2---5---
D ---5-----------------5--------------------------5--5----------
G ------------------------------------------------------------

We all loved true. We will sail the salt sea o-ver, and we'll
```

```
  Em      C   D    G   Em      C           G
E -0-----2---3--2-------3---2-0------0-----------------       Em
A 5-------------5----------------5-------5---2-------0----    G E B G
D ---------------------------------------------5---------      ② ②
G -----------------------------------------------------        ③

Return for shore, to see a-gain the girls we love, and the
```

```
          D           G
E -----------------------------------
A 2--5---5---3---2-0------------------
D 5-----------------5----------------
G -----------------------------------

Holy Ground once more... FINE GIRL YOU ARE!
```

CHORUS

```
  G                 Em    C  D     G     Em       C         G
E -----------------0--2-3--2-------3----2-0------0-----------------    C
A 5-----5---5----5--------------5-----------5--------5---2------      G E C E
D ---------------------------------------------------------------     
G ---------------------------------------------------------------     ②
                                                                    ③
You're the girl I do a-dore, and still I live in hopes to see,
```

```
              D         G
E --------------------------------
A ----2-5---5---3--2-0------------
D 5-------------------5----------
G --------------------------------

The Holy Ground once more... FINE GIRL YOU ARE!
```

83

The Holy Ground
(continued)

Melody & Chords

Key of G

```
     G                 D        G            D        G            G
E ───────────────────────────────────────────────────────────────
A ──────0───────2──────5──5──3──2─0─────0─2──5───────5──────2──────
D 5─────0───────0──────0──0──0──0─0─5───5────0─0─────0──────0─5────
G 0─────────────0──────2────────0─────0──────0──────2────0────────
```
Fare thee well my lo-ve-l-y Dinah, a thousand times a-dieu,

```
                          Em           C  D           G
E ──────────────────0───2─────2────3─3──2────────0───0──────
A 2────2──────5──5──5─2──2────2────3─3──0─────────0───0─5────
D 0────0──────0──0──2─2────────────2────0─────────0────0─────
G 0────────0──────────────────────0────2────────────0───────
```
For we're sailing a-way from the Holy Ground, and the girls

```
           D           G       D       G
E ───────────────────────────────────────────────────────────────
A 2───────2───────0───────0──2──5───5──3──2─0──────2───5─────
D 0──5────0───────0────5───0──0───0──0─0──0─0─5─5──0───0──────
G 0──0────0───────2───────2──────0──────2────2─0─0────0───0──
```
We all loved true. We will sail the salt sea o-ver, and we'll

```
  Em      C  D    G    Em      C          G
E ─0───2──3──2────────3──2─0───────0──────────────
A 5─2─────2──3──0──5──2────0─2──5──3───────5─2─────
D 0─2────────2──0──0───0──────2────2──2────2─0─────
G ───────────0──2──2───0──────0────────0────0──────
```
Return for shore, to see a-gain the girls we love, and the

```
          D           G
E ────────────────────────────
A 2─5──5──3─────2─0────────────
D 0─0──0──0─────0─0──5─────────
G 0───────2────────────0──────
```
Holy Ground once more... FINE GIRL YOU ARE!

CHORUS

```
  G                  Em   C  D     G       Em       C          G
E ──────────────────0──2─3──2──────3──────2─0──────0─────────────
A 5────────5───5────5─2──2──3──0──5───2───2─2──────5──3──────5─2──
D 0────────0───0────0─2────2──0──0────0───2─2──────2─2──────2─0───
G 0────────────0──────────0──2──0──0──────0───────0─────────0─────
```
You're the girl I do a-dore, and still I live in hopes to see,

```
          D           G
E ────────────────────────────
A ─────2─5──5───3──2─0─────────
D 5────0─0──0───0──0─0──5──────
G 0────0────2──────────0───────
```
The Holy Ground once more... FINE GIRL YOU ARE!

I'll Tell Me Ma

Basic Melody
Key of G

Words and Music
Traditional

"I'll Tell Me Ma" Is a traditional Irish song that was originally part of a children's game from the 19th century, reportedly in the city of Belfast. Today it enjoys a regular spot in Irish music sessions, having been covered by many notable Irish bands and Performers such as The Dubliners, Van Morrison, The Chieftains, Bradigan and The Clancy Brothers with Tommy Makem.

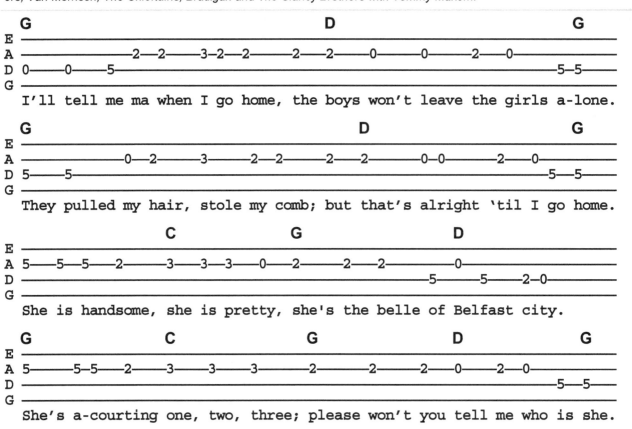

I'll tell me ma when I go home, the boys won't leave the girls a-lone.

They pulled my hair, stole my comb; but that's alright 'til I go home.

She is handsome, she is pretty, she's the belle of Belfast city.

She's a-courting one, two, three; please won't you tell me who is she.

Chord Forms

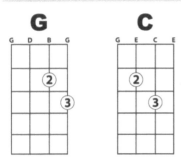

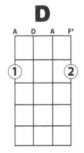

Additional Verses

Albert Mooney says he loves her,
All the boys are fighting for her.
Knock on the door and ring the bell,
Oh my true love are ye well?
There she goes, as white as snow,
Rings on her fingers, bells on her toes.
Ole Jenny Murray says she'll die
If she doesn't get the fella with the roving eye.

Let the wind and the rain and the hail blow high,
Snow come tumblin' from the sky.
She's as nice as an apple pie,
She'll get her own love by and by.
When she gets a love of her own,
She won't tell 'er ma when she comes home.
Let them all come as they will,
For it's Albert Mooney she loves still.

I'll Tell Me Ma (continued)

Melody & Chords
Key of G

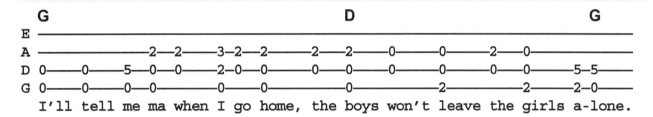

```
          G                              D                         G
E ----------------------------------------------------------------------------------
A ------------2--2----3-2--2-------2---2-----0----0----2--0--------------------------
D 0----0----5--0--0----2-0--0------0---0-----0----0----0--0----5-5------------------
G 0----0-------0--0-------0--------0---------0----2---------2---2-0------------------
```
I'll tell me ma when I go home, the boys won't leave the girls a-lone.

```
          G                              D                         G
E ----------------------------------------------------------------------------------
A ------------0--2----3------2--2------2---2------0-0--------2--0---------------------
D 5----5-------0--0----2------0--0-----0---0------0-0--------0--0-5--5---------------
G 0----0----------0-------0--------0------------2-----------2-2--0-------------------
```
They pulled my hair, stole my comb; but that's alright 'til I go home.

```
                    C            G           D
E ----------------------------------------------------------------------------------
A 5----5--5---2------3---3--3----0--2----2--2----------0-----------------------------
D 0----0--0---0------2---2--2----2--0----0--0----5---0-5----2-0----------------------
G 0--------0--0---------0-----0-----0----0--0----0-2--2-----2-2----------------------
```
She is handsome, she is pretty, she's the belle of Belfast city.

```
          G          C           G           D           G
E ----------------------------------------------------------------------------------
A 5--------5-5---2---3---3--3------2------2----2--0----2--0---------------------------
D 0-------0-0---0----2---2--2------0------0----0--0----0--0-5---5--------------------
G 0----------0------0--------0----0----------2----2-2----2--0-----------------------
```
She's a-courting one, two, three; please won't you tell me who is she.

Chord Forms

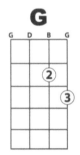 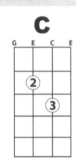 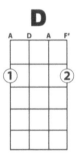

I'll Tell Me Ma (continued)

Basic Melody
Key of C (Low)

```
       C                                    G                          C
E -----------------------------------------------------------------------------------
A -----------------------------------------------------------------------------------
D -------------2--2------3-2--2------2----2------0-------0------2---0-------------------
G 0------0-----5----------------------------------------------------------5--5---------
```
I'll tell me ma when I go home, the boys won't leave the girls a-lone.

```
       C                                    G                          C
E -----------------------------------------------------------------------------------
A -----------------------------------------------------------------------------------
D --------------0--2------3------2--2------2----2------0--0------2---0-----------------
G 5------5-------------------------------------------------------------5--5------------
```
They pulled my hair, stole my comb; but that's alright 'til I go home.

```
               F              C                  G
E -----------------------------------------------------------------------------------
A -----------------------------------------------------------------------------------
D 5----5--5----2------3---3--3----0---2-----2--2------0-------------------------------
G ----------------------------------------------5------5----2--0----------------------
```
She is handsome, she is pretty, she's the belle of Belfast city.

```
       C              F              C              G              C
E -----------------------------------------------------------------------------------
A -----------------------------------------------------------------------------------
D 5------5--5----2----3----3----3------2------2----2---0------2--0--------------------
G ---------------------------------------------------------------5--5------------------
```
She's a-courting one, two, three; please won't you tell me who is she.

Chord Forms

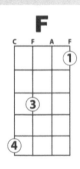

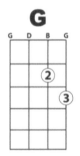

I'll Tell Me Ma (continued)

```
      C                                G                            C
E ——————————0—0———1—0—0————0———0————————————0—————————————————
A —————3——————————————————————————5———5————5———3—3————————————
D 5———5———————————————————————————————————————————————————————
G ———————————————————————————————————————————————————————————
```
I'll tell me ma when I go home, the boys won't leave the girls a-lone.

```
      C                                G                            C
E ——————————————0———1————0—0————0———0————————————0—————————————
A 3———3—————5—————————————————————5—5————5—3———3——————————————
D ———————————————————————————————————————————————————————————
G ———————————————————————————————————————————————————————————
```
They pulled my hair, stole my comb; but that's alright 'til I go home.

```
                  F           C              G
E 3———3—3———0———1———1—1————0———0———0———————————————————————————
A ————————————————5——————————————3—5—3———0———————————————————
D ————————————————————————————————————————5—————————————————
G ———————————————————————————————————————————————————————————
```
She is handsome, she is pretty, she's the belle of Belfast city.

```
      C            F           C              G            C
E 3———————3—3———0———1———1———1————0———0———0———0—————————————————
A ————————————————————————————————————5———5—3———3————————————
D ———————————————————————————————————————————————————————————
G ———————————————————————————————————————————————————————————
```
She's a-courting one, two, three; please won't you tell me who is she.

Chord Forms

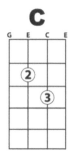

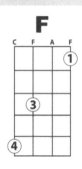

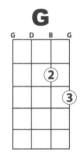

I'll Tell Me Ma (continued)

Melody & Chords
Key of C (High)

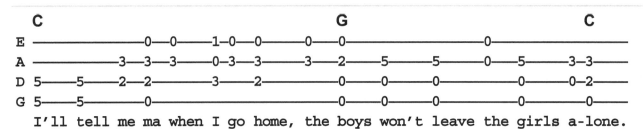

I'll tell me ma when I go home, the boys won't leave the girls a-lone.

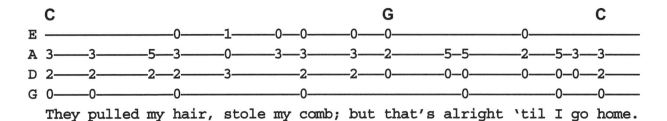

They pulled my hair, stole my comb; but that's alright 'til I go home.

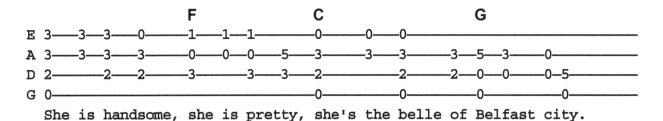

She is handsome, she is pretty, she's the belle of Belfast city.

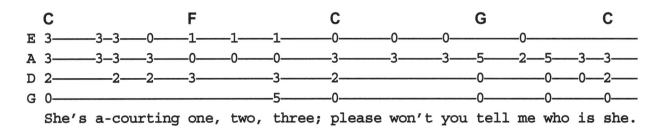

She's a-courting one, two, three; please won't you tell me who is she.

Chord Forms

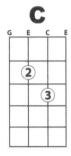
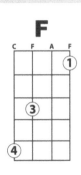
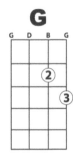

I'm A Man You Don't Meet Every Day (Jock Stewart)

Basic Melody

Key of C

This old folk song is of either Scottish or Irish origin, and is written from the point of view of a wealthy landowner buying rounds of drinks in a pub. This is one of the gentler of the traditional drinking songs, but very beautiful in its own right.

Words and Music

Traditional

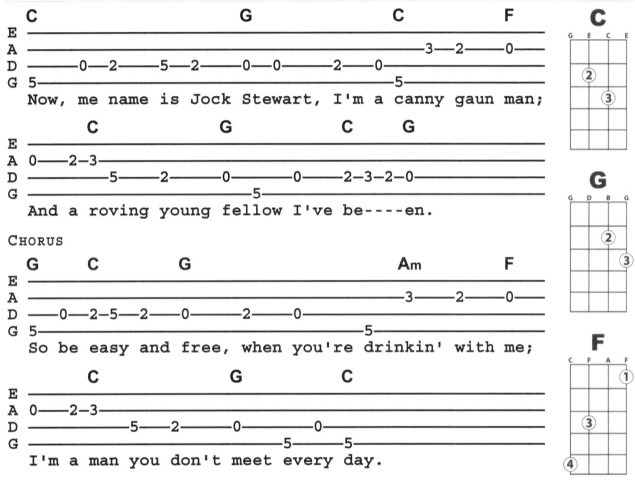

CHORUS

Additional Verses

I have acres of land, and men at command;
And I've always a shilling to spare...

I'm a piper by trade, I'm a roving young blade;
And it's many the tunes I do play...

Let us catch well the hours, and the minutes that fly;
And we'll share them together this day...

I go out with my dogs, and my gun for to shoot;
All down by the River Kildare...

So come fill up your glass, with whiskey or wine;
And whatever the cost, I will pay...

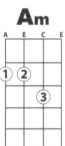

90

I'm A Man You Don't Meet Every Day (Jock Stewart)

Melody & Chords

Key of C

(continued)

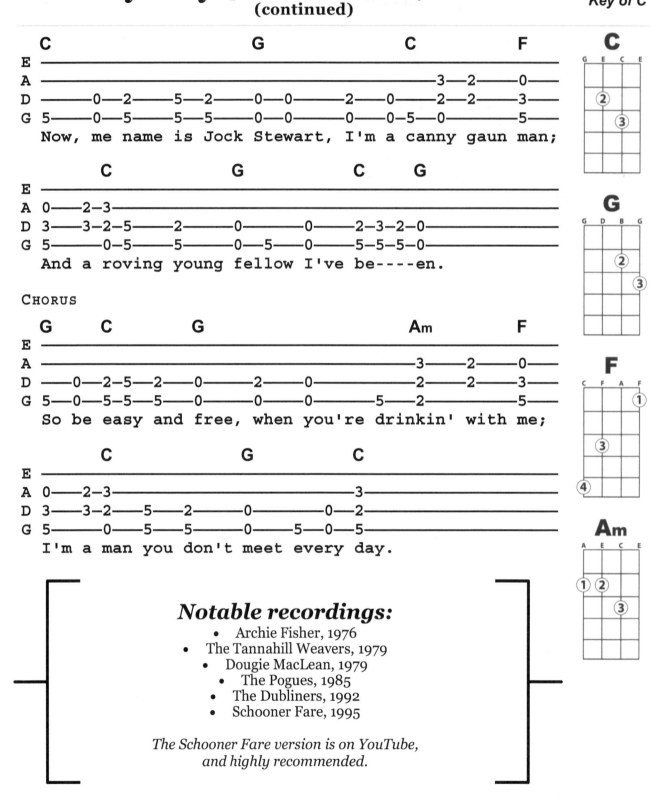

C   G   C   F

```
E ----------------------------------------------------------------
A ---------------------------------------------3---2------0--------
D -------0---2------5---2------0---0------2---0------2---2------3---
G 5------0---5------5---5------0---0------0---0-5---0----------5----
```
Now, me name is Jock Stewart, I'm a canny gaun man;

C   G   C   G

```
E ----------------------------------------------------------------
A 0------2-3------------------------------------------------------
D 3------3-2-5------2--------0--------0------2-3-2-0--------------
G 5--------0-5------5--------0---5----0------5-5-5-0--------------
```
And a roving young fellow I've be----en.

CHORUS

G   C   G   Am   F

```
E ----------------------------------------------------------------
A ---------------------------------------------3-----2------0-----
D ------0---2-5---2------0--------2--------0---------2------2-----3---
G 5--0--5-5--5------0--------0--------0------5----2----------5----
```
So be easy and free, when you're drinkin' with me;

C   G   C

```
E ----------------------------------------------------------------
A 0------2-3--------------------------3--------------------------
D 3------3-2------5------2--------0--------0---2-----------------
G 5--------0---5------5--------0---5---0---5--------------------
```
I'm a man you don't meet every day.

Notable recordings:

- Archie Fisher, 1976
- The Tannahill Weavers, 1979
- Dougie MacLean, 1979
- The Pogues, 1985
- The Dubliners, 1992
- Schooner Fare, 1995

The Schooner Fare version is on YouTube, and highly recommended.

91

I'm A Man You Don't Meet Every Day (Jock Stewart)

Basic Melody

Key of G (Low)

(continued)

```
        G                    D              G           C
E ————————————————————————————————————————————————————————————
A ————————————————————————————————————————————————————————————
D ——————————————————0——————————————————————————5——4————2——————
G 0————2——4—————————4————2——2————4——2—0————————————————————————
  Now, me name is Jock Stewart,  I'm a canny gaun man;
```

```
        G              D            G        D
E ————————————————————————————————————————————————————————————
A ————————————————————————————————————————————————————————————
D 2————4—5—0—————————————————————————————————————————————————
G ——————————————————4————2——0——2————4—5—4—2—————————————————————
  And a roving young fellow I've be————en.
```

CHORUS

```
    D    G       D                       Em        C
E ————————————————————————————————————————————————————————————
A ————————————————————————————————————————————————————————————
D ——————————0————————————————————————————5——————4————2————————
G 0——2——4—————4——2————4——2——————————0—————————————————————————
  So be easy and free, when you're drinkin' with me;
```

```
        G              D          G
E ————————————————————————————————————————————————————————————
A ————————————————————————————————————————————————————————————
D 2————4—5————0———————————————————————————————————————————————
G ——————————————————4————2——0—2——0——————————————————————————
  I'm a man you don't meet every day.
```

Chord Forms

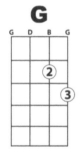

G

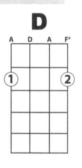

D

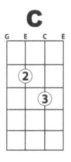

C

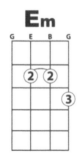

Em

92

I'm A Man You Don't Meet Every Day (Jock Stewart)

Basic Melody

Key of G (High)

(continued)

```
       G                      D                  G            C
E ────────────────────────────────────────────3──2────0───────
A ────0──2────5──2─────0──0──────2──0──────────────────────────
D 5────────────────────────────────────5──────────────────────
G ─────────────────────────────────────────────────────────────
```
Now, me name is Jock Stewart, I'm a canny gaun man;

```
       G                  D              G      D
E 0────2─3────────────────────────────────────────────────────
A ──────────5──────2──────0──────0──────2─3─2─0────────────────
D ───────────────────────5─────────────────────────────────────
G ─────────────────────────────────────────────────────────────
```
And a roving young fellow I've be----en.

CHORUS

```
   D      G       D                    Em        C
E ──────────────────────────────────3──2────0───────
A ──0──2─5──2─────0──────2──────0──────────────────────
D 5──────────────────────────────5────────────────────
G ─────────────────────────────────────────────────────
```
So be easy and free, when you're drinkin' with me;

```
       G           D          G
E 0────2─3──────────────────────────────────────
A ──────────5──────2──────0──────0───────────────
D ───────────────────────5──────5────────────────
G ───────────────────────────────────────────────
```
I'm a man you don't meet every day.

Chord Forms

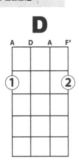

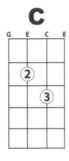

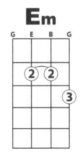

Em

I'm A Man You Don't Meet Every Day (Jock Stewart)
(continued)

Melody & Chords

Key of G (High)

```
      G                         D              G           C
E ——————————————————————————————————————————————3—2——————0—————
A ——————0—2————5—2——————0—0——————2——0——————2—2——————3—————
D 5——————0—0——————0—0——————0—0——————0——0—5——0—0————2—————
G 0——————————0—0——————0—0——————2——————2————0—0—0——————0—————
```
Now, me name is Jock Stewart, I'm a canny gaun man;

```
      G                D            G    D
E 0——————2—3—————————————————————————————————————————————————
A 3——0—2—5——————2——————0——————0——————2—3—2—0———————————————
D 2——————0—0——————0——————0—5——0——————0—0—0—0———————————————
G ——————————0—0——————0——————2—2——————2——————0————————2—————
```
And a roving young fellow I've be----en.

CHORUS

```
      D   G       D                         Em        C
E ——————————————————————————————————————————3——————2——————0—————
A ——————0—2—5——2——————0——————2——————0——————2——————2——————3—————
D 5—0——0—0——0—0——————0——————0——————0——————5——2——————————2—————
G 0——2—0——————0——————2——————2——————————————0——————————————0—————
```
So be easy and free, when you're drinkin' with me;

```
      G                D            G
E 0——————2—3—————————————————————————————————————————————————
A 3——0—2——————5——————2————————————0——————0—————————————————————
D 2——————0——————0——————0——————5—0——5——————————————————————————
G 0——————————0——————0——————2——————2——————0————————————————————
```
I'm a man you don't meet every day.

Chord Forms

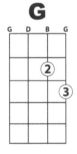
G

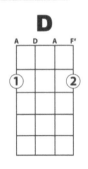
D

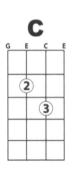
C

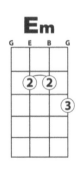
Em

94

The Irish Rover

Basic Melody
Key of G (Low)

Words and Music

Traditional

This lively song tells the story of the mythical ship the Irish Rover and its crew, and its sad demise. It is a good example of the Irish tendency towards exaggeration when spinning a tale. This song has been recorded at one time or another by most of the well-known Irish bands, including The Clancy Brothers with Tommy Makem, and also (not surprisingly) by the band that took their name from the song: The Irish Rovers.

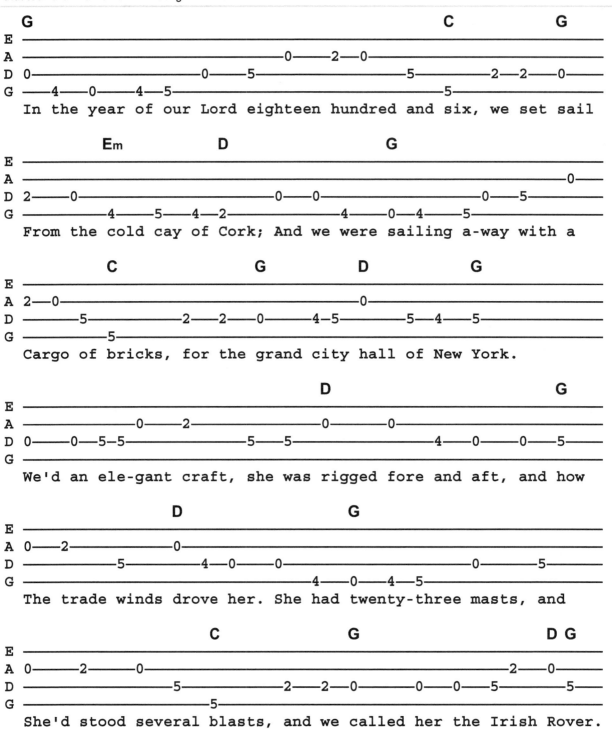

```
        G                                              C              G
E ───────────────────────────────────────────────────────────────────────────
A ────────────────────────────0────2──0───────────────────────────────────────
D 0─────────────────0─────5────────────────────5──────────2──2────0────────────
G ────4───0────4──5──────────────────────────────5────────────────────────────
```
In the year of our Lord eighteen hundred and six, we set sail

```
        Em        D                      G
E ───────────────────────────────────────────────────────────────────────────
A ──────────────────────────────────────────────────────────────────0──────────
D 2────0─────────────────────0────0──────────────────0────5────────────────────
G ──────────4────5──4──2──────────────4───0──4────5────────────────────────────
```
From the cold cay of Cork; And we were sailing a-way with a

```
        C              G        D        G
E ───────────────────────────────────────────────────────────────────────────
A 2──0─────────────────────────────0───────────────────────────────────────────
D ──────5────────2──2──0────4─5─────────5──4────5───────────────────────────────
G ──────────5───────────────────────────────────────────────────────────────────
```
Cargo of bricks, for the grand city hall of New York.

```
                              D                    G
E ───────────────────────────────────────────────────────────────────────────
A ──────────────0───2──────────────0─────0─────────────────────────────────────
D 0───0──5─5───────────────5────5──────────────4───0─────0────5─────────────────
G ───────────────────────────────────────────────────────────────────────────────
```
We'd an ele-gant craft, she was rigged fore and aft, and how

```
              D              G
E ───────────────────────────────────────────────────────────────────────────
A 0────2─────────────0──────────────────────────────────────────────────────────
D ──────────5────────4──0────0──────────────────────0────5──────────────────────
G ─────────────────────────4───0──4──5──────────────────────────────────────────
```
The trade winds drove her. She had twenty-three masts, and

```
              C              G                D  G
E ───────────────────────────────────────────────────────────────────────────
A 0────2─────────0────────────────────────────2──0─────────────────────────────
D ──────────5──────────2──2──0─────0──0──5────────5─────────────────────────────
G ─────────────5────────────────────────────────────────────────────────────────
```
She'd stood several blasts, and we called her the Irish Rover.

See Chords and Additional Verses on Next Page

The Irish Rover
(continued)

Additional Verses

We had one million bags of the best Sligo rags,
We had two million barrels of stone.
And we had three million bales of old nanny goats' tails
We had four million barrels of bone.
We had five million hogs, and six million dogs,
And seven million barrels of porter.
We had eight million sides of old blind horses' hides,
In the hold of the Irish Rover!

And there was Barney McGee from the banks of the Lee,
There was Hogan from County Tyrone,
And there was Johnny McGirk, who was scared stiff of work,
And a chap from Westmeath named Malone.
There was Slugger O'Toole who was drunk as a rule,
And fightin' Charlie Boyle from Dover,
And yer man Mick McGann, from the banks of the Ban,
Was the skipper of the Irish Rover.

We had sailed seven years when the measles broke out,
And the ship lost her way in a fog (GREAT FOG!)
And the whole of the crew was reduced down to two,
Just meself and the captain's old dog.
And then the ship struck a rock, oh Lord what a shock,
I nearly tumbled over... turned nine times around,
And the poor old dog was drowned...
I'm the last of the Irish Rover!

Chord Forms

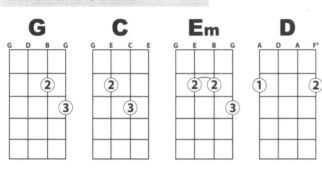

The Irish Rover
(continued)

Basic Melody

Key of G (High)

```
        G                                                    C           G
E ————————————————————————————3———5———7—5———3——————————————0——0—————————
A 5—2——————————2—3——5————————————————————————————————3————————————————5——
D ————————5——————————————————————————————————————————————————————————————
G ———————————————————————————————————————————————————————————————————————
```
In the year of our Lord eighteen hundred and six, we set sail

```
          Em          D               G
E 0———————————————————————————————————————————————————————3———5——
A ————5———2———3———2—0———5———5—2—————————2———3—5———————————————————
D ————————————————————————————————————5——————————————————————————
G ———————————————————————————————————————————————————————————————
```
From the cold cay of Cork; And we were sailing a-way with a

```
        C               G         D           G
E 7—5—3——————————————0——0—————————2—3—5———3—2———3——————————————————
A ————————3——————————————5————————————————————————————————————————
D ———————————————————————————————————————————————————————————————
G ———————————————————————————————————————————————————————————————
```
Cargo of bricks, for the grand city hall of New York.

```
                                    D                       G
E ——————3-3—5———7———3———3———5———5———2————————————————3——————
A 5———5——————————————————————————————————5———5———————————————
D ———————————————————————————————————————————————————————————
G ———————————————————————————————————————————————————————————
```
We'd an ele-gant craft, she was rigged fore and aft, and how

```
          D           G
E 5———7———3———5—2——————————————————————————————3———————
A ——————————————5———5———2—————2—3———5————————————————————
D ——————————————————————————5————————————————————————————
G ———————————————————————————————————————————————————————
```
The trade winds drove her. She had twenty-three masts, and

```
              C               G               D G
E 5———7———5—3——————————0——0——————————————3—7——5—3——
A 0———5———0—2———3——————3—3—5—————5—5——2—5——0—2——
D —————————————————————————————————————————————————
G —————————————————————————————————————————————————
```
She'd stood several blasts, and we called her the Irish Rover.

See Chords and Additional Verses on Previous Page

The Irish Rover
(continued)

Melody & Chords

Key of G (High)

```
      G                                              C          G
E ──────────────────────3──5───7─5───3──────────────0──0──────────
A 5─2───────────2─3──5──2──0───5─0──2───3──────3─2──5──────────────
D 0─0──5───0──0──0───0─────5─────────2────2──────────0─────────────
G 0──────0───0────0───────────────────────0────0───0──────────────
```
In the year of our Lord eighteen hundred and six, we set sail

```
          Em          D                 G
E 0──────────────────────────────────────────────3──5──
A 2───5──2───3──2─0──5──5─2───────2───3─5──2───────0───
D 0───0─2───2──2─0─────0──0─0───5─0───0─0──0──────────
G ──────4────────2───2───2──0─0───0───────────────────
```
From the cold cay of Cork; And we were sailing a-way with a

```
      C              G        D          G
E 7─5─3──────────0───0──────2─3─5──3─2──3──────────
A 5─0─0─3────3──3──5────5─5─0──0─0──2──────────────
D 5────2──────2─────0───────4─────0────────────────
G ──────0────────0───────────────────0────────────
```
Cargo of bricks, for the grand city hall of New York.

```
                                       D             G
E ───────3─3─5───7───3──3─5────5──2──────────3──────
A 5────5─2─2─0──5───2──2─0───0──0─5──5─2────────────
D 0───0─0─0──5──0──4────4──0──0──0─0────────────────
G 0─────0────0───────────────────2───2─0──────────
```
We'd an ele-gant craft, she was rigged fore and aft, and how

```
            D           G
E 5──7──3──5─2────────────────────────3────
A 0──5──2──0─0─5──5─2───2─3──5────2────────
D ──5──0──4──0──0─0──5─0─0────0─────────────
G ──0────────2──────0─────0────────────────
```
The trade winds drove her. She had twenty-three masts, and

```
            C          G             D G
E 5───7─5─3───────0──0───────────3─7─5─3──
A 0───5─0─2─3──3─3─5──5─5─2─5─0─2──0─2────
D ──5─0──0─2──2─2─0──0─0─0─5─4─0────────────
G ───────0────0───0──────0───0─────────────
```
She'd stood several blasts, and we called her the Irish Rover.

See Chords and Additional Verses Two Pages Previous

The Irish Rover
(continued)

Basic Melody

Key of C

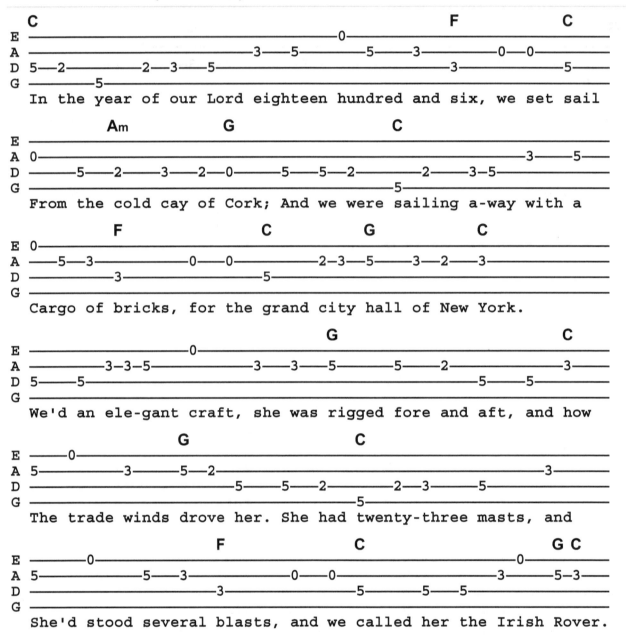

In the year of our Lord eighteen hundred and six, we set sail

From the cold cay of Cork; And we were sailing a-way with a

Cargo of bricks, for the grand city hall of New York.

We'd an ele-gant craft, she was rigged fore and aft, and how

The trade winds drove her. She had twenty-three masts, and

She'd stood several blasts, and we called her the Irish Rover.

Chord Forms

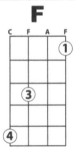
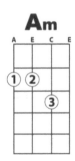
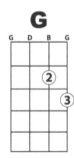

99

The Irish Rover
(continued)

Melody & Chords

Key of C

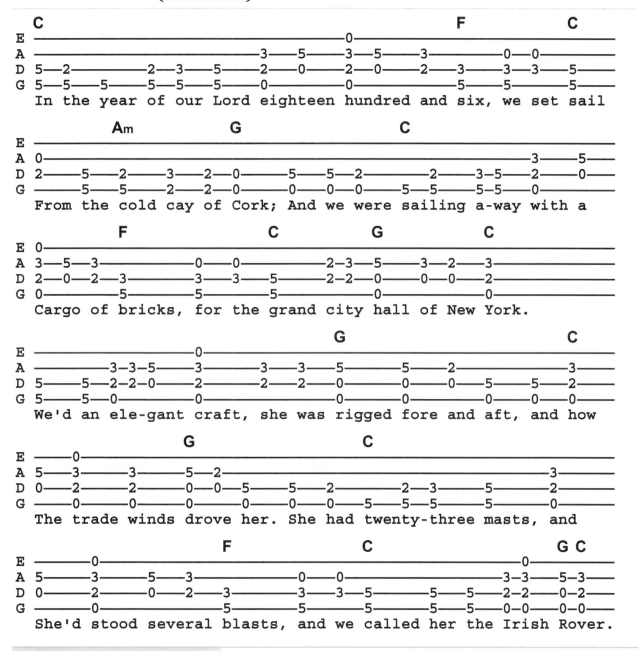

In the year of our Lord eighteen hundred and six, we set sail

From the cold cay of Cork; And we were sailing a-way with a

Cargo of bricks, for the grand city hall of New York.

We'd an ele-gant craft, she was rigged fore and aft, and how

The trade winds drove her. She had twenty-three masts, and

She'd stood several blasts, and we called her the Irish Rover.

Chord Forms

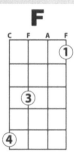
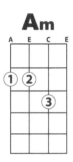
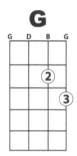

Isn't It Grand Boys

Basic Melody
Key of C

This song is one of the best examples of the Irish irreverence towards death. It tells the humorous tale of a dead man looking around his own funeral, and ending at the declaration that being dead isn't so bad after all. It is best sung at the top of your lungs while holding a pint of Guinness.

Words and Music

Traditional

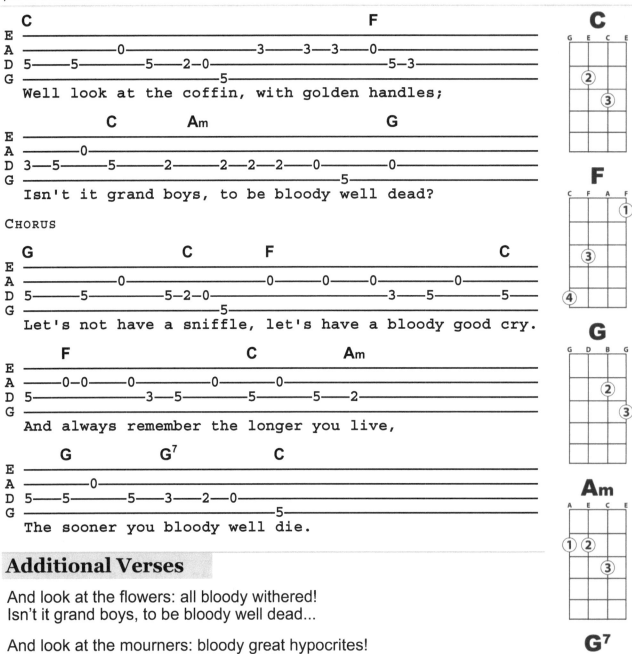

```
     C                                    F
E _____
A _____0_____3___3__3____0_____
D 5_____5_____5___2_0_____5_3_____
G _____5_____
     Well look at the coffin, with golden handles;
```

```
           C       Am                    G
E _____
A _____0_____
D 3__5_____5_____2_____2_2_2___0_____0_____
G _____5_____
     Isn't it grand boys, to be bloody well dead?
```

CHORUS

```
     G           C       F                    C
E _____
A _____0_____0_____0_____0_____0_____
D 5_____5_____5_2_0_____3__5_____5____
G _____5_____
     Let's not have a sniffle, let's have a bloody good cry.
```

```
        F                 C       Am
E _____
A ____0_0____0_____0_____0_____
D 5_____3_5____5_____5_____2_____
G _____
     And always remember the longer you live,
```

```
        G       G7      C
E _____
A _____0_____
D 5__5_____5__3__2_0_____
G _____5_____
     The sooner you bloody well die.
```

Additional Verses

And look at the flowers: all bloody withered!
Isn't it grand boys, to be bloody well dead...

And look at the mourners: bloody great hypocrites!
Isn't it grand boys, to be bloody well dead...

And look at the preacher: bloody sanctimonious!
Isn't it grand boys, to be bloody well dead...

And look at the widow: bloody great female!
Isn't it grand boys, to be bloody well dead...

Isn't It Grand Boys
(continued)

Melody & Chords

Key of C

```
    C                                    F
E ─────────────────────────────────────────────────────
A ──────────0────────────3────3──3──────0──────────────
D 5─────5───3──5────2─0──────2─────2──2───3─5─3────────
G 0─────0──────0───5─5─5────0─────0──────2─2─2────────
  Well  look   at  the coffin,   with  golden handles;
```

```
          C        Am                    G      G⁷
E ─────────────────────────────────────────────────────
A ──────────0─────────────────────────────────────────
D 3──5──3──5──────2──────2──2──2────0──────────0───────
G 2──2──2──5──────5──────2──2──2──2─5──────0──────────
  Isn't it grand boys, to  be bloody well dead?
```

CHORUS

```
  G⁷              C        F                          C
E ─────────────────────────────────────────────────────
A ──────────0──────────────0─────0──────0────────0────
D 5─────5───3──5─2─0──────3─────3─────3─3───5──3────5──
G 0─────0───0──0─5─5─5──2──────2────2──2──────────5──
  Let's not have a sniffle,  let's  have a bloody good cry.
```

```
  F                     C        Am
E ─────────────────────────────────────────────────────
A ───0─0─────0───────────0─────0───────────────────────
D 5──3─3───3─3──5──3───5──5───5──2─────────────────────
G 5──2─────2─2───2──5──0───0──2────────────────────────
  And always remember the longer you live,
```

```
  G        G⁷       C
E ─────────────────────────────────────────────────────
A ──────0───────────3──────────────────────────────────
D 5──5──0──5──3───2─0──2────────────────────────────────
G 2──0─────0──0──0─0──5─────────────────────────────────
  The sooner you bloody well die.
```

Chord Forms

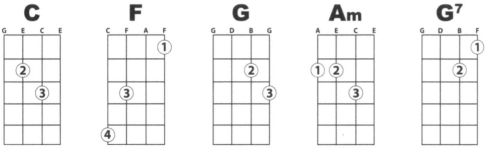

Isn't It Grand Boys

(continued)

Basic Melody

Key of G (Low)

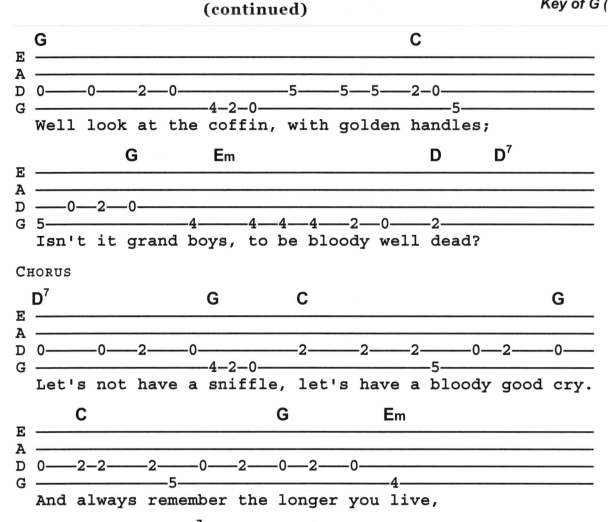

```
G                                        C
E ────────────────────────────────────────────────────────
A ────────────────────────────────────────────────────────
D 0────0────2─0────────────5────5──5────2─0────────────────
G ──────────────4─2─0──────────────────────────5──────────
  Well look at the coffin, with golden handles;

         G      Em                    D     D7
E ────────────────────────────────────────────────────────
A ────────────────────────────────────────────────────────
D ──0──2─0─────────────────────────────────────────────────
G 5────────────4────4──4──4──2──0────2─────────────────────
  Isn't it grand boys, to be bloody well dead?
```

CHORUS

```
D7               G      C                         G
E ────────────────────────────────────────────────────────
A ────────────────────────────────────────────────────────
D 0────────0──2─────0────────2──────2────2────0──2────0────
G ──────────────4─2─0──────────────────────5──────────────
  Let's not have a sniffle, let's have a bloody good cry.

         C                  G      Em
E ────────────────────────────────────────────────────────
A ────────────────────────────────────────────────────────
D 0──2─2────2─────0──2──0──2──0────────────────────────────
G ──────────5─────────────────────4───────────────────────
  And always remember the longer you live,

         D      D7      G
E ────────────────────────────────────────────────────────
A ────────────────────────────────────────────────────────
D 0──0──2──0───────────────────────────────────────────────
G ──────────5──4──2────0───────────────────────────────────
  The sooner you bloody well die.
```

Chord Forms

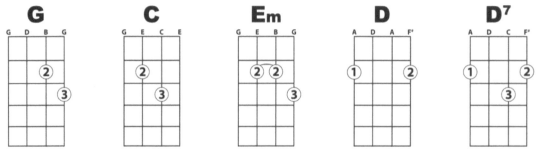

103

Isn't It Grand Boys
(continued)

Basic Melody

Key of G (High)

```
    G                                      C
E ───────────────0─────────────3────3──3────0────────────────
A 5─────5──────────────5───2─0─────────────────5─3───────────
D ───────────────────────────5────────────────────────────
G ──────────────────────────────────────────────────────────
```
Well look at the coffin, with golden handles;

```
         G      Em                    D     D⁷
E ──────0────────────────────────────────────────────────────
A 3──5──────5──────2────2──2──2──0────────0──────────────────
D ────────────────────────────5────────────────────────────
G ──────────────────────────────────────────────────────────
```
Isn't it grand boys, to be bloody well dead?

CHORUS

```
  D⁷              G       C                             G
E ──────────0────────────────0────0─────0──────0──────────────
A 5─────5───────5─2─0────────────────3─────5──────5────────
D ────────────────5──────────────────────────────────────
G ──────────────────────────────────────────────────────────
```
Let's not have a sniffle, let's have a bloody good cry.

```
     C                      G      Em
E ─────0─0────0──────────0────0───────────────────────────────
A 5────────────3─5────────5──────5──2──────────────────────
D ────────────────────────────────────────────────────────
G ──────────────────────────────────────────────────────────
```
And always remember the longer you live,

```
     D         D⁷       G
E ─────────0──────────────────────────────────────────────────
A 5────5───────5──3──2──0────────────────────────────────
D ────────────────────────5───────────────────────────────
G ──────────────────────────────────────────────────────────
```
The sooner you bloody well die.

Chord Forms

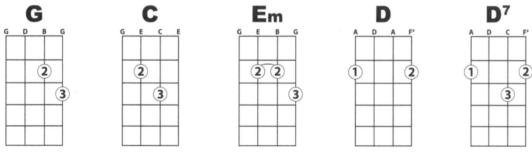

104

Isn't It Grand Boys

Melody & Chords

Key of G (High)

(continued)

```
     G                                              C
E ——————————0———————————————————3———3——3———0———————————————————
A 5———————5———0—5——2-0————————2———2——2———3-5-3———————————————————
D 0———————0———————0-0-0-5———————0———————0———————2-2-2——————————————
G 0———————0———————————0———0——————————0———————0——0———————————————
```
Well look at the coffin, with golden handles;

```
           G           Em                    D        D7
E —————————0———————————————————————————————————————————————————————
A 3———5—3—5———————2———————2—2—2———0———————————0——————————————————
D 2—2—2———0———————0———————2—2—2———2—5———————0————————————————————
G 0———————0———————0———4———————4————————4———2———————————————————————
```
Isn't it grand boys, to be bloody well dead?

Chorus

```
   D7                    G            C                                G
E ——————————0———————————————————0———————0———0————————————0—————————————
A 5———————5———0———————5-2-0——————3———————3———3-3————5—3———5——————
D 4———————4———0———————0-0-0-5——2————————2———2-2———2—2————0——————
G 2———————2————————————0————0———0————————————0————————————0——————
```
Let's not have a sniffle, let's have a bloody good cry.

```
      C                          G            Em
E ——————0—0————————0—————————————0————————0————————————————————
A 5———3-3————————3-3——5———3——5—2———5———2——————————————————
D 0———2————————————2—2———2———0———————0———2————————————————————
G 0———0————————————0———————————0———————0———0————————————————————
```
And always remember the longer you live,

```
      D            D7            G
E ——————————0————————————————————————————————————————————————————
A 5———5—0——5———3——2—0———————————————————————————————————————
D 2———0—0——0———0—0—0—0———5————————————————————————————————————
G ——————2————————2———0—0———0———————————————————————————————————
```
The sooner you bloody well die.

Chord Forms

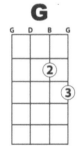

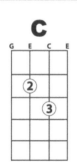

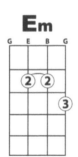

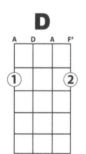

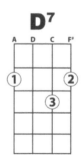

Jug of Punch

Basic Melody
Key of C (Low)

Words and Music

Traditional

This old song was one of the staples of The Clancy Brothers' live shows, with Patrick Clancy beautifully performing it. As he would say, the course of the song follows the same timeline of a good night of drinking: starting off softly and gently and progressively deteriorating. The lines starting with "Toora loora lo" are technically the chorus, but note the last line changes each time through to reflect the verse.

```
       C                                                    G
E ----------------------------------------------------------------------------
A ----------------------------------------------------------------------------
D 5---2----2----2--2---------------------------------0-0----0---0-------
G -------------------5--0--5------5--5------4-5----------------------------
  One pleasant evening in the month of June, a-s I was sitting
```

```
          C                                           F
E ----------------------------------------------------------------------------
A ------------------------------------------------------0------------------
D ------0--2----2----2-------2-5------5------5--3--2----3-0--------------
G 5---------------------------------------------------------------------------
  With my glass and spoon; a small bird sat on an ivy bush,
```

```
          C    F    C       G    C
E ----------------------------------------------------------------------------
A --------------0-------------------------------------------------------------
D 2---3--5----2-------5--3--2--0-------------------------------------------
G ----------------------------------5---------------------------------------
  And the song he sang was the Jug of Punch.
```

Chorus

```
       C                     F                G
E ----------------------------------------------------------------------------
A ----------------------------------------------------------------------------
D 5--5--2--2--2----0--2--3--3--3------3--2--0--0--0-----------------
G ----------------------------------------------------------------------------
  Toora loora lo, toora loora lay, toora loora lo,
```

```
          C                                           F
E ----------------------------------------------------------------------------
A ------------------------------------------------------0------------------
D ----0--2--2--2-------2-5------5------5--3--2----3-0--------------------
G 5---------------------------------------------------------------------------
  Toora loora lay, a small bird sat on an ivy bush,
```

```
          C    F    C       G    C
E ----------------------------------------------------------------------------
A --------------0-------------------------------------------------------------
D 2---3--5----2-------5--3--2--0-------------------------------------------
G ----------------------------------5---------------------------------------
  And the song he sang was the Jug of Punch.
```

See Chords and Additional Verses on Next Page

Jug of Punch
(continued)

Additional Verses

What more diversion can a man desire,
Than to sit him down by an alehouse fire;
Upon his knee a pretty wench,
And on the table a jug of punch.
And toora loora lo, toora loora lay,
Toora loora lo, toora loora lay;
Upon his knee a pretty wench,
And on the table a jug of punch.

Let the doctors come with all their art,
They'll make no impression on my heart.
Even the cripple forgets his crutch,
When he's got outside of a jug of punch!
And toora loora lo, toora loora lay,
Toora loora lo, toora loora lay;
Even the cripple forgets his crutch,
When he's got outside of a jug of punch.

And if I get drunk, well me money's me own,
And them don't like me they can leave me 'lone;
I'll tune me fiddle and I'll rosin me bow,
And I'll be welcome where're I go!
And toora loora lo, toora loora lay,
Toora loora lo, toora loora lay,
I'll tune me fiddle and I'll rosin me bow,
And I'll be welcome wherever I go!

And when I'm dead and in my grave,
No costly tombstone will I have;
Just lay me down in my native peat,
With a jug of punch at my head and feet!
And toora loora lo, toora loora lay,
Toora loora lo, toora loora lay,
Just lay me down in my native peat...
With a jug of punch at my head and feet!

Chord Forms

C

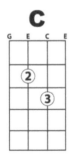

G

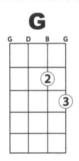

F

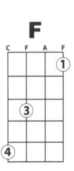

Jug of Punch
(continued)

Basic Melody

Key of C (High)

```
     C                                              G
E 3——0——0——0—0————————————————————————————————————————————————————————
A ——————————————————3———————3———————3—3——————2-3-5-5——5—5——
D ——————————————5——————————————————————————————————————————
G ——————————————————————————————————————————————————————————
```

One pleasant evening in the month of June, a-s I was sitting

```
          C                                      F
E ——————0———————0——0————————0-3——————3———3——1—0—5-1——————
A 3——5——————————————————————————————————————————————5———
D ———————————————————————————————————————————————————————
G ———————————————————————————————————————————————————————
```

With my glass and spoon; a small bird sat on an ivy bush,

```
         C      F   C      G      C
E 0——1——3——0—5——3——1——0—————————————————————
A ——————————————————————5——3————————————————
D ———————————————————————————————————————————
G ———————————————————————————————————————————
```

And the song he sang was the Jug of Punch.

CHORUS

```
     C                  F            G
E 3——3——0—0—0————————0—1—1—1——1—0——————————————————
A ——————————————5——————————————————5—5—5——————————
D ——————————————————————————————————————————————————
G ——————————————————————————————————————————————————
```

Toora loora lo, toora loora lay, toora loora lo,

```
          C                              F
E ——————0—0—0————————0-3——————3———3——1—0—5-1——————
A 3—5————————————————————————————————————————5———
D ————————————————————————————————————————————————
G ————————————————————————————————————————————————
```

Toora loora lay, a small bird sat on an ivy bush,

```
         C      F   C      G      C
E 0——1——3——0—5——3——1——0—————————————————————
A ——————————————————————5——3————————————————
D ———————————————————————————————————————————
G ———————————————————————————————————————————
```

And the song he sang was the Jug of Punch.

See Chords and Additional Verses on Previous Page

Jug of Punch
(continued)

Melody & Chords

Key of C (High)

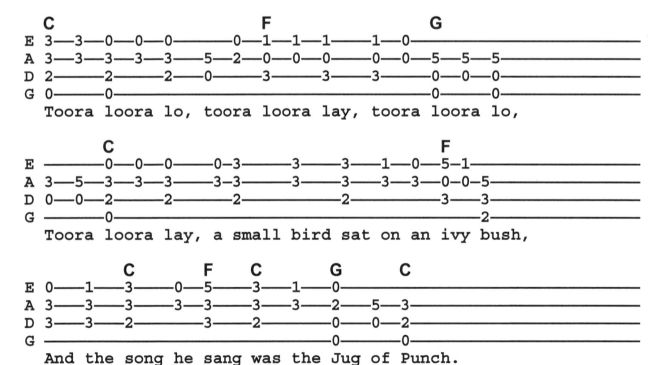

```
      C                                              G
E  3——0——0——————0——0——————————————————————————————————————————————
A  3——3——3——————3——3——————3—————————3——3——————2-3-5-5——5——5——————
D  2——2——————————2——5——————2—————————2——2——————2-2-0-0————0——0———
G  0——0——————————————0——0——————0——————————0——————0——0————————0———
   One pleasant evening in the month of June, a-s I was sitting
```

```
              C                                              F
E  ——————————0——————0——0——————0-3——————3——————3——1—0——5-1—————————
A  3————5——3——————3——3——————3-3——————3——————3——3—3—3——3-0-5————————
D  0——————0——2——————2——————————2——————————————2——————3——3————————
G  ——————————0————————————————————————————————————————————2——————
   With my glass and spoon; a small bird sat on an ivy bush,
```

```
              C     F     C     G     C
E  0——1——3——————0—5——3——1——0————————————————————————————————————
A  3——3——3——————3—3——3——3——2—5——3——————————————————————————————
D  3——————2——————3————————————0——0——2————————————————————————————
G  ——————————————————————————————0————————————————————————————————
   And the song he sang was the Jug of Punch.
```

CHORUS

```
      C                    F           G
E  3——3——0——0——0——————————0——1—1—1——————1——0——————————————————————
A  3——3——3——3——3——————5——2——0——0——0——————0——0—5——5——5——————————————
D  2——————2——————0——————————3——————3——————3——0——0——0————————————
G  0——————0——————————————————————————————————0——————0————————————
   Toora loora lo, toora loora lay, toora loora lo,
```

```
              C                                              F
E  ——————————0——0——0——————0-3——————3——————3——1—0——5-1—————————————
A  3——5——3——3——3——————3-3——————3——————3——3—3—3——0-0-5——————————————
D  0——0——2——————2——————————2——————————————2——————3——3————————————
G  ——————————0————————————————————————————————————————2——————————
   Toora loora lay, a small bird sat on an ivy bush,
```

```
              C     F     C     G     C
E  0——1——3——————0—5——3——1——0————————————————————————————————————
A  3——3——3——————3—3——3——3——2—5——3——————————————————————————————
D  3——3——2——————3——2——————————0——0——2————————————————————————————
G  ——————————————————————————————0——0————————————————————————————
   And the song he sang was the Jug of Punch.
```

See Chords and Additional Verses Two Pages Previous

Jug of Punch
(continued)

Basic Melody

Key of G

```
            G                                                    D
E  ──────────────────────────────────────────────────────────────────────────
A  5──2──2────2──2──────────────────────────────────────0─0──0──0──
D  ───────────────5──0──5─────5─5──────4─5────────────
G  ──────────────────────────────────────────────────────────────────────────
```
One pleasant evening in the month of June, a-s I was sitting

```
            G                                          C
E  ──────────────────────────────────────────────0──────────
A  ────0──2────2──2──────2─5────5────5──3──2───3─0──
D  5──────────────────────────────────────────────────────────
G  ──────────────────────────────────────────────────────────
```
With my glass and spoon; a small bird sat on an ivy bush,

```
            G      C    G      D      G
E  ──────────────0──────────────────────────
A  2──3──5────2──────5──3──2──0──────────
D  ──────────────────────────5──────────────
G  ──────────────────────────────────────────
```
And the song he sang was the Jug of Punch.

CHORUS
```
            G                        C                    D
E  ──────────────────────────────────────────────────────
A  5──5──2──2──2────0──2──3──3──3────3──2──0──0──0──
D  ──────────────────────────────────────────────────────
G  ──────────────────────────────────────────────────────
```
Toora loora lo, toora loora lay, toora loora lo,

```
            G                                          C
E  ──────────────────────────────────────────────0──────────
A  ────0──2──2──2──────2─5────5────5──3──2───3─0──
D  5──────────────────────────────────────────────────────────
G  ──────────────────────────────────────────────────────────
```
Toora loora lay, a small bird sat on an ivy bush,

```
            G      C    G      D      G
E  ──────────────0──────────────────────────
A  2──3──5────2──────5──3──2──0──────────
D  ──────────────────────────5──────────────
G  ──────────────────────────────────────────
```
And the song he sang was the Jug of Punch.

Chord Forms

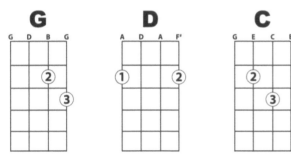

Jug of Punch

(continued)

Melody & Chords

Key of G

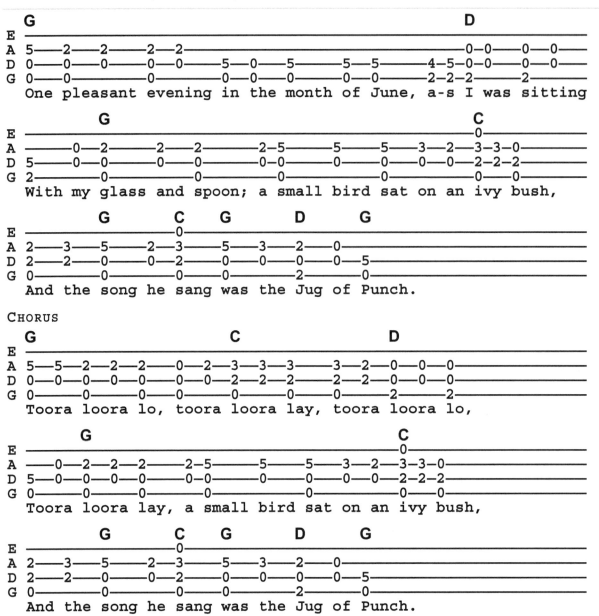

```
        G                                                      D
E ────────────────────────────────────────────────────────────────────────────
A 5──2──2────2──2──────────────────────────────────0─0──0──0──
D 0──0──0────0──0────5──0──5────5──5──────4─5─0─0──0──0──
G 0──0───────0───────0──0──0────0──0──────2─2─2────2──
One pleasant evening in the month of June, a-s I was sitting
```

```
              G                                        C
E ──────────────────────────────────────────────0──────────────────
A ───0──2───2──2──────2─5──────5────5──3─2─3─3─0──────
D 5───0──0──0──0──────0─0─────0────0──0─0─2─2─2──────
G 2──────0──────0──────0──────0──────0──0──
With my glass and spoon; a small bird sat on an ivy bush,
```

```
        G     C   G     D     G
E ────────────0──────────────────────
A 2──3──5──2──3────5──3──2──0──
D 2──2──0──0──2────0──0──0──0──5──
G 0─────0─────0──────0──────2──────0──
And the song he sang was the Jug of Punch.
```

CHORUS

```
        G                    C              D
E ────────────────────────────────────────────────
A 5──5──2──2──2──0──2──3──3──3────3──2──0──0──0──
D 0──0──0──0──0──0──0──2──2──2────2──2──0──0──0──
G 0─────0─────0─────0──────0─────0──────2──────2──
Toora loora lo, toora loora lay, toora loora lo,
```

```
              G                                        C
E ──────────────────────────────────────────────0──────────────────
A ───0──2──2──2──────2─5──────5────5──3─2─3─3─0──────
D 5───0──0──0──0──────0─0─────0────0──0─0─2─2─2──────
G 0──────0──────0──────0──────0──────0──0──
Toora loora lay, a small bird sat on an ivy bush,
```

```
        G     C   G     D     G
E ────────────0──────────────────────
A 2──3──5──2──3────5──3──2──0──
D 2──2──0──0──2────0──0──0──0──5──
G 0─────0─────0──────0──────2──────0──
And the song he sang was the Jug of Punch.
```

Chord Forms

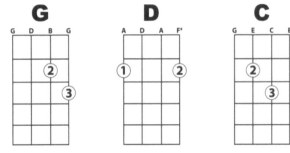

The Juice Of the Barley

Basic Melody
Key of C

The first line of the chorus of this song is a phonetic rendering of an Irish Gaelic line which goes "bainne na mbó ar na gamhna." Translated, it means "the cow's milk is alright for the calf." The next line points out that while milk might be alright for calves, it's the juice of the barley (in other words, beer) that's best for the singer. The Clancy Brother and Tommy Makem's version of this on YouTube, sung by Liam Clancy, is definitive.

Words and Music

Traditional

```
    C                             F           C
E ————————————————————————————————————————————————————————
A ——————————————————————————————————0—2——————3———————————
D 5——3——2——————0——2——————2——2——3—————————————————————————
G ——————————————————5—————————————————————————————————————
  In the sweet county Lim'rick, one cold winter's night;
```

```
    C                                   F           G
E ————————————————————————————————————————————————————————
A ————————————————————————————————————————————————————————
D 5———3——2——————0——————2————2——5——5-3——————2——3——0————————
G ——————————————————5—————————————————————————————————————
  All the turf fires were burning when I first saw the light.
```

```
    G    C                     F         C
E ————————————————————————————————————————————————————————
A ——————————————————————————0—2——————3———————————————————
D 5———3——2—0——2————2—————2——3—————————————————————————————
G ——————————————5—————————————————————————————————————————
  And a drunken old midwife went tipsy with joy;
```

```
    C       0                      F      G
E —————————0——————————————————————————————————————————————
A 3——5—————————5——————3——0————————————————————————————————
D ——————————————————————————5——2——3——2—3-0————————————————
G ————————————————————————————————————————————————————————
  As she danced round the floor with her slip of a boy.
```

CHORUS

```
    G       C
E ————————————————————————————————————————————————————————
A ————————————————————————3————————————————————————————————
D 5———3——2——0—2————2—5——————————5—————————————————————————
G ——————————————5—————————————————————————————————————————
  Singing ban-ya-na mo if an-gawn-ya,
```

```
    C                G⁷         C
E ————————————————————————————————————————————————————————
A ————————————————————————————————————————————————————————
D 5———3——2——————0——2——3——0—————————————————————————————————
G ——————————————————————————4——5——————————————————————————
  And the juice of the barley for me.
```

See Chords and Additional Verses on Next Page

The Juice Of the Barley
(continued)

Additional Verses

Well when I was a gossoon of eight years or so,
With me turf and me primer to school I did go;
To a dusty old school house without any door,
Where lay the school master blind drunk on the floor...

At the learning I wasn't such a genius I'm thinking,
But I soon beat the master entirely at drinking;
Not a wake or a wedding for five miles around,
But meself in the corner was sure to be found.

One Sunday the priest thread me out from the altar,
Saying you'll end up your days with your neck in a halter;
And you'll dance a fine jig between heaven and hell,
And his words they did frighten me the truth for to tell.

So the very next morning as the dawn it did break,
I went down to the vestry the pledge for to take;
And there in that room sat the priests in a bunch,
Round a big roaring fire drinking tumblers of punch.

Well from that day to this I have wandered alone,
I'm a jack of all trades and a master of none;
With the sky for me roof and the earth for me floor,
And I'll dance out my days drinking whiskey galore.

Chord Forms

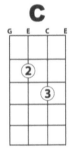
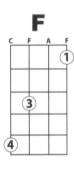
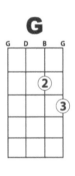

The Juice Of the Barley

Melody & Chords

(continued)

Key of C

```
     C                                      F            C
E ----------------------------------------------------------------
A ------------------------------------------0--2------3-----------
D 5--3----2--------0--2--------2------2--3--3--3------2-----------
G 5--5----5--------0--5--5--5--5------5--5--5---------0-----------
  In the sweet county Lim'rick, one cold winter's night;
```

```
     C                                      F            G
E ----------------------------------------------------------------
A ----------------------------------------------------------------
D 5------3----2----0------2--------2----5----5-3------2--3----0----
G 5------5----5----0------5----5-5-5----5----5-5------5--5----0----
  All the turf fires were burning when I first saw the light.
```

```
     G     C                              F          C
E ----------------------------------------------------------------
A --------------------------------------0--2------3---------------
D 5----3--2--0----2--------2------2--3--3--3------2---------------
G 0----0--5--0----5----5--5--5----5-----5--2------0---------------
  And a drunken old midwife went tipsy with joy;
```

```
     C                                      F          G
E ----------0-----------------------------------------------------
A 3--5----3--------5------3----0----------------------------------
D 2--2----2--------2------2----2------5----2--3------2--3-0--------
G 0---------0---------------------5----5--5--5------5--5-0--------
  As she danced round the floor with her slip of a boy.
```

CHORUS

```
     G        C
E ----------------------------------------------------------------
A --------------------------3-------------------------------------
D 5----3----2----0--2------2--5--2------5-------------------------
G 0----0----5----0--5--5--5--5--5--0----5------------------------
  Singing ban-ya-na mo if an-gawn-ya,
```

```
     C                    G⁷          C
E ----------------------------------------------------------------
A ------------------------------------3---------------------------
D 5----3----2------0--2----3--0----0--2---------------------------
G 5----5----5------0--0----0--0----4--5--------------------------
  And the juice of the barley for me.
```

See Chords Forms on Previous Page

> *Here's to the land of the shamrock so green,*
> *Here's to each lad and his darlin' colleen,*
> *Here's to the ones we love dearest and most,*
> *May God bless old Ireland, that's this Irishman's toast!*

The Juice Of the Barley

(continued)

Basic Melody

Key of G

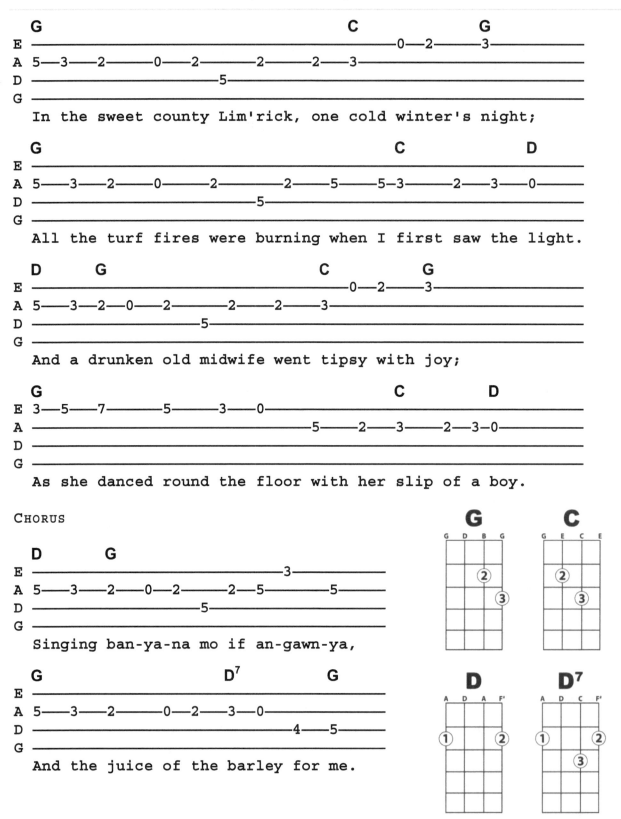

```
         G                                        C              G
E  ──────────────────────────────────────────────0──2───────3─────────────
A  5───3───2───────0───2───────2───────2───3──────────────────────────────
D  ────────────────────────5───────────────────────────────────────────────
G  ──────────────────────────────────────────────────────────────────────
```

In the sweet county Lim'rick, one cold winter's night;

```
         G                                        C              D
E  ──────────────────────────────────────────────────────────────────────
A  5───3───2───────0───────2───────2───5───5─3───────2───3───0────────────
D  ────────────────────────5───────────────────────────────────────────────
G  ──────────────────────────────────────────────────────────────────────
```

All the turf fires were burning when I first saw the light.

```
   D    G                                 C        G
E  ─────────────────────────────────0───2───3──────────────────────────────
A  5───3─2─0───2───────2───────2───3────────────────────────────────────────
D  ───────────────5──────────────────────────────────────────────────────
G  ──────────────────────────────────────────────────────────────────────
```

And a drunken old midwife went tipsy with joy;

```
   G                                        C        D
E  3───5───7───────5───────3───0──────────────────────────────────────────
A  ──────────────────────────────────5───2───3───2─3─0────────────────────
D  ──────────────────────────────────────────────────────────────────────
G  ──────────────────────────────────────────────────────────────────────
```

As she danced round the floor with her slip of a boy.

CHORUS

```
   D    G                                    
E  ──────────────────────────────────3─────────────────
A  5───3───2───0─2───────2───5───────5──────────────────
D  ────────────────5─────────────────────────────────
G  ──────────────────────────────────────────────────
```

Singing ban-ya-na mo if an-gawn-ya,

```
   G                          D⁷       G
E  ──────────────────────────────────────────────────
A  5───3───2───────0───2───3───0─────────────────────
D  ───────────────────────────────4───5─────────────
G  ──────────────────────────────────────────────────
```

And the juice of the barley for me.

The Juice Of the Barley

(continued)

Basic Melody

Key of G

```
      G                                           C              G
E ─────────────────────────────────────────────0──2───────3──────────────
A 5──3────2────────0──2──────2─────2──3────3──3────2───────────────────────
D 0──0────0────────0──0──5───0──────0──2────2──────0───────────────────────
G 0──────────0─────────0──0────────0─────────────0────────────────────────
```
In the sweet county Lim'rick, one cold winter's night;

```
      G                                           C              D
E ─────────────────────────────────────────────────────────────────────────
A 5────3───2────0──2──────2────5───5─3──────2───3───0──────────────────────
D 0────0───0────0────0──5──0────0──0─2──────2───2───0──────────────────────
G 0──────────0──────────0────0────0────────0──────2──────────────────────
```
All the turf fires were burning when I first saw the light.

```
      D    G                                      C              G
E ─────────────────────────────────────────────0──2───────3──────────────
A 5────3─2──0────2──────2────2──3──3──3───2──────────────────────────────
D 0────0─0──0──0──0──5──0────0──2──2────0───────────────────────────────
G 2─────────0──────0────0──2──────────0──────────0────────────────────────
```
And a drunken old midwife went tipsy with joy;

```
      G                                           C          D
E 3──5────7──────5──────3────0──────────────────────────────────────────
A 2──0────5──────0──────2──2──5───2──3────2──3─0──────────────────────────
D 0──0────5──────0──────0──0──────0──0──2──2──2─0──────────────────────────
G 0───────────────────────────0──────0──────2────────────────────────────
```
As she danced round the floor with her slip of a boy.

CHORUS

```
      D    G
E ─────────────────────────────────────3──────────────────
A 5────3───2──0──2──────2──5──2──────5────────────────────
D 0────0───0──0──0──5───0──0──0──────0────────────────────
G 2────────0──────0──0──0──────0─────0────────────────────
```
Singing ban-ya-na mo if an-gawn-ya,

```
      G                            D⁷         G
E ──────────────────────────────────────────────────────────
A 5────3───2──────0──2──3──0────────────────────────────────
D 0────0───0──────0──0──0──0──4───5─────────────────────────
G 0──────────0────────────2───────2──0─────────────────────
```
And the juice of the barley for me.

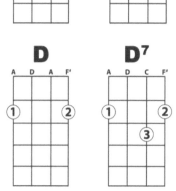

Landlord Fill the Flowing Bowl (Three Jolly Coachmen)

Basic Melody

Key of G

This old convivial drinking song has been around for hundreds of years, and is believed to be of English origin. It has also been known as "Three Jolly Coachmen" and "For Tonight We'll Merry Merry Be", amongst other titles. There are plenty of versions on YouTube you can listen to for a reminder of how the song is supposed to go.

Words and Music

Traditional

```
      G                                         D7              G
E ————————————————————————————————————————————————————————————————————————————————
A ——————————————————————————————————————————0—0——0——0——————2——2—————————————————————
D 0——————5——————0—————————0——5—5————5——————————————————————————————————5—————————————
G ———————————————————————4—————————————————————————————————————————————————————————
```
Come landlord fill the flowing bowl, until it does run o-ver;

```
                                            D7              G
E ————————————————————————————————————————————————————————————————————————————————
A ——————————————————————————————————————————0—0——0——0——————2——2—————————————————————
D 5——————0—————————0——5—5————5——————————————————————————————————5—————————————————————
G ———————————————4—————————————————————————————————————————————————————————————————
```
Landlord fill the flowing bowl, until it does run o-ver.

```
                      C               D7                  G
E ——————————————————————————————————————————————————————————————————————————————————
A 2——2—2————————5————5—3——3—3——3————0——0—0——————3————3—2——2——2—2—————————————————————
D ————————————————————————————————————————————————————————————————————————————————
G ——————————————————————————————————————————————————————————————————————————————————
```
For tonight we'll merry merry be, for tonight we'll merry merry be,

```
  Em                            Am      D7                G
E ——————————————————————————————————————————————————————————————————————————————————
A —————————————2————2—2—0——0—3————0——————————————————————————————————————————————————
D 5——5—5——————————————————————————4——0——2——————4——5—5————————————————————————————————
G ——————————————————————————————————————————————————————————————————————————————————
```
For tonight we'll merry merry be... tomorrow we'll be sober.

Chord Forms

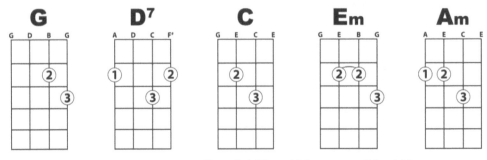

See Additional Verses on Next Page

117

Landlord Fill the Flowing Bowl
(Three Jolly Coachmen) (continued)

Melody & Chords

Key of G

```
     G                              D7              G
E ----------------------------------------------------------------
A --------------------------------0-0---0--0----2----2-----------
D 0------5----0----------0---5--5------5---0-0--0--0----0---0-5---
G 0------0----0----4-----0---0--0------0---2------2-----0-0-------
  Come landlord fill  the flowing bowl,  until it does run o-ver;

                                    D7              G
E ----------------------------------------------------------------
A --------------------------------0-0--0--0----2----2------------
D 5----0----------0---5--5----5-------0-0--0--0----0---0-5-------
G 0----0----4-----0---0--0----0-------2------2-----0-0-----------
  Landlord fill the flowing bowl, until it does run o-ver.

               C           D7              G
E ----------------------------------------------------------------
A 2----2-2----5----5--3--3--3--3---0---0-0------3-------3-2--2--2--2-
D 0----0-0----0----2--2--2--2--2---0---0-0------0-------0-0--0--0--0-
G 0----------0--------------0------0---2------2-------0------0------0-
  For tonight we'll merry merry be, for tonight we'll merry merry be,

  Em                        Am    D7              G
E ----------------------------------------------------------------
A --------2-------2--2--0--0--3-------0--------------------------
D 5----5-5----2-------2--2--2--2--2-----0-4--0----2-----4---5-5---
G 4----4-4----4----4----4-----2-----2-2-2--2----2----2---0-0-----
  For tonight we'll merry merry be... tomorrow we'll be sober.
```

Additional Verses

For each verse, repeat the first two lines twice each time through, then repeat the third line three times, as spelled out in the first verse below.

Three jolly coachmen sat in an English tavern
Three jolly coachmen sat in an English tavern,
And they decided,
And they decided,
And they decided...
To have another flagon!

Here's to the man who drinks weak ale,
And goes to bed quite sober; (2X)
He fades as the leaves do fade, (3X)
That drop off in October.

Here's to the man who drinks strong beer,
And goes to bed right mellow; (2X)
He lives as he ought to live, (3X)
And dies a jolly good fellow.

Here's to the maid who steals a kiss,
And runs to tell her mother; (2X)
She's a foolish, foolish thing, (3X)
She'll never get another!

Here's to the girl who steals a kiss,
And comes to steal another; (2X)
She's a boon to all mankind, (3X)
Soon she'll be a mother!

Here's to the one who drinks our ale,
And never does repay us; (2X)
Soon he will drink alone, (3X)
And learn to be more generous!

Landlord Fill the Flowing Bowl
(Three Jolly Coachmen) (continued)

Basic Melody

Key of C

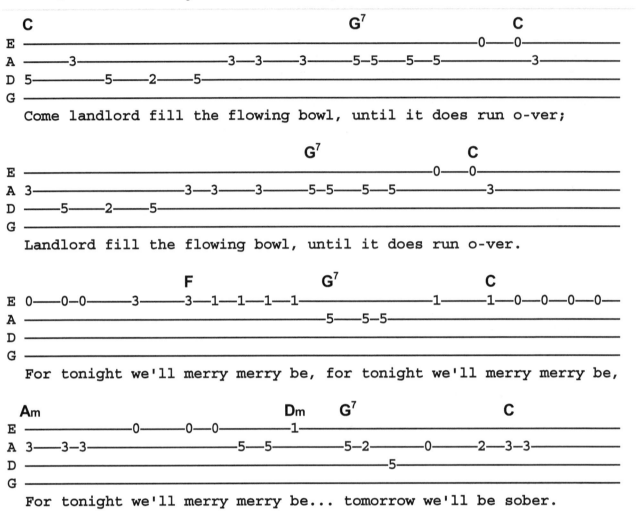

Come landlord fill the flowing bowl, until it does run o-ver;

Landlord fill the flowing bowl, until it does run o-ver.

For tonight we'll merry merry be, for tonight we'll merry merry be,

For tonight we'll merry merry be... tomorrow we'll be sober.

Chord Forms

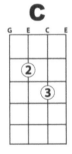
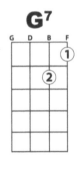
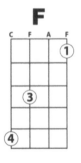
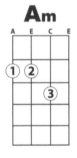
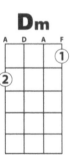

Landlord Fill the Flowing Bowl
(Three Jolly Coachmen) (continued)

Melody & Chords

Key of C

```
        C                                    G7                C
E ─────────────────────────────────────────────────────0───0──────────────
A ─────3─────────────────3───3────3──────5─5──5─5────3───3─3────────────────
D 5─────2────5─────2────5───2─2────2──────3─3──3─3────2─2──────────────────
G 0──────0────0─────0────0──0────────0──────0────0──────0─0────────────────
```
Come landlord fill the flowing bowl, until it does run o-ver;

```
                                    G7                C
E ─────────────────────────────────────────────────0───0──────────────────
A 3───────────────────3───3────3──────5─5──5─5────3───3─3──────────────────
D 2────5─────2────5────2─2────2──────3─3──3─3────2─2───────────────────────
G 0─────0─────0────0────0──────0──────0────0──────0─0─────────────────────
```
Landlord fill the flowing bowl, until it does run o-ver.

```
            F                G7                C
E 0────0─0──────3──────3─1──1─1──1──────────1──────1─0──0──0──0────
A 3────3─3──────3──────0─0──0─0──0──5──5─5────2──────3──3──3─3──3─3─
D 2──────2──────────3──────3──────3─3──3─3────0──────2──────2──────2─
G 0────────────────────────────0──────0────────────────────────0──
```
For tonight we'll merry merry be, for tonight we'll merry merry be,

```
    Am                        Dm    G7                C
E ──────────────0──────0──0────────1──────────────────────────────
A 3───3─3──────0──────0─0──5─5──0────5─2──────0──────2─3─3─────────
D 2───2─2──────2──────2────5─5──0────0─0──5────3──────0─2─2────────
G 2─────2──────────2──────────2──────0──────0──0──────0─0──────────
```
For tonight we'll merry merry be... tomorrow we'll be sober.

Chord Forms

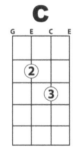 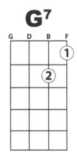 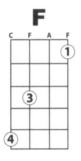 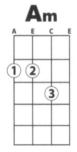 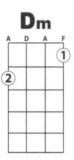

Let Your Back And Sides Go Bare

Basic Melody

Key of C

The origins of this piece, also known as "The Beggar's Song", go back into the 1500's. It tells of some of the hardships of the beggar's life, though in an upbeat and humorous way. This is one of the more obscure of the old folks songs, not heard so much these days and without many professional recordings to refer to - but you can find some good examples on YouTube.

Words and Music

Traditional

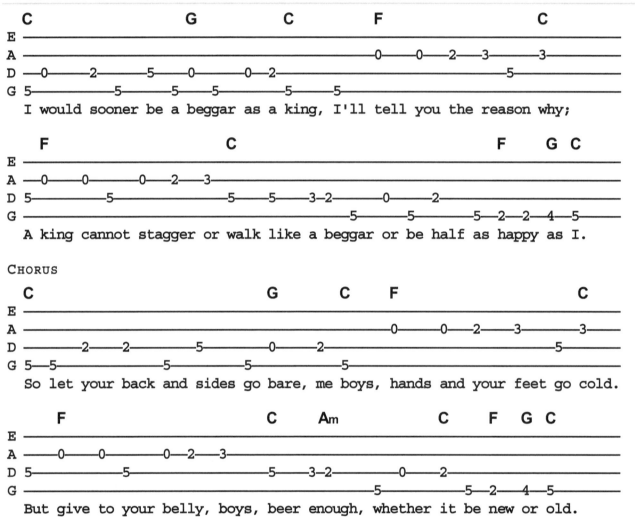

```
      C                 G           C           F                       C
E ————————————————————————————————————————————————————————————————————————————————
A ————————————————————————————————————————0———0———2———3———————3—————————————————————
D ——0———————2———————5———0———————0—2——————————————————————————————5———————————————————
G 5—————————————5———————5———5———————5———5————————————————————————————————————————————
      I would sooner be a beggar as a king, I'll tell you the reason why;
```

```
      F                       C                           F       G  C
E ————————————————————————————————————————————————————————————————————————————————
A ——0———0———————0———2———3————————————————————————————————————————————————————————————
D 5—————————5————————————————5———5———3—2——————0———————2——————————————————————————————
G ——————————————————————————————5———————5——————————5———————5—2———2———4———5————————————
      A king cannot stagger or walk like a beggar or be half as happy as I.
```

CHORUS

```
      C                          G       C   F                       C
E ————————————————————————————————————————————————————————————————————————————————
A ————————————————————————————————————————0———0———2———3———————3———————————————————————
D ——————2———————2———————5———0———————2——————————————————————————5——————————————————————
G 5———5—————————————5———————5———————5————————————————————————————————————————————————
      So let your back and sides go bare, me boys, hands and your feet go cold.
```

```
      F                       C       Am          C   F   G  C
E ————————————————————————————————————————————————————————————————————————————————
A ——0———0———————0———2———3————————————————————————————————————————————————————————————
D 5—————————5————————————5———3—2——————0———————2——————————————————————————————————————
G ——————————————————————————5———————————5——————5—2———4———5————————————————————————————
      But give to your belly, boys, beer enough, whether it be new or old.
```

Chord Forms

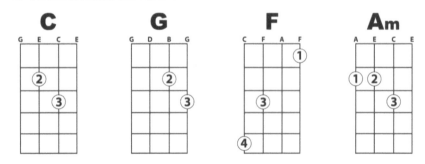

See Additional Verses on Next Page

Let Your Back And Sides Go Bare (continued)

Basic Melody

Key of G

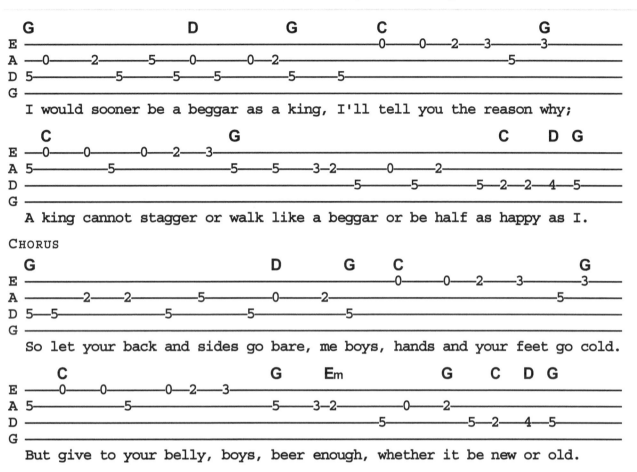

I would sooner be a beggar as a king, I'll tell you the reason why;

A king cannot stagger or walk like a beggar or be half as happy as I.

CHORUS

So let your back and sides go bare, me boys, hands and your feet go cold.

But give to your belly, boys, beer enough, whether it be new or old.

Chord Forms

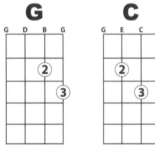

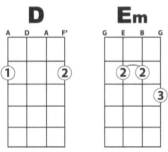

Additional Verses

I've sixpence in me pocket,
And I worked hard for that,
Landlord, here it is;
There isn't any Turk going to make me work,
While the beggin' is as good as it is.

Sometimes we call at a nobleman's house,
Beg for bread and beer;
Sometimes we are lame,
Sometimes we are blind,
Sometimes too deaf to hear.

Sometimes we lie like hogs in a sty,
Frost and snow on the ground;
Sometimes eat a crust that's rolled in the dust,
And be thankful if that can be found.

Let Your Back And Sides Go Bare (continued)

Melody & Chords

Key of G

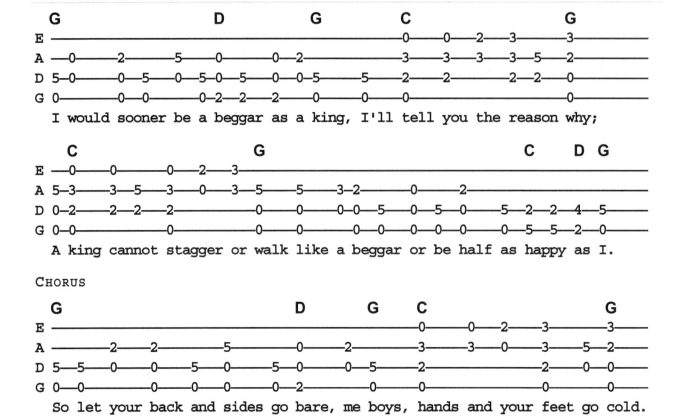

I would sooner be a beggar as a king, I'll tell you the reason why;

A king cannot stagger or walk like a beggar or be half as happy as I.

CHORUS

So let your back and sides go bare, me boys, hands and your feet go cold.

But give to your belly, boys, beer enough, whether it be new or old.

Chord Forms

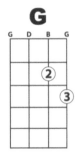
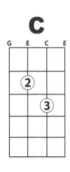
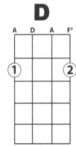
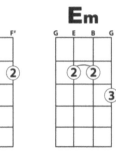

123

Molly Malone

Basic Melody
Key of C (Low)

Words and Music

Traditional

This is one of the best-known of all the old traditional Irish ballads. It tells the story of Molly Malone, a Dublin street seafood vendor who died of a fever. While the song's historical roots are uncertain, its popularity caused the city of Dublin to erect a bronze statue commemorating Molly Malone.

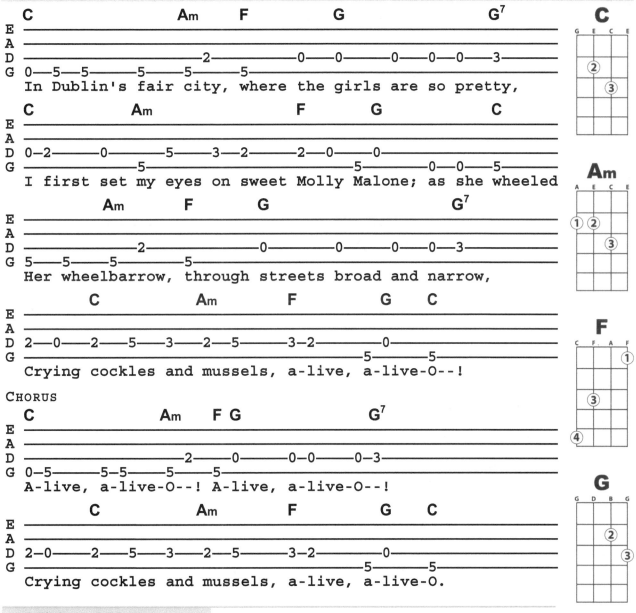

Additional Verses

She was a fishmonger,
And sure 'twas no wonder,
For so were her father
And mother before.
And they both wheeled their barrows,
Through streets broad and narrow,
Crying "Cockles, and mussels,
Alive, alive-o."

She died of a fever,
And no one could save her,
And that was the end
Of sweet Molly Malone.
Now her ghost wheels her barrow,
Through streets broad and narrow,
Crying "Cockles, and mussels,
Alive, alive-o."

Molly Malone (continued)

Basic Melody
Key of C (High)

```
      C                 Am      F         G              G7
E ——————————————————————0————————————————————————————————1——————
A ———3—3—————————3————3————3—————5————5—————5———5——5—————————————
D 5——————————————————————————————————————————————————————————————
G ————————————————————————————————————————————————————————————————
```

In Dublin's fair city, where the girls are so pretty,

```
      C           Am                F      G            C
E ——0——————————————————3————1——0————0——————————————————————————————
A 5——————5————3——————————————————————5——3—5——————————3——————————————
D ——————————————————————————————————————————5——5————————————————————
G ————————————————————————————————————————————————————————————————
```

I first set my eyes on sweet Molly Malone; as she wheeled

```
          Am       F        G              G7
E ——————————0————————————————————————————————1——————
A 3———3———3————————3—————5————5———5——5————————————————
D ————————————————————————————————————————————————————
G ————————————————————————————————————————————————————
```

Her wheelbarrow, through streets broad and narrow,

```
    C        C   Am     F        G    C
E 0————————0——3——1——0——3——1—0——————————————————
A ——5——————————————————————————3—5————3——————————
D ————————————————————————————————————————————————
G ————————————————————————————————————————————————
```

Crying cockles and mussels, a-live, a-live-O--!

CHORUS

```
      C           Am    F G         G7
E ——————————————————0————————————————1——————
A ——3——————3—3——————3————3—5————5—5——————5————
D 5——————————————————————————————————————————
G ————————————————————————————————————————————
```

A-live, a-live-O--! A-live, a-live-O--!

```
        C        Am     F        G    C
E 0————————0——3——1——0——3——1—0——————————————————
A ——5——————————————————————————3—5————3——————————
D ————————————————————————————————————————————————
G ————————————————————————————————————————————————
```

Crying cockles and mussels, a-live, a-live-O.

Additional Verses

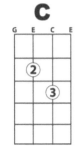
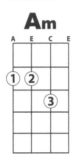
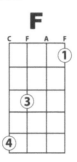
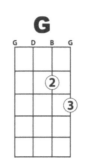
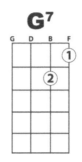

Molly Malone (continued)

Melody & Chords
Key of C (High)

```
     C                    Am       F          G              G7
E ————————————————————————0———————————————————————————————1————————
A ———3——3————————3————3—0——3———————3————5——————5——5——5——2—————————
D 5—2——2—————————2————2—2——————3————3————0——————0——0——0———0————————
G 5—0————————————————2———2—————————0——————————0————0——0———0————————
  In  Dublin's  fair  city,   where  the  girls  are  so  pretty,
```

```
     C              Am            F          G              C
E ———0————————————————3——————1—0——————0—————————————————————————————
A 5—3————————5———3—2————0——0—————0—5——3—5——————————3————————
D 0—2——————2———2——2——————————3———3—3—0—————5——5———2————————
G ———0————————————2——————————————————0——————0——0——0———————
  I first  set  my  eyes  on  sweet  Molly  Malone;  as  she  wheeled
```

```
            Am       F          G                      G7
E ——————————————0———————————————————————————————————1————————
A 3——3————3—0——3——————5———————5——————5——5——2—————————
D 2——2————2—2——————3————0——————0——————0——0——0————————
G ————0————————2——————————0————————0————0——0—————————
  Her  wheelbarrow,  through  streets  broad  and  narrow,
```

```
            C         Am         F            G    C
E 0—————————0———3——1——0—3————————1—0————————————————————
A 2—5——————3———3——3——0—0————————0—0——————3—5————3————————
D 0—0——————2——————————2————————3—3——————3—0————2————————
G ————————0————————————2—————————————2—0————0————————
  Crying  cockles  and  mussels,  a-live,  a-live-O--!
```

CHORUS

```
     C              Am      F G              G7
E ——————————————————0——————————————————————1————————
A ——3————————3—3——3—0——3—5————5—5————5—2————————
D 5—2—————2—2——2—2——3—0————0—0————0—0————————
G 5—0——————————0————2—2——0——————0————0—0————————
  A-live,  a-live-O--!  A-live,  a-live-O--!
```

```
            C         Am         F            G    C
E 0—————————0———3——1——0—3————————1—0————————————————————
A 2—5——————3———3——3——0—0————————0—0——————3—5————3————————
D 5—0——————2——————————2————————3—3——————3—0————2————————
G ————————0————————————2—————————————2—0————0————————
  Crying  cockles  and  mussels,  a-live,  a-live-O.
```

Additional Verses

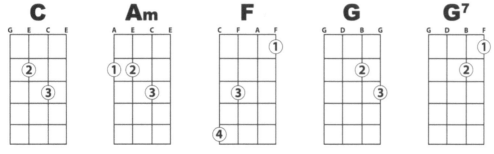

Molly Malone (continued)

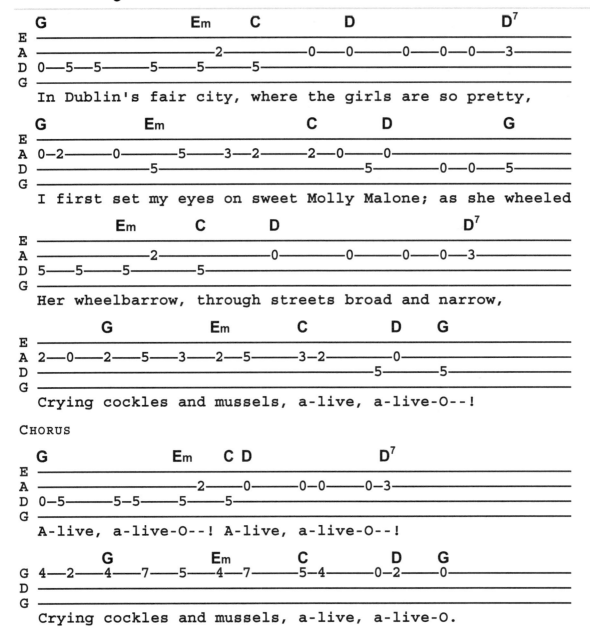

In Dublin's fair city, where the girls are so pretty,

I first set my eyes on sweet Molly Malone; as she wheeled

Her wheelbarrow, through streets broad and narrow,

Crying cockles and mussels, a-live, a-live-O--!

CHORUS

A-live, a-live-O--! A-live, a-live-O--!

Crying cockles and mussels, a-live, a-live-O.

Chord Forms

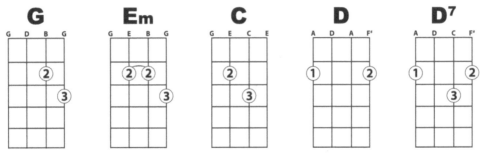

Molly Malone (continued)

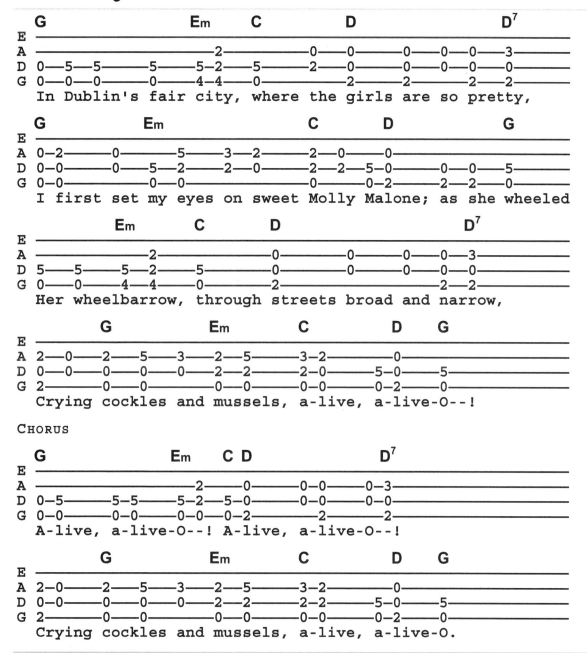

```
     G                Em      C           D                  D7
E ----------------------------------------------------------------------
A -------------------------2-------0---0-------0---0---0---3-------------
D 0---5---5------5-----5-2---5-----2---0-------0---0---0---0-------------
G 0---0---0------0-----4-4---0-------------2-------2-------2---2---------
     In Dublin's fair city, where the girls are so pretty,

     G               Em                C       D            G
E ----------------------------------------------------------------------
A 0-2-------0--------5---3-2-----2---0-----0----------------------------
D 0-0-------0----5-2-----2---0---2-2---5-0-------0---0---5--------------
G 0-0----------0---0-------------0-------0-2-----2---2---0--------------
     I first set my eyes on sweet Molly Malone; as she wheeled

          Em       C       D                  D7
E ----------------------------------------------------------------------
A -----------2-------------0-------0-------0---0---3--------------------
D 5---5-----5-2-----5------0-------0-------0---0---0--------------------
G 0---0---4-4-------0------2-------------------2---2-------------------
     Her wheelbarrow, through streets broad and narrow,

          G        Em       C         D    G
E ----------------------------------------------------------------------
A 2---0---2---5---3---2---5--------3-2-------0-------------------------
D 0---0---0---0---0---2-2----2-0-------5-0-----5----------------------
G 2-------0---0---------0-0-------0-0------0-2-----0------------------
     Crying cockles and mussels, a-live, a-live-O--!
```

CHORUS

```
     G                Em     C D           D7
E ----------------------------------------------------------------------
A -------------------------2-----0-----0-0-----0-3--------------------
D 0-5-------5-5-----5-2---5-0-------0-0-----0-0-----------------------
G 0-0-------0-0-----0-0---0-2----------2-------2--------------------
     A-live, a-live-O--! A-live, a-live-O--!

          G        Em       C         D    G
E ----------------------------------------------------------------------
A 2-0-----2---5---3---2---5--------3-2-------0-----------------------
D 0-0-----0---0---0---2-2----2-2-------5-0-----5-------------------
G 2-------0---0---------0-0-------0-0------0-2-----0--------------
     Crying cockles and mussels, a-live, a-live-O.
```

Chord Forms

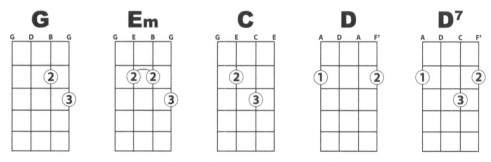

The Moonshiner

Basic Melody
Key of G

This is another traditional Irish drinking song, a favorite at singing sessions both in Ireland and abroad. You are very likely to hear the Duffy boys sing this one in full voice when things get going down at Charlie's Greenhouse in Dover, New Hampshire.

Words and Music
Traditional

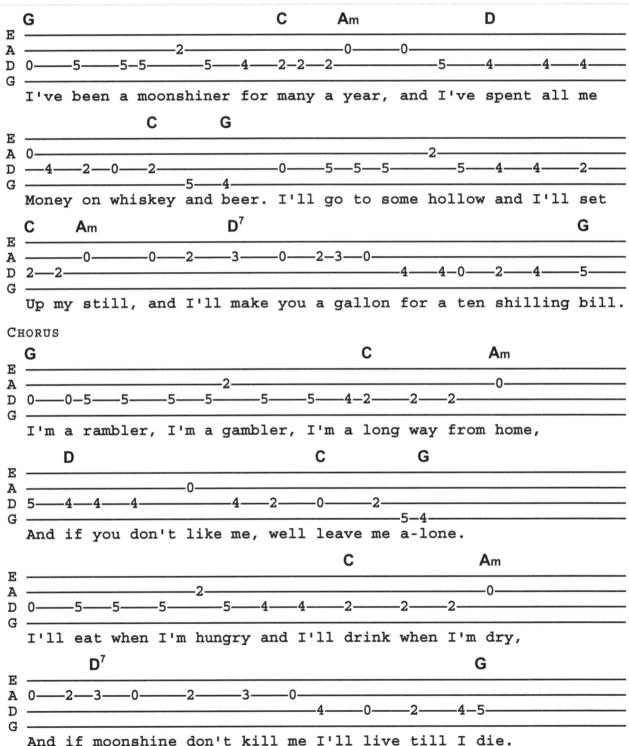

CHORUS

See Chord Forms and Additional Verses on Next Page

The Moonshiner (continued)

Chord Forms (Key of G)

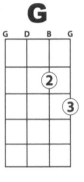
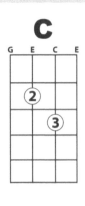
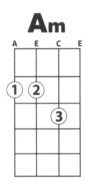
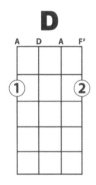
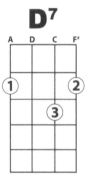

Additional Verses

I'll go to some hollow in this coun--try,
Ten gallons of wash I can go on a spree;
No women to follow, the world is all mine,
I love none so well as I love the moonshine.

Oh, moonshine, dear moonshine, oh, how I love thee,
You killed me old father, but dare you try me;
Now bless all moonshiners and bless all moonshine,
Their breath smells as sweet as the dew on the vine.

Chord Forms (Key of C)

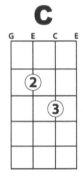
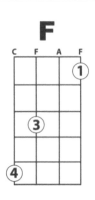
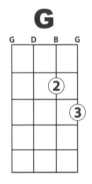
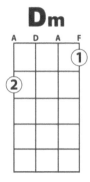
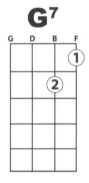

The Moonshiner (continued)

Melody & Chords
Key of G

```
      G                          C     Am          D
E ──────────────────────────────────────────────────────────────
A ────────────────2─────────────────0─────0──────────────────────
D 0───5─────5─5───0──5───4──2─2──2─2────2───5───4────4───4────────
G 0───0───0─0───0───0──0──5─5──5─5───────5──0───2────2───2────────
```
I've been a moonshiner for many a year, and I've spent all me

```
                    C       G
E ──────────────────────────────────────────────────────────────
A 0────────────────────────────────────────2─────────────────────
D 0─4───2──0──2────────0───────0──5──5─5──────0─5───4──4───2───────
G 2─2──2─2──5──5───4─────4────0─0──0────0─0──0──0───0──0───0───────
```
Money on whiskey and beer. I'll go to some hollow and I'll set

```
  C    Am                 D⁷                                    G
E ──────────────────────────────────────────────────────────────
A ─────0──────0──2───3───0──2─3──0────────────────────────────────
D 2───2──2───2──2───0────0──0─0──0───4───4─0──2───4────5──────────
G 0─5─5───5─────2───2────2────2─2─2──2───2──2───0─────
```
Up my still, and I'll make you a gallon for a ten shilling bill.

CHORUS

```
  G                              C          Am
E ──────────────────────────────────────────────────────────────
A ────────────────2────────────────────────0─────────────────────
D 0───0─5──5────5───5─0──5───5──4─2──2───2──2─────────────────────
G 0───0─0──0────0───0─0──0───0──0─5──5───5──5─────────────────────
```
I'm a rambler, I'm a gambler, I'm a long way from home,

```
  D                         C      G
E ──────────────────────────────────────────────────────────────
A ────────────────0───────────────────────────────────────────────
D 5───4──4───4────0───4──2───0───2───0────────────────────────────
G 5───2─2───2────2───2─2───0───5─5─4──────────────────────────────
```
And if you don't like me, well leave me a-lone.

```
                                C          Am
E ──────────────────────────────────────────────────────────────
A ────────────────2────────────────────────0─────────────────────
D 0───5───5───5───0─5───4──4───2───2───2──2───────────────────────
G 4───0───0───0───0─0───0──0───0─5─────5───5──5───────────────────
```
I'll eat when I'm hungry and I'll drink when I'm dry,

```
        D⁷                                      G
E ──────────────────────────────────────────────────────────────
A 0──2──3───0────2───3───0────────────────────────────────────────
D 2──2──0───0────0───0──0──4───0───2───4─5────────────────────────
G 5────2────────2────2──2───2──2──2─0─────────────────────────────
```
And if moonshine don't kill me I'll live till I die.

See Chord Forms and Additional Verses on Previous Page

The Moonshiner (continued)

Basic Melody
Key of C

```
      C                           F     Dm            G
E _____0_____
A _____3____3-3_____3___2__0-0__0-5_____5___3___2_____2___2_____
D 5_____
G _____
```
I've been a moonshiner for many a year, and I've spent all me

```
                 F     C
E _____0_____
A 5-2___0_____0_____3__3-3_____3___2___2____0_____
D _____5_____3__2_____5_____
G _____
```
Money on whiskey and beer. I'll go to some hollow and I'll set

```
  F    Dm                 G7                              C
E _____0____1_____0-1_____
A 0___0-5_____5_____5_____5___2__2_____0__2___3_____
D _____5_____
G _____
```
Up my still, and I'll make you a gallon for a ten shilling bill.

CHORUS

```
   C                           F     Dm
E _____0_____
A _____3___3___3___3_____3___3__2-0____0___0___5_____
D 5___5_____
G _____
```
I'm a rambler, I'm a gambler, I'm a long way from home,

```
     G                      F     C
E _____
A 3___2__2___2_____5___2__0_____0_____
D _____5_____3-2_____
G _____
```
And if you don't like me, well leave me a-lone.

```
                              F     Dm
E _____0_____
A _____3___3___3_____3__2__2___0___0___0___5_____
D 5_____
G _____
```
I'll eat when I'm hungry and I'll drink when I'm dry,

```
     G7                           C
E _____0__1_____0___1_____
A 5_____5_____5__2_____0___2-3_____
D _____5_____
G _____
```
And if moonshine don't kill me I'll live till I die.

See Chord Forms and Additional Verses Two Pages Previous

The Moonshiner (continued)

Melody & Chords
Key of C

```
        C                           F       Dm              G
E _____0_____
A _____3____3-3____3__3___2___0-0__0-5_____5___3___2_____2__2__
D 5___2____2-2___2__2___2___3-3__3-3_____3___3___0_____0__0__
G 5___0_____0_____5_____2___2_____0___0_____
  I've been a moonshiner for many a year, and I've spent all me
```

```
              F    C
E _____0_____
A 5-2___0_____0_____3__3-3___3-3__2__2___0__
D 0-0__0-5__3__3__2___5___2-2__2___2-2__2__2___3__
G 0_____0__2__2__5___5___0_____0_____2__
  Money on whiskey and beer. I'll go to some hollow and I'll set
```

```
  F    Dm           G7                              C
E _____0___1____0-1_____
A 0___0-5___5__3__2___5__0-2-5___2__2___0__2__3__
D 3___3-3____3_____0_____0__0___0__0-5__0__0__2__
G 2___2_____2_____0_____0_____0__0__0_____0__
  Up my still, and I'll make you a gallon for a ten shilling bill.
```

CHORUS

```
  C                           F       Dm
E _____0_____
A ___3__3___3__3-3__3__3__2-0__0__0__5__
D 5__5-2__2__2__2-2__2__2__2-3__3__3__3__
G 0__0-0_____0_____0_____0__5_____2__
  I'm a rambler, I'm a gambler, I'm a long way from home,
```

```
  G                     F    C
E _____
A 3__2-2__2___5__2__0_____0_____
D 0__0-0__0__0____0__0__5__3__3-2__
G 0__0____0__0__0_____0__5__5-5__
  And if you don't like me, well leave me a-lone.
```

```
                        F       Dm
E _____0_____
A ___3__3___3__3-3__2__2___0__0__0__5__
D 5__2__2__2__2-2__2__2___3__3__3__3__
G 0__0_____0_____5_____2__
  I'll eat when I'm hungry and I'll drink when I'm dry,
```

```
        G7                              C
E _____0__1_____0___1_____
A 5__3__2-5___0__2__5-2_____0__2-3__
D 3__0__0_____0__0-0__5__0__0-2__
G 2__0__0_____0__0-0__0_____0__
  And if moonshine don't kill me I'll live till I die.
```

See Chord Forms and Additional Verses Three Pages Previous

The Morning Glory (page 1)

Basic Melody
Key of G

This is another "love" song that does not entirely follow the traditional form. In it a sailor tells the story of the results of his courtship of the four daughters of the landlord of a local pub. When he returns from sea, the results of his amorous adventures await him.

Words and Music

Traditional

```
    G                      D     G            C          G
E ——————————————————————————————————————————————————————————————————
A 5——5——————————————————0——0—2————2-2—2————3————————3—5——————5—5——————
D ————————5——5—5————————————————————————————————————————————————————
G ——————————————————————————————————————————————————————————————————
```
At the end of the day I like a little drink to raise my voice

```
    C  G          C                      G                    A
E ——————————————————————————0——0————————————————————————————————————
A 3——2——————2——2-3-3————————————————5—3-2————5—5——————5——2——0——0——————
D ——————————————————————————————————————————————————————————————————
G ——————————————————————————————————————————————————————————————————
```
And sing; and another or two of a pint of brew and I'm ready

```
              D            G            D            G     C
E ——————————————————————————————————————————————————————————————————
A 0——2——0————5—5————————————————0——————0————————0————2—2————3————————
D ——————5——————————————5————————5————————————————————————————————————
G ——————————————————————————————————————————————————————————————————
```
For anything. At the Cross Keys Inn there were sisters four,

```
        G                C  G    C
E ————————————————————————————————0——0——————————————————————————————
A 3——5——5————————5————3————2————2——3————————5——————3—————————————————
D ——————————————————————————————————————————————————————————————————
G ——————————————————————————————————————————————————————————————————
```
The landlord's daughters fair; and every night when they'd

```
    G                      A            D
E ——————————————————————————————————————————————————————————————————
A 2————5——5——5————————2——0——0——2—4————5————————5—5——————————————————
D ——————————————————————————————————————————————————————————————————
G ——————————————————————————————————————————————————————————————————
```
Turn out the light I'd tip toe up the stairs, singin':

Chord Forms

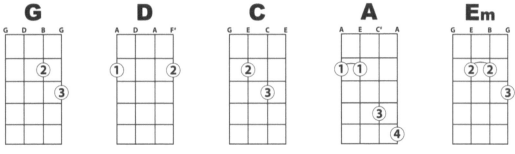

The Morning Glory (page 2)

Basic Melody
Key of G

CHORUS

```
         G                    C  G   D                 G
E ——————————————————————0——————————————————————————————————————————
A ——————————————2——5————————5————0———0———0———0——————2————————————————
D 5————5————5————————————————————————————————————————————5———————————
G ———————————————————————————————————————————————————————————————————
```
One for the morning glory,   two for the early dew;

```
  C                    G              C          G            C
E ——————————————————————————————————0———————2———3———————————————————————
A 3————————3————3————2————2————5————————————————————————2————3———————————
D ——————————————————————————————————————————————————————————————————————
G ——————————————————————————————————————————————————————————————————————
```
Three for the man who would stand his round, and four

```
            G    D  G   D Em       C              G       D  G
E —————————————————————————————————————————————————————————————————————
A 3————3————2————0——————0———2———3————————3————3————2————0————————————————
D ——————————————————5———————————————————————————————————————5————————————
G ——————————————————————————————————————————————————————————————————————
```
For the love of you my girl, four for the love of you.

Additional Verses

Well I got the call from foreign shores, to go and fight the foe;
Though I thought no more of the sisters four, still I was sad to go.
We sailed away on a ship, the Morning Glory was her name;
And we'd all fall down when the rum went 'round,
Then we'd get up and start again... singin':

Well we sailed once more to our native shore, farewell to the rolling sea;
The Cross Keys Inn it was beckonin', and my heart was full of glee.
But there on the shore were the sisters four, with a bundle on each knee;
There were three little girls and a bouncin' boy,
And they all looked just like me... singing':

Chord Forms (Key of C)   *(For arrangements that follow - see Key of G forms on previous page)*

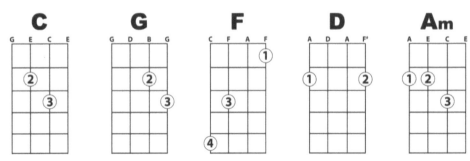

The Morning Glory

(continued)

Melody & Chords

Key of C

```
        G                    D      G              C          G
E ——————————————————————————————————————————————————————————————————
A 5——5———————————————————————0——0—2——2—2——2———3———3—5———5——5————
D 0——0———5———5—5————0———0—0———0—0——0———2———2—0———0—0———
G 0———————0———0—0———2———0——————————0—————————0————————0——————
At the end of the day I like a little drink to raise my voice
```

```
  C   G          C                      G              A
E ——————————————————————0——0—————————————————————————————————
A 3———2————2———2—3—3———3—3———5—3—2——5—5———5——2——0—0————
D 2———0————0——0—2—2———2——2——2—0——0——0——0——2—2——
G 0———0————0—————————0—————————0——————0————2————
And sing; and another or two of a pint of brew and I'm ready
```

```
        D            G           D          G      C
E ——————————————————————————————————————————————————————————————
A 0——2——0———5—5———————————0——0————0———2—2———3———
D 2——2—5—0———0—0——5———5———0——0————0——0—0———2———
G ———2—2—2———2——————0———0——2———————————0——————0——
For anything. At the Cross Keys Inn there were sisters four,
```

```
      G              C   G     C
E ———————————————————————————0——0——————————————————
A 3——5—5———————5———3——2——2—3—3—3———5——3———
D 2——0—0———————0——2——0———0—2——2——2——2——
G ———0———————0————————0—0—0——0——
The landlord's daughters fair; and every night when they'd
```

```
  G                      A            D
E ——————————————————————————————————————————————————————
A 2——5—5——5———2——0——0—2—4——5———5—5———
D 0——0——0—0———0——2——2——2—2——0———0—0——
G 0——0——0——0——2——2——2—2——2——2——
Turn out the light I'd tip toe up the stairs, singin':
```

CHORUS

```
  G                C   G   D            G
E ——————————————————0———————————————————————————————
A ——————2—5——3—5——0——0——0——0——2———
D 5——5—5—0—0——2—0——0——0——0—0—5—0——
G 0——0—0—0——————0—0——2——2—2—0——
One for the morning glory,   two for the early dew;
```

```
  C            G          C      G      C
E ——————————————————————0——2—3———————————
A 3———3—3——2—2——5——3——3—2——2—3—.——
D 2———2—2—0—0——0——2——0—0—2——
G 0———0——0——0——0——0—0——
Three for the man who would stand his round, and four
```

```
        G   D G   D Em   C         G   D G
E ——————————————————————————————————————————————————
A 3——3—2——0——0—2——3——3—3—2——0——
D 2——2—0——0—5—0—2——2——2—2—0——0—5—
G 0——————0—2—0——4——0———————0——0——
For the love of you my girl, four for the love of you.
```

See Chord Forms on Previous Page

The Morning Glory (continued)

Basic Melody
Key of C

```
        C                 G     C            F         C
E ----------------------------------------------------------------
A ----------------------------------------------------------------
D 5---5---------------0---0-2---2-2---2---3-----3---5-----5---5----
G ----------5---5---5----------------------------------------------
  At  the  end  of  the  day  I  like  a  little  drink  to  raise  my  voice
```

```
  F   C        F                    C                   D
E ----------------------------------------------------------------
A -------------------0---0-----------------------------------------
D 3---2-----2---2-3-3---------5---3-2---5---5-----5---2---0---0-----
G ----------------------------------------------------------------
  And  sing;  and  another  or  two  of  a  pint  of  brew  and  I'm  ready
```

```
            G           C         G             C    F
E ----------------------------------------------------------------
A ----------------------------------------------------------------
D 0---2---0-----5---5-------------0---0-----0---2---2---3----------
G ----------5---------5-----5-------------------------------------
  For  anything.  At  the  Cross  Keys  Inn  there  were  sisters  four,
```

```
        C               F   C         F
E ----------------------------------------------------------------
A -----------------------------------0---0------------------------
D 3---5---5-------5---3-----2-----2---3-------5---3----------------
G ----------------------------------------------------------------
  The  landlord's  daughters  fair;  and  every  night  when  they'd
```

```
  C                       D           G
E ----------------------------------------------------------------
A ----------------------------------------------------------------
D 2-----5---5---5-----2---0---0---2-4---5-------5---5--------------
G ----------------------------------------------------------------
  Turn  out  the  light  I'd  tip  toe  up  the  stairs,  singin':
```

CHORUS

```
  C                   F   C   G               C
E ----------------------------------------------------------------
A -------------------0--------------------------------------------
D -------------2---5-----5---0---0---0---0-------2-----------------
G 5---5---5----------------------------------5--------------------
  One  for  the  morning  glory,    two  for  the  early  dew;
```

```
  F               C           F           C           F
E ----------------------------------------------------------------
A -------------------------0-----2---3----------------------------
D 3-------3---3---2---2---5-----------------2---3------------------
G ----------------------------------------------------------------
  Three  for  the  man  who  would  stand  his  round,  and  four
```

```
            C   G C   G Am    F           C   G C
E ----------------------------------------------------------------
A ----------------------------------------------------------------
D 3-------3---2---0-----0-2---3-----3---3---2---0------------------
G ----------------5-------------------------------------5---------
  For  the  love  of  you  my  girl,  four  for  the  love  of  you.
```

See Chord Forms Two Pages Previous

The Morning Glory

Melody & Chords

(continued)

Key of C

```
    C              G      C           F       C
E _____
A _____
D 5—5——————————0——0-2———2-2—2——3———3—5———5—5——————
G 5—5——5——5—5——0——0-5———5-5—5——5———5-5———5—5——————
At the end of the day I like a little drink to raise my voice
```

```
  F   C        F                  C                D
E _____
A _____0—0_____
D 3——2————2——2-3-3——3—3——5—3-2——5—5———5——2——0—0——
G 5——5————5——5-5-5——5—5——5-5-5——5—5———5——5—2—2——
And sing; and another or two of a pint of brew and I'm ready
```

```
        G              C        G          C    F
E _____
A _____
D 0——2——0——5—5—————————0——0——0——2—2———3——
G 2——2-5-0——0—0—5————5————0——0——0——5-5———5——
For anything. At the Cross Keys Inn there were sisters four,
```

```
    C              F   C        F
E _____
A _____0—0_____
D 3——5——5————5——3——2——2——3—3-3———5——3——
G 5——5—5————5——5——5——5——5-5———5—5——
The landlord's daughters fair; and every night when they'd
```

```
  C                   D          G
E _____
A _____
D 2——5——5——5——2——0——0——2-4——5———5—5——
G 5——5——5——5——5——2——2——2-2——0———0—0——
Turn out the light I'd tip toe up the stairs, singin':
```

CHORUS

```
  C           F C  G            C
E _____
A _____0_____
D ————————2—5——3-5——0——0——0——0——2——
G 5——5——5——5-5——5—5——0——0——0——0-5—5——
One for the morning glory,  two for the early dew;
```

```
  F          C        F        C         F
E _____
A _____0_____2—3_____
D 3——————3——3——2——2——5——3——3——2——2——3——
G 5——5——5—5—5—5——5——5————0——0—5——
Three for the man who would stand his round, and four
```

```
      C  G C  G Am      F        C  G  C
E _____
A _____3_____
D 3——3——2——0——0—2——3——3-3—2——0—2——
G 5—5——5——0-5——0-2——5——5-5—5——0-5——
For the love of you my girl, four for the love of you.
```

See Chord Forms Three Pages Previous

Nancy Whiskey

Basic Melody
Key of G

There have been many different versions of this song over the years, and it has gone by a number of names. It has long been a part of both the Irish and the Scottish folk traditions. It tells the tale of a weaver from Carlton in Scotland (a small town long ago absorbed by Glasgow) who lets his love of whiskey get the better of him.

Words and Music

Traditional

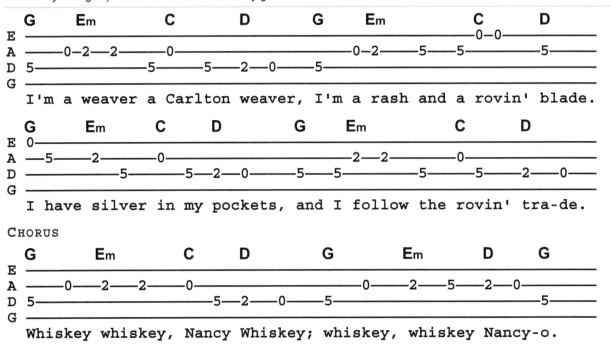

I'm a weaver a Carlton weaver, I'm a rash and a rovin' blade.

I have silver in my pockets, and I follow the rovin' tra-de.

CHORUS

Whiskey whiskey, Nancy Whiskey; whiskey, whiskey Nancy-o.

Additional Verses

As I walked out in Glasgow City,
Nancy Whiskey I chanced to smell;
I went in, sat down beside her.
Seven long years, I loved her well.

The more I kissed her, the more I loved her.
The more I kissed her, the more she smiled;
I forgot my mother's teaching,
Nancy soon had me beguiled.

When I rose early in the morning,
To quench my thirst it was my need.
I tried to rise but was not able,
Nancy had me by the knees.

Well I'll go back to the Carlton weaving,
I'll surely make those shuttles fly;
For I'll make more at the Carlton weaving,
Than every I did in the roving way.

So come all you weavers, you Carlton weavers;
Come all you weavers where ere you be;
Beware of whiskey, Nancy Whiskey,
She'll ruin you as she ruined me.

Chord Forms

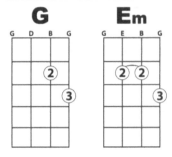

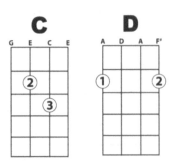

Nancy Whiskey (continued)

Melody & Chords
Key of G

```
       G    Em        C        D        G    Em            C        D
E ──────────────────────────────────────────────────────────0─0─────────────
A ────0─2──2────────0───────────────────────0─2─────5────5─3─3──────5────────
D 5────0─2──2────5─2────5────2───0────5────0─2───────2────2─2─2──────0────────
G 0─────4─────────4─5────5────2──2────0──────4──────────0────────2──────────
```
I'm a weaver a Carlton weaver, I'm a rash and a rovin' blade.

```
       G    Em        C        D        G    Em            C        D
E 0──────────────────────────────────────────────────────────────────────────
A 0─5─────2────────0───────────────────────2─2────────0────────────────────
D 0─0─────2─5────2─5─2───0────5───5─2──2───5────2─5──────2───0───
G ───────4─4────5─5──2──2────0──0─4──────4──5─5──────2────2──
```
I have silver in my pockets, and I follow the rovin' tra-de.

CHORUS

```
       G      Em        C        D        G         Em        D      G
E ────────────────────────────────────────────────────────────────────────────
A ────0────2────2──────0──────────────0──────2────5────2──0──────────────
D 5────0────2────2────2─5──2───0──────5────0──────2────2────0─0──5──────
G 0──────4──────5─5──2──2────0──────────4──────────2──────0──
```
Whiskey whiskey, Nancy Whiskey; whiskey, whiskey Nancy-o.

Chord Forms

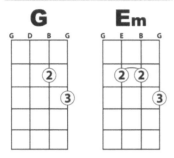

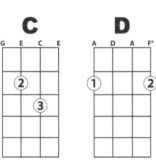

Nancy Whiskey (continued)

Basic Melody
Key of C (Low)

```
     C      Am         F        G       C      Am             F       G
E  ─────────────────────────────────────────────────────────────────────────
A  ─────────────────────────────────────────────────────────0─0──────────────
D  ──────0─2──2───────0────────────────────0─2────5──5────────────5──────────
G  5───────────────5──────5──2─0────5─────────────────────────────────────────
     I'm a weaver a Carlton weaver, I'm a rash and a rovin' blade.


     C      Am         F        G          C      Am           F        G
E  ─────────────────────────────────────────────────────────────────────────
A  0───────────────────────────────────────────────────────────────────────
D  ──5────2─────────0──────────────────────2──2─────────0────────────────────
G  ────────────5──────5─2─0────5──5──────────────5──────5──2───0──────────────
     I have silver in my pockets, and I follow the rovin' tra-de.
```

CHORUS

```
     C       Am         F       G       C       Am         G        C
E  ─────────────────────────────────────────────────────────────────────────
A  ─────────────────────────────────────────────────────────────────────────
D  ──────0───2──2──────0──────────────────0─────2──5───2─0────────────────────
G  5───────────────────────5─2─0────5──────────────────────────5──────────────
     Whiskey whiskey, Nancy Whiskey; whiskey, whiskey Nancy-o.
```

Chord Forms

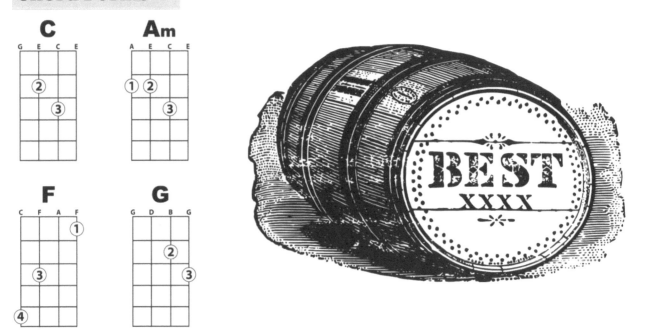

Nancy Whiskey (continued)

Basic Melody
Key of C (High)

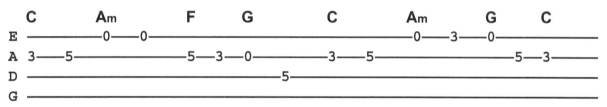

```
      C    Am       F     G       C    Am          F         G
E ———————0———0———————————————————————————0———3———3-5-5———————3—————————
A 3———5——————————3-5———3———0——————3———5———————————————————————————————
D —————————————————————————————5———————————————————————————————————————
G —————————————————————————————————————————————————————————————————————
```
I'm a weaver a Carlton weaver, I'm a rash and a rovin' blade.

```
      C    Am       F     G       C    Am          F         G
E 5-3——————0————————————————————————————0———0———————————————————————————
A ——————————3———5———3———0——————3———3——————————3———5-3————————0——————————
D ————————————————————————5————————————————————————————————————5————————
G —————————————————————————————————————————————————————————————————————
```
I have silver in my pockets, and I follow the rovin' tra-de.

CHORUS

```
      C      Am      F     G       C      Am       G       C
E ——————————0———0———————————————————————————0———3———0——————————————————
A 3———5————————————5———3———0——————3———5——————————————————————5———3——————
D ——————————————————————————5—————————————————————————————————————————
G —————————————————————————————————————————————————————————————————————
```
Whiskey whiskey, Nancy Whiskey; whiskey, whiskey Nancy-o.

Chord Forms

C
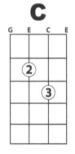

Am
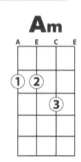

F
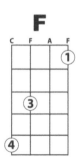

G
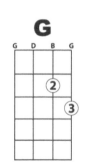

Nancy Whiskey (continued)

Melody & Chords
Key of C (High)

```
     C        Am          F        G          C        Am              F        G
E ——————————0———0——————————————————————————————————0———3———3—5—5——————3————————
A 3——————5—0———0——————3—5——3———0——————————3——————5—0———3———3—3—3——————2————————
D 2——————2—2———2——————2—3——3———0———5——————2——————2—2————————————3——————0————————
G 0——————2——————————2——————————0———————0——————2——————————————————————0————————
```
I'm a weaver a Carlton weaver, I'm a rash and a rovin' blade.

```
     C        Am          F        G          C            Am              F        G
E 5—3———————0————————————————————————————————————0———0—————————————————————————————
A 3—3———————0———3——5——3———0——————————3——————3—0———0———3——————5—3——————0——————————————
D 2—2———————2———2——3——3———0———5——————2——————2—2———2———2——————3—3——————0———5——————————
G ——————————2——————————0———0——————0——————2——————————2——————————————0———0———
```
I have silver in my pockets, and I follow the rovin' tra-de.

CHORUS

```
     C        Am          F        G          C            Am          G        C
E ——————————0———0——————————————————————————————————0———3———0——————————————————————
A 3——————5———0———0——————5——3———0——————————3——————5———0———3———2—5—3——————————————————
D 2——————2———2———2——————3——3———0———5——————2——————2———2——————0—0—2——————————————————
G 0——————2——————————2——————————0———0——————0——————2——————————0—0——————————————————
```
Whiskey whiskey, Nancy Whiskey; whiskey, whiskey Nancy-o.

Chord Forms

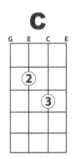

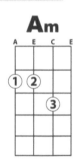

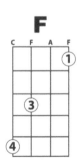

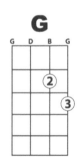

The Night That Paddy Murphy Died (page 1)

Basic Melody

Key of G

This great old traditional song is thought to have originated among Irish immigrants in Newfoundland in the late 1800's. It tells the tale of a raucous group of Irish folks holding a wake for their deceased friend Paddy Murphy. The band Great Big Sea's recording of this classic has helped revive its popularity.

Words and Music

Traditional

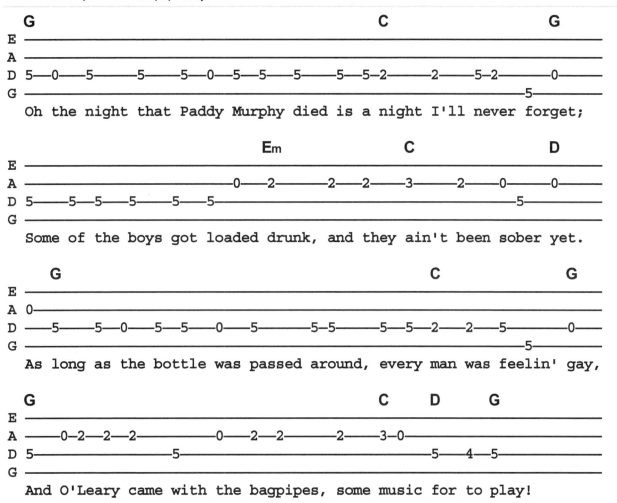

Oh the night that Paddy Murphy died is a night I'll never forget;

Some of the boys got loaded drunk, and they ain't been sober yet.

As long as the bottle was passed around, every man was feelin' gay,

And O'Leary came with the bagpipes, some music for to play!

Chord Forms

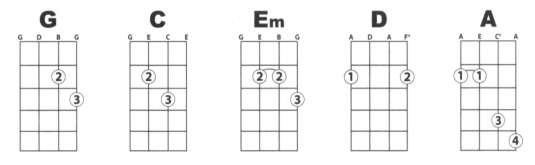

See Chorus and Additional Verses on Next Page

The Night That Paddy Murphy Died (page 2)

Basic Melody

Key of G

CHORUS

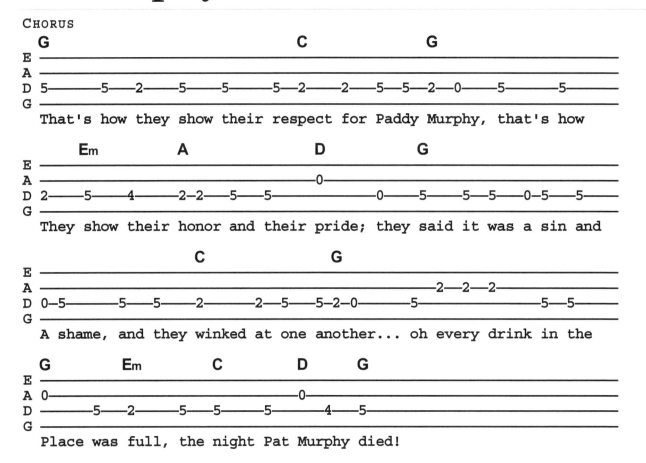

That's how they show their respect for Paddy Murphy, that's how

They show their honor and their pride; they said it was a sin and

A shame, and they winked at one another... oh every drink in the

Place was full, the night Pat Murphy died!

Additional Verses

As Mrs. Murphy sat in the corner, pourin' out her grief;
Kelly and his gang came tearing down the street.
They went into an empty room, and a bottle of whiskey stole;
They put the bottle with the corpse, to keep the whiskey cold!

At two o'clock in the morning, after emptyin' the jug;
Doyle lifts up the icebox lid, to see poor Paddy's mug.
They stopped the clock so Mrs. Murphy couldn't tell the time,
And at quarter after two they argued it was nine!

Well they emptied out the jugs, but still they had a thirst;
The next thing they had done, well you'll think it was the worst;
And Mrs. Murphy fainted when the news fell on her ears,
They scraped the ice right off the corpse, and put it in their beers!

Well we stopped the hearse on George's Street, outside some damn saloon;
We all went in and half-past eight, and staggered out at noon.
We went down to the graveyard, so holy and sublime...
Found out when we got there, we'd left the corpse behind!

The Night That Paddy Murphy Died (continued)

Melody & Chords

Key of G

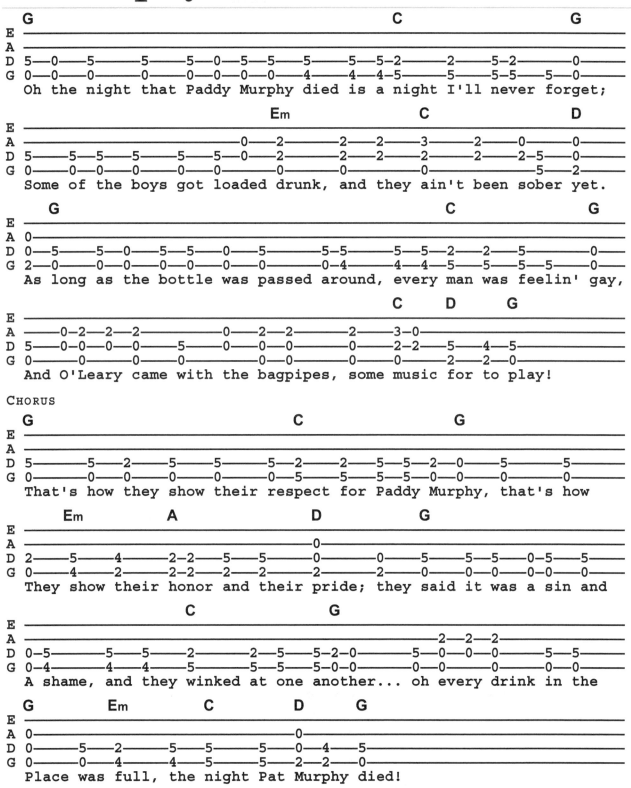

See Chord Forms Two Pages Previous

The Night That Paddy Murphy Died (continued)

Basic Melody

Key of C

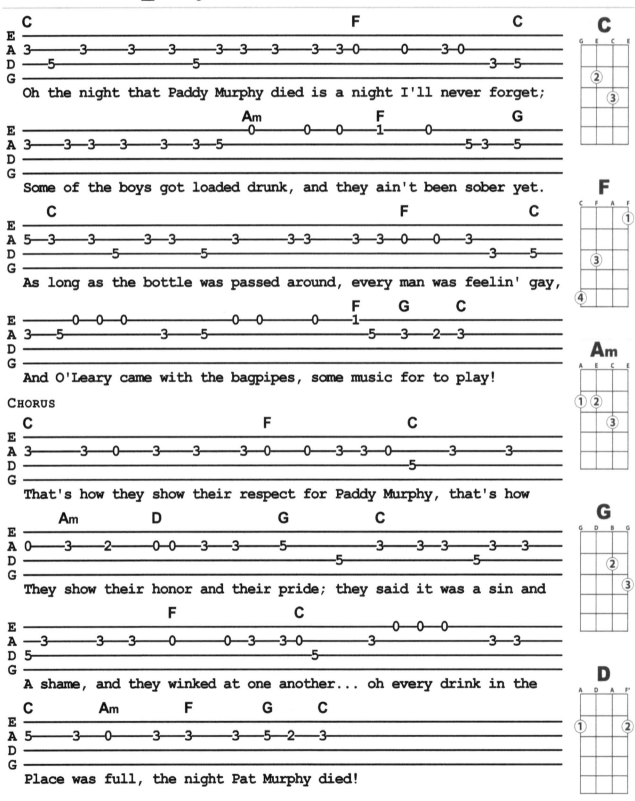

C   F   C

Oh the night that Paddy Murphy died is a night I'll never forget;

Some of the boys got loaded drunk, and they ain't been sober yet.

As long as the bottle was passed around, every man was feelin' gay,

And O'Leary came with the bagpipes, some music for to play!

CHORUS

That's how they show their respect for Paddy Murphy, that's how

They show their honor and their pride; they said it was a sin and

A shame, and they winked at one another... oh every drink in the

Place was full, the night Pat Murphy died!

Irish Pub Favorites Mandolin Tablature Songbook · Copyright 2020 by Hobo Music Works LLC · All Rights Reserved

The Night That Paddy Murphy Died (continued)

Melody & Chords

Key of C

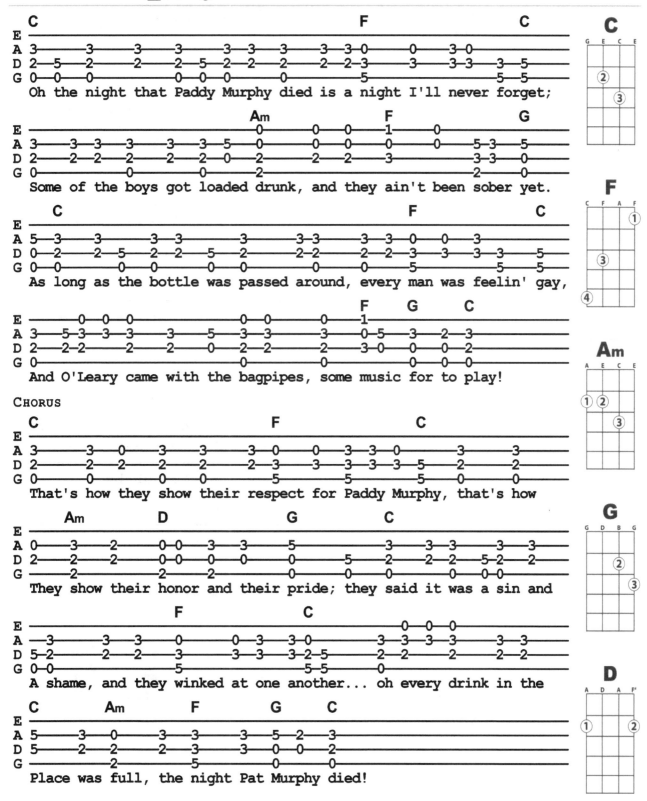

Oh the night that Paddy Murphy died is a night I'll never forget;

Some of the boys got loaded drunk, and they ain't been sober yet.

As long as the bottle was passed around, every man was feelin' gay,

And O'Leary came with the bagpipes, some music for to play!

CHORUS

That's how they show their respect for Paddy Murphy, that's how

They show their honor and their pride; they said it was a sin and

A shame, and they winked at one another... oh every drink in the

Place was full, the night Pat Murphy died!

The Old Dun Cow (page 1)

Basic Melody

Key of Am

The full name of this song is "When the Old Dun Cow Caught Fire", and it was written in 1893 by Harry Wincott. A singer by the name of Harry Champion first had commercial success with it. While not strictly a Scottish song, the shouting of the name "MacIntyre" helps suit it to the genre, and it is often performed by Scottish and Irish singers. The melody and chords given below are just a suggestion - this song is usually performed acapella.

Words and Music

by Harry Wincott

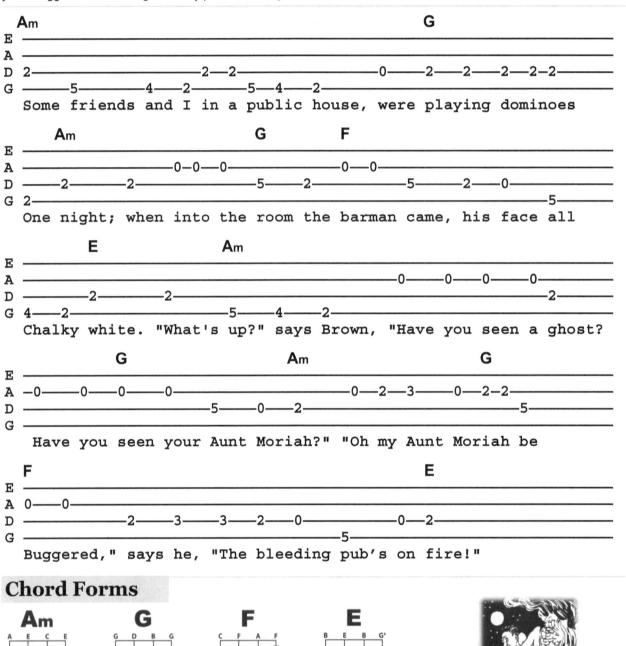

Some friends and I in a public house, were playing dominoes

One night; when into the room the barman came, his face all

Chalky white. "What's up?" says Brown, "Have you seen a ghost?

Have you seen your Aunt Moriah?" "Oh my Aunt Moriah be

Buggered," says he, "The bleeding pub's on fire!"

Chord Forms

Am G F E

The Old Dun Cow (page 2)

Basic Melody
Key of Am

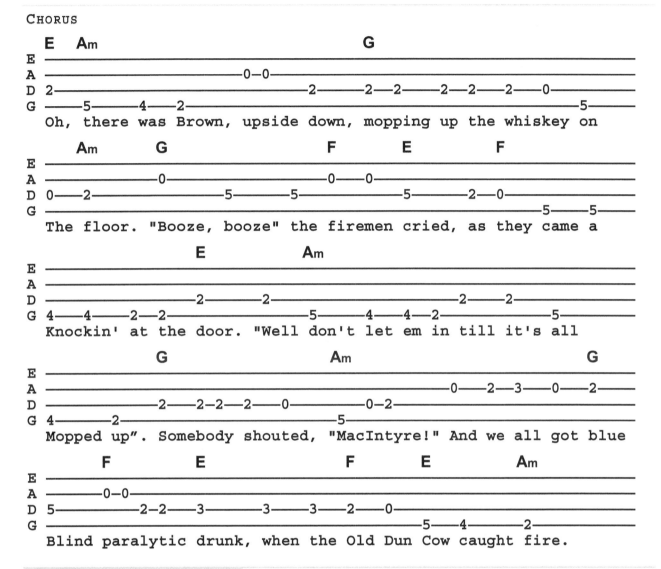

CHORUS

Oh, there was Brown, upside down, mopping up the whiskey on
The floor. "Booze, booze" the firemen cried, as they came a
Knockin' at the door. "Well don't let em in till it's all
Mopped up". Somebody shouted, "MacIntyre!" And we all got blue
Blind paralytic drunk, when the Old Dun Cow caught fire.

Additional Verses

"A fire," says Brown, "What a bit of luck,
Everybody follow me;
It's down to the cellar if the fire's not there,
Then we'll have a grand old spree."
So we all went down with good old Brown,
And the booze we could not miss.
And we hadn't been there ten minutes or more,
'Til we were bloody pissed...

Then Smith ran over to the port wine tub,
And gave it just a few hard knocks;
He started taking off his pantaloons,
Likewise his shoes and socks.

"Oh no," says Brown, "That's not allowed,
You canna do that in here...
Don't be washing your trotters in the port wine tub,
When there's plenty of English beer."

Then there came a mighty crash,
Half the bloody room caved in;
And we were drownded by the fireman's hose,
But we were going to stay.
So we got some tacks and some wet old sacks,
And we packed ourselves inside;
And we sat there drinking the finest rum,
'Til we were bleary-eyed...

The Old Dun Cow
(continued - page 1)

Basic Melody

Key of Em

```
      Em                                              D
E ──────────────────────────────────────────────────────────────────────
A 2─────────────────────2──2──────────────0────2────2────2──2─2──────────
D ─────5─────4────2──────5──4──2──────────────────────────────────────────
G ──────────────────────────────────────────────────────────────────────
```
Some friends and I in a public house, were playing dominoes

```
        Em                       D        C
E ──────────────────0─0──0──────────0──0──────────────────────────────────
A ──────2────────2───────────5────2──────5────2────0──────────────────────
D 2──────────────────────────────────────────────────────────5────────────
G ──────────────────────────────────────────────────────────────────────
```
One night; when into the room the barman came, his face all

```
        B              Em
E ──────────────────────────────────0────0────0────0──────────────────────
A ──────2────────2──────────────────────────────────2──────────────────────
D 4──2───────────────5────4────2──────────────────────────────────────────
G ──────────────────────────────────────────────────────────────────────
```
Chalky white. "What's up?" says Brown, "Have you seen a ghost?

```
            D                      Em                    D
E ─0────0────0────0──────────────────0──2──3────0──2─2──────────────────────
A ──────────────────5────0────2─────────────────────────5──────────────────
D ──────────────────────────────────────────────────────────────────────
G ──────────────────────────────────────────────────────────────────────
```
Have you seen your Aunt Moriah?" "Oh my Aunt Moriah be

```
      C                                      B
E 0────0──────────────────────────────────────────────────────────────────
A ──────────2────3────3────2────0──────────0──2────────────────────────────
D ──────────────────────────────────5──────────────────────────────────────
G ──────────────────────────────────────────────────────────────────────
```
Buggered," says he, "The bleeding pub's on fire!"

Chord Forms

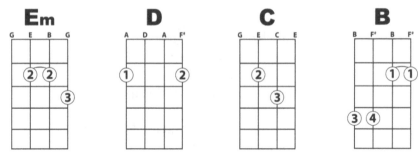

The Old Dun Cow
(continued - page 2)

Basic Melody

Key of Em

CHORUS

```
   B  Em                                    D
E ─────────────────────0─0─────────────────────────────────────────────
A 2─────────────────────────2────2─2────2─2──2───0──────────────────────
D ──────5──────4─────2────────────────────────────────────5─────────────
G ──────────────────────────────────────────────────────────────────────
```
Oh, there was Brown, upside down, mopping up the whiskey on

```
   Em      D              C     B     C
E ──────────0─────────────────0────0────────────────────────────────────
A 0───2──────────────5──────5──────────5──────2─0───────────────────────
D ──────────────────────────────────────────────────5──────5────────────
G ──────────────────────────────────────────────────────────────────────
```
The floor. "Booze, booze" the firemen cried, as they came a

```
            B         Em
E ──────────────────────────────────────────────────────────────────────
A ──────────2─────────2─────────────────2────2──────────────────────────
D 4──4────2─2───────────────5───4──4──2──────────5───────────────────────
G ──────────────────────────────────────────────────────────────────────
```
Knockin' at the door. "Well don't let em in till it's all

```
            D              Em                                        D
E ──────────────────────────────────────0───2──3───0──2────────────────
A ──────────2──2─2─2───0─────────0─2─────────────────────────────────────
D 4───────2──────────────────5───────────────────────────────────────────
G ──────────────────────────────────────────────────────────────────────
```
Mopped up". Somebody shouted, "MacIntyre!" And we all got blue

```
     C       B           C      B      Em
E ──────0─0────────────────────────────────────────────────────────────
A 5─────────2─2───3──────3────3──2──0───────────────────────────────────
D ──────────────────────────────────────5────4─────2────────────────────
G ──────────────────────────────────────────────────────────────────────
```
Blind paralytic drunk, when the Old Dun Cow caught fire.

The Old Dun Cow
(continued - page 1)

Melody & Chords

Key of Em

```
      Em                                              D
E ————————————————————————————————————————————————————————————————————
A 2————————————————————2—2————————————————0———2———2———2—2-2————————————
D 2———5————4———2-2———2-5—4———2——————2———0———0———0—0-0————————————————————
G 4———4———4———4-4———4—4———4——————4———2————————2———2————————————————————
  Some friends and I in a public house, were playing dominoes
```

```
      Em                          D        C
E ————————————————0-0—0————————————0———0————————————————————————————————
A ————2———2———2-2-2———5———2———3—3———5———2———0—————————————————————————————
D 2———2———2———2——————0———0———2———2———2———2———5————————————————————————————
G 2———4———4———0——————2———2———0———0——————0———2—————————————————————————————
  One night; when into the room the barman came, his face all
```

```
        B              Em
E ——————————————————————————————————————0———0———0———0——————————————————————
A ————2————2———————————————————————2———2———2———2-2—————————————————————————
D 4—2-4———4———————5———4———2———2———2———2—————————————————————————————————————
G 2—2-4———4———4———4———4———4————————0——————0———4————————————————————————————
  Chalky white. "What's up?" says Brown, "Have you seen a ghost?
```

```
          D                      Em                  D
E -0———0———0———0————————————————————0—2—3———0—2-2————————————————————————
A -2———2———0———0———5———0———2———2—2—2———2-0-0-5————————————————————————————
D -2———————0———0———0———0———2———2———2————————0———0————————————————————————
G -0————————2————————2————4———0———0—————————2———2————————————————————————
   Have you seen your Aunt Moriah?" "Oh my Aunt Moriah be
```

```
    C                                        B
E 0———0————————————————————————————————————————————————————————————————
A 3———3———————2———3———3—2———0——————————0—2——————————————————————————————
D 2————————2———2———2-2———2———5———0———4——————————————————————————————————
G 0————————————0———0——————————0————————4———————————————————————————————
  Buggered," says he, "The bleeding pub's on fire!"
```

Chord Forms

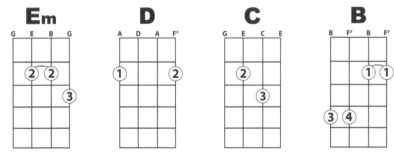

153

The Old Dun Cow
(continued - page 2)

Melody & Chords

Key of Em

CHORUS

```
    B   Em                                      D
E ------------------------0-0---------------------------------------
A 2-----------------2-2----2----2--2----2--2----2--0-----------------
D 4----5-----4--2---2-2----2----0--0----0--0----0--0----5-----------
G 4----4-----4--4---0------0----2------2------2--------2-------------
```
Oh, there was Brown, upside down, mopping up the whiskey on

```
    Em      D               C    B      C
E ----------0-------------------0----0-----------------------------
A 0---2-----0----5-----5---3---3--5---2--0-------------------------
D 0---2-----0----0-----0---2---2--4----4--2---5-----5--------------
G -----4------2-----2-------0------4------0-----0-----0------------
```
The floor. "Booze, booze" the firemen cried, as they came a

```
            B         Em
E ---------------------------------------------------------------
A --------------2-------2------------------2-----2----------------
D 4---4----2--2--4------4-----5----4--4--2--2-----2----5----------
G 2---2----4--4--4------4-----4----4--4--4--4----------4----------
```
Knockin' at the door. "Well don't let em in till it's all

```
            D             Em                          D
E -----------------------------------------0----2--3----0---2------
A --------------2----2-2---2----0------0-2----2----2--2----2--0-----
D 4------2-----0----0-0--0----0------5--2-2---2------2----2--0------
G 4------4-----2------2------4----4------0------0--------2----------
```
Mopped up". Somebody shouted, "MacIntyre!" And we all got blue

```
        C       B               C    B      Em
E -------0-0-----------------------------------------------------
A 5------3-3-2-2----3-------3---3--2--0---------------------------
D 0------2-2-2--4------4----4--2--2--5----4-----2-----------------
G 2------0--------4-------------5--0--4---4-----4----------------
```
Blind paralytic drunk, when the Old Dun Cow caught fire.

Paddy Doyle's Boots

Basic Melody
Key of G

According to folk history, this was a sea shanty specifically for "bunting" the main sail of the old sailing ships. The rhythm and words were timed to the men's' movements, and the "yah" on each line was where the sailors would have to perform a particularly heavy heave of the bundled sail. Each of the lines below is technically a separate verse.

Words and Music
Traditional

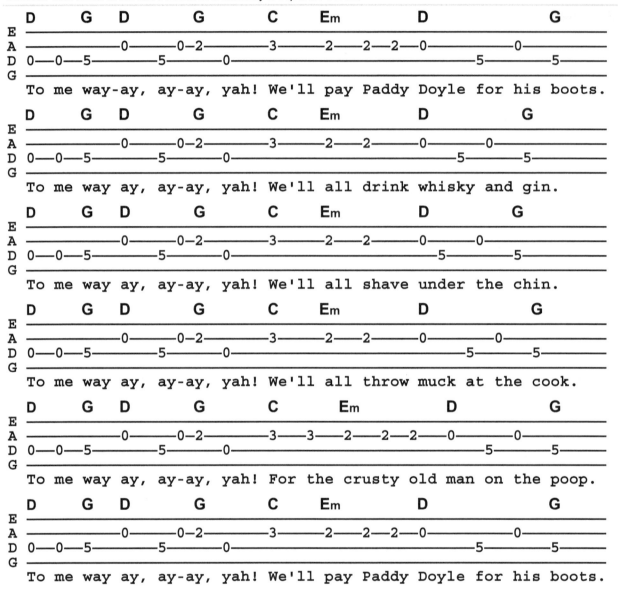

To me way-ay, ay-ay, yah! We'll pay Paddy Doyle for his boots.

To me way ay, ay-ay, yah! We'll all drink whisky and gin.

To me way ay, ay-ay, yah! We'll all shave under the chin.

To me way ay, ay-ay, yah! We'll all throw muck at the cook.

To me way ay, ay-ay, yah! For the crusty old man on the poop.

To me way ay, ay-ay, yah! We'll pay Paddy Doyle for his boots.

Chord Forms

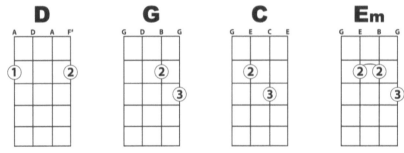

Paddy Doyle's Boots
(continued)

Melody & Chords

Key of G

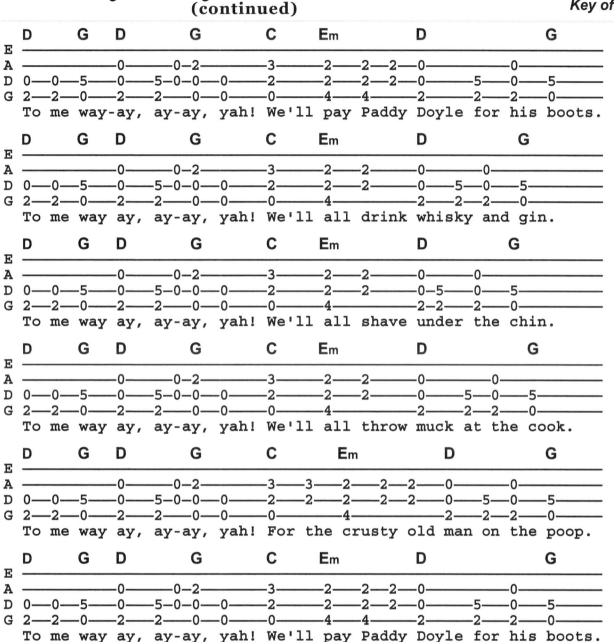

```
     D     G   D        G      C     Em      D            G
E ─────────────────────────────────────────────────────────────
A ──────────────0─────────0─2──────3─────2──2──2──0───────0──────
D 0──0──5──────0─────5─0─0──0──────2─────2──2──2──0────5──0──5────
G 2──2──0──────2─────2─────0──0────0────4──4────────2──2──2──0────
```
To me way-ay, ay-ay, yah! We'll pay Paddy Doyle for his boots.

```
     D     G   D        G      C     Em      D          G
E ─────────────────────────────────────────────────────────────
A ──────────────0─────────0─2──────3─────2──2───────0─────0───────
D 0──0──5──────0─────5─0─0──0──────2─────2──2───────0──5──0──5─────
G 2──2──0──────2─────2─────0──0────0────4────────2──2──2──0───────
```
To me way ay, ay-ay, yah! We'll all drink whisky and gin.

```
     D     G   D        G      C     Em      D          G
E ─────────────────────────────────────────────────────────────
A ──────────────0─────────0─2──────3─────2──2───────0─────0───────
D 0──0──5──────0─────5─0─0──0──────2─────2──2───────0─5──0──5──────
G 2──2──0──────2─────2─────0──0────0────4────────2─2──2──0────────
```
To me way ay, ay-ay, yah! We'll all shave under the chin.

```
     D     G   D        G      C     Em      D            G
E ─────────────────────────────────────────────────────────────
A ──────────────0─────────0─2──────3─────2──2───────0────────0────
D 0──0──5──────0─────5─0─0──0──────2─────2──2───────0────5──0──5───
G 2──2──0──────2─────2─────0──0────0────4────────2──2──2──0───────
```
To me way ay, ay-ay, yah! We'll all throw muck at the cook.

```
     D     G   D        G      C      Em       D          G
E ─────────────────────────────────────────────────────────────
A ──────────────0─────────0─2──────3──3──2──2──2──0────────0──────
D 0──0──5──────0─────5─0─0──0──────2─────2──2──2──2──0──5──0──5────
G 2──2──0──────2─────2─────0──0────0────4────────2──2──2──0───────
```
To me way ay, ay-ay, yah! For the crusty old man on the poop.

```
     D     G   D        G      C     Em      D             G
E ─────────────────────────────────────────────────────────────
A ──────────────0─────────0─2──────3─────2──2──2──0────────0──────
D 0──0──5──────0─────5─0─0──0──────2─────2──2──2──0────5──0──5─────
G 2──2──0──────2─────2─────0──0────0────4──4────────2──2──2──0─────
```
To me way ay, ay-ay, yah! We'll pay Paddy Doyle for his boots.

Chord Forms

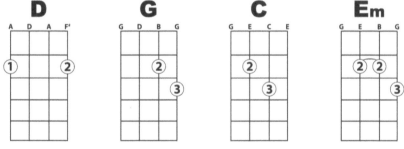

156

Paddy Doyle's Boots
(continued)

Basic Melody

Key of C (Low)

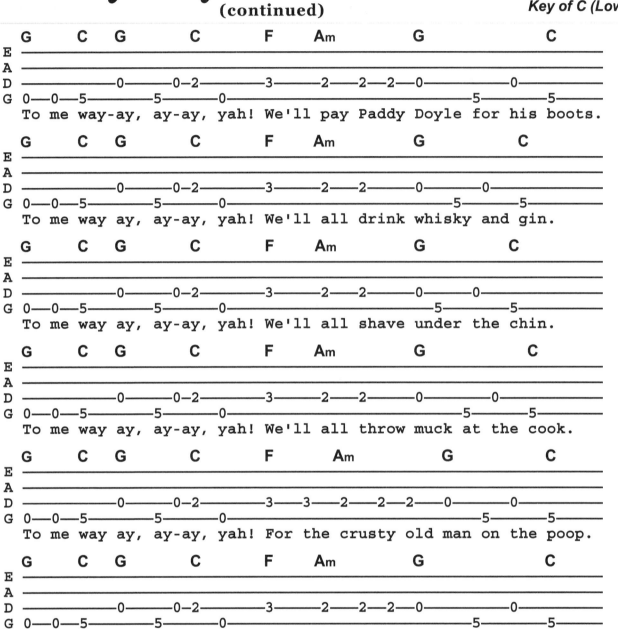

```
     G      C   G       C          F      Am        G              C
E ------------------------------------------------------------------------------
A ------------------------------------------------------------------------------
D -----------0------0-2-------3------2---2---2---0----------0---------------------
G 0--0--5-------5-------0-----------------------------5-------5-----------------
  To me way-ay, ay-ay, yah! We'll pay Paddy Doyle for his boots.

     G      C   G       C          F      Am        G              C
E ------------------------------------------------------------------------------
A ------------------------------------------------------------------------------
D -----------0------0-2-------3------2---2---2---0----------0---------------------
G 0--0--5-------5-------0-----------------------------5-------5-----------------
  To me way ay, ay-ay, yah! We'll all drink whisky and gin.

     G      C   G       C          F      Am        G              C
E ------------------------------------------------------------------------------
A ------------------------------------------------------------------------------
D -----------0------0-2-------3------2---2---2---0----------0---------------------
G 0--0--5-------5-------0-----------------------------5-------5-----------------
  To me way ay, ay-ay, yah! We'll all shave under the chin.

     G      C   G       C          F      Am        G              C
E ------------------------------------------------------------------------------
A ------------------------------------------------------------------------------
D -----------0------0-2-------3------2---2---2---0----------0---------------------
G 0--0--5-------5-------0-----------------------------5-------5-----------------
  To me way ay, ay-ay, yah! We'll all throw muck at the cook.

     G      C   G       C          F      Am        G              C
E ------------------------------------------------------------------------------
A ------------------------------------------------------------------------------
D -----------0------0-2-------3---3---2---2---2---0----------0--------------------
G 0--0--5-------5-------0-----------------------------5-------5-----------------
  To me way ay, ay-ay, yah! For the crusty old man on the poop.

     G      C   G       C          F      Am        G              C
E ------------------------------------------------------------------------------
A ------------------------------------------------------------------------------
D -----------0------0-2-------3------2---2---2---0----------0---------------------
G 0--0--5-------5-------0-----------------------------5-------5-----------------
  To me way ay, ay-ay, yah! We'll pay Paddy Doyle for his boots.
```

Chord Forms

G
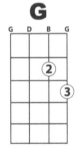

C
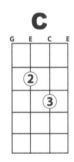

F
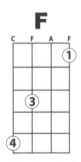

Am
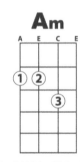

Paddy Doyle's Boots
(continued)

Basic Melody

Key of C (High)

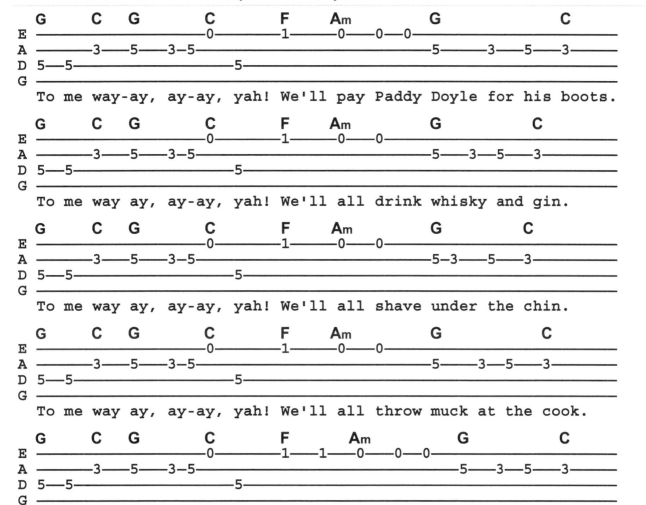

```
     G       C   G         C       F   Am          G           C
E ─────────────────────────0───────1───0───0───0─────────────────────────
A ───────3───5───3─5─────────────────────────────────5───3───5───3───────
D 5───5─────────────────────5─────────────────────────────────────────────
G ─────────────────────────────────────────────────────────────────────────
```
To me way-ay, ay-ay, yah! We'll pay Paddy Doyle for his boots.

```
     G       C   G         C       F   Am          G           C
E ─────────────────────────0───────1───0───0───0─────────────────────────
A ───────3───5───3─5─────────────────────────────────5───3───5───3───────
D 5───5─────────────────────5─────────────────────────────────────────────
G ─────────────────────────────────────────────────────────────────────────
```
To me way ay, ay-ay, yah! We'll all drink whisky and gin.

```
     G       C   G         C       F   Am          G           C
E ─────────────────────────0───────1───0───0─────────────────────────────
A ───────3───5───3─5───────────────────────────────5─3───5───3───────────
D 5───5─────────────────────5─────────────────────────────────────────────
G ─────────────────────────────────────────────────────────────────────────
```
To me way ay, ay-ay, yah! We'll all shave under the chin.

```
     G       C   G         C       F   Am          G           C
E ─────────────────────────0───────1───0───0─────────────────────────────
A ───────3───5───3─5─────────────────────────────────5───3───5───3───────
D 5───5─────────────────────5─────────────────────────────────────────────
G ─────────────────────────────────────────────────────────────────────────
```
To me way ay, ay-ay, yah! We'll all throw muck at the cook.

```
     G       C   G         C       F     Am          G           C
E ─────────────────────────0───────1───1───0───0───0─────────────────────
A ───────3───5───3─5───────────────────────────────────5───3───5───3─────
D 5───5─────────────────────5─────────────────────────────────────────────
G ─────────────────────────────────────────────────────────────────────────
```
To me way ay, ay-ay, yah! For the crusty old man on the poop.

```
     G       C   G         C       F   Am          G           C
E ─────────────────────────0───────1───0───0───0─────────────────────────
A ───────3───5───3─5─────────────────────────────────5───3───5───3───────
D 5───5─────────────────────5─────────────────────────────────────────────
G ─────────────────────────────────────────────────────────────────────────
```
To me way ay, ay-ay, yah! We'll pay Paddy Doyle for his boots.

Chord Forms

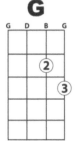
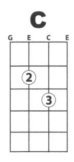
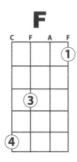
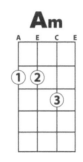

Paddy Doyle's Boots
(continued)

Melody & Chords

Key of C (High)

```
    G     C   G      C        F    Am        G              C
E ─────────────────────0───────1────0────0──0─────────────────────────────
A ────────3───5───3─5─3────────0────2──2──2──5──────3───5────3────────────
D 5───5───2───0───0─0─2────5────3────2──2──────0──────0────0────2─────────
G 0───0───0───0───────0──5─────────────────────0──────0────0────0────────
```
To me way-ay, ay-ay, yah! We'll pay Paddy Doyle for his boots.

```
    G     C   G      C        F    Am        G              C
E ─────────────────────0───────1────0────0─────────────────────────────────
A ────────3───5───3─5─3────────0────2──2──2──5──────3───5────3────────────
D 5───5───2───0───0─0─2────5────3────2──2──────0──────0────0────2─────────
G 0───0───0───0───────0──5─────────────────────0──────0────0────0────────
```
To me way ay, ay-ay, yah! We'll all drink whisky and gin.

```
    G     C   G      C        F    Am        G              C
E ─────────────────────0───────1────0────0─────────────────────────────────
A ────────3───5───3─5─3────────0────2──2──2──5─3────5────3─────────────────
D 5───5───2───0───0─0─2────5────3────2──2──────0─0────0────2───────────────
G 0───0───0───0───────0──0────────────────────0─0────0────0───────────────
```
To me way ay, ay-ay, yah! We'll all shave under the chin.

```
    G     C   G      C        F    Am        G              C
E ─────────────────────0───────1────0────0─────────────────────────────────
A ────────3───5───3─5─3────────0────2──2──2──5──────3───5────3────────────
D 5───5───2───0───0─0─2────5────3────2──2──────0──────0────0────2─────────
G 0───0───0───0───────0──5─────────────────────0──────0────0────0────────
```
To me way ay, ay-ay, yah! We'll all throw muck at the cook.

```
    G     C   G      C        F    Am        G              C
E ─────────────────────0───────1──1─0────0──0─────────────────────────────
A ────────3───5───3─5─3────────0──0─2──2──2──5──────3───5────3────────────
D 5───5───2───0───0─0─2────5────3────2──────2──0──────0────0────2─────────
G 0───0───0───0───────0──5─────────────────────0──────0────0────0────────
```
To me way ay, ay-ay, yah! For the crusty old man on the poop.

```
    G     C   G      C        F    Am        G              C
E ─────────────────────0───────1────0────0──0─────────────────────────────
A ────────3───5───3─5─3────────0────2──2──2──5──────3───5────3────────────
D 5───5───2───0───0─0─2────5────3────2──2──────0──────0────0────2─────────
G 0───0───0───0───────0──5─────────────────────0──────0────0────0────────
```
To me way ay, ay-ay, yah! We'll pay Paddy Doyle for his boots.

Chord Forms

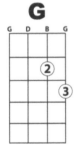
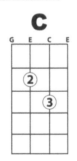
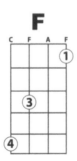
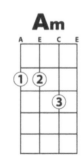

The Parting Glass

Basic Melody
Key of Em

This beautiful Scottish song first appeared In print in the 1770's, and remains a favorite parting and farewell song at Irish and Scottish parties and sessions. It is often performed acapella. The words below are somewhat modernized from the earlier Scottish versions.

Words and Music
Traditional

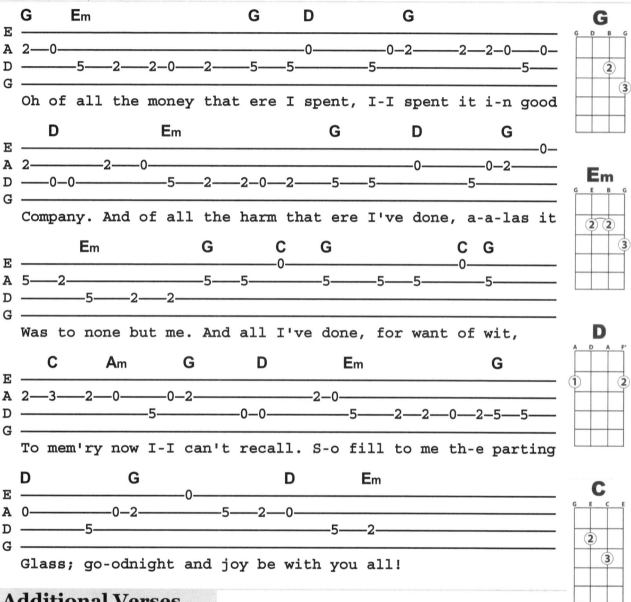

Additional Verses

Oh if I had money enough to spend,
And leisure for to sit a while.
There is a fair maid in this town,
Who surely has my heart beguiled.
Her rosy cheeks, and ruby lips,
Alas she has my heart in thrall;
So fill to me the parting glass,
Goodnight and joy be with you all.

Of all the comrades that e're I had,
They were sorry for my going away.
And of all the sweethearts that ere I had,
They'd wish me one more day to stay.
But since it falls unto my lot,
That I should rise, and you should not,
I'll gently rise, and I'll softly call,
Goodnight and joy be with you all!

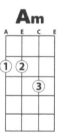

The Parting Glass
(continued)

Melody & Chords

Key of Em

```
      G    Em                        G      D         G
E  ─────────────────────────────────────────────────────────────
A  2──0──────────────────────────0──────0─2───────2──2─0────0─
D  0──0──5────2──────2─0────2─────5──5─0───────5─0─0────0──0─0─5─0─
G  0─────4──4──4─0────4──────0──0─2─────2────0──────0────0─
   Oh of all the money that ere I spent, I-I spent it i-n good
```

```
      D                Em                      G      D      G
E  ──────────────────────────────────────────────────────────────0─
A  2─────────2────0──────────────────────0───────0─2─────2─
D  0──0─0────0────0──5────2────2─0────2────5────5─────0───────5─0─0──────0─
G  0──2─2────2──────4────4────4─0──4────0────0────2──────2────0────0─
   Company. And of all the harm that ere I've done, a-a-las it
```

```
            Em            G       C     G              C   G
E  ──────────────────────────────0───────────────────────0─────
A  5────2───────────5────5────3────5────5────5────3──5──────
D  0────0──5────2────2────0────0────2────0────0──0────2──0──────
G  0────0──4────4────4────0────0────0────0────0──0────0──0──────
   Was to none but me. And all I've done, for want of wit,
```

```
      C     Am     G        D         Em                 G
E  ───────────────────────────────────────────────────────────────
A  2──3──2──0───────0─2───────────2─0───────────────────────
D  0──2──2──2────5─2─0────0─0──────0─0─5────2──2──0──2─5──5─
G  0──0──────2──5────0───────0─2────2────4───4─4──0─4─0──0─
   To mem'ry now I-I can't recall. S-o fill to me th-e parting
```

```
      D              G               D       Em
E  ───────────────────0───────────────────────────────────────
A  0───────────0─2────2──5────2──0──────────────────────
D  0───────5─0─0──────0────0──0──0────5────2────────────
G  2────────2────0──────0──0──0─2────2────4──────────────
   Glass; go-odnight and joy be with you all!
```

Chord Forms

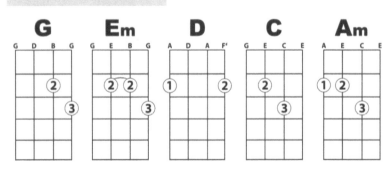

The Parting Glass
(continued)

Basic Melody

Key of Am (Low)

```
       C      Am                    C        G          C
E _____
A _____
D 2——0——————————————————————0————————0—2————2—2—0———0—
G ——————5———2——2-0——2——5——5——————————5——————————————5——
  Oh of all the money that ere I spent, I-I spent it i-n good
```

```
       G            Am                    C        G          C
E _____
A _____0—
D 2————————————2——0————————————————————0————————0-2————
G ——0-0————————————5———2——2-0—2——5——5——————————5——————
  Company. And of all the harm that ere I've done, a-a-las it
```

```
          Am          C        F      C              F    C
E _____
A _____0_____0_____
D 5——2—————————————5——5————————5——————5——5————5————
G ————————5———2——2—————————————————————————————————
  Was to none but me. And all I've done, for want of wit,
```

```
       F     Dm      C        G          Am                  C
E _____
A _____
D 2——3——2——0—————————0-2——————————————2-0————————————
G ——————————5————————0-0——————————5——2——2—0—2-5——5——
  To mem'ry now I-I can't recall. S-o fill to me th-e parting
```

```
       G            C            G        Am
E _____
A _____0_____
D 0————————————0-2————————5——2—0————————————————————
G ————————5————————————————————5——2————————————————
  Glass; go-odnight and joy be with you all!
```

Chord Forms

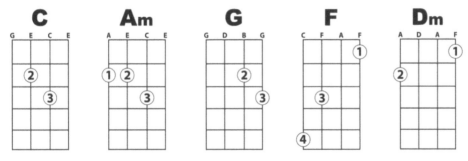

The Parting Glass
(continued)

Basic Melody

Key of Am (High)

```
   C    Am                    C      G        C
E 0—————————————————————————————————————0——————0——0————
A ———5——3——0——0————0——3——3—5————3—5————————————5—3—5—
D ———————————————5————————————————————————————————————
G —————————————————————————————————————————————————————
```
Oh of all the money that ere I spent, I-I spent it i-n good

```
   G          Am                    C      G        C
E 0—————————0———————————————————————————————————0———5—
A ——————————————5——3——0——0————0——3——3————5————3—5————
D ———5—5———————————————————5———————————————————————————
G —————————————————————————————————————————————————————
```
Company. And of all the harm that ere I've done, a-a-las it

```
   Am          C      F   C           F   C
E 3——0—————————3——3——5——3————3——3————5——3————
A ———————3——0——0——————————————————————————————
D ————————————————————————————————————————————
G ————————————————————————————————————————————
```
Was to none but me. And all I've done, for want of wit,

```
   F    Dm     C      G        Am                C
E 0—1——0————————0——————————0——————————————————————————
A ———————5——3—5——————————————5—3——0——0————0—3——3——
D ———————————————5—5—————————————————————5—————————
G ————————————————————————————————————————————————————
```
To mem'ry now I-I can't recall. S-o fill to me th-e parting

```
   G          C           G      Am
E ————————————0——5——3——0———————————————
A 5————3—5———————————————5——3——0————————
D —————————————————————————————————————
G —————————————————————————————————————
```
Glass; go-odnight and joy be with you all!

Chord Forms

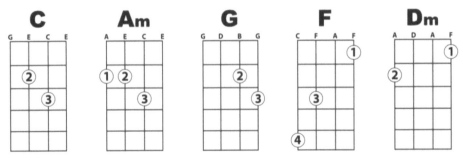

Irish Pub Favorites Mandolin Tablature Songbook · Copyright 2020 by Hobo Music Works LLC · All Rights Reserved

The Parting Glass
(continued)

Melody & Chords

Key of Am (High)

```
        C     Am                      C     G          C
E  0------------------------------------------------0------0---0-------
A  3---5---3----0----0------0----3----3-5------3-5-3----3---3-5-3-5-
D  2---2---2----2----2-5----2----2----2-0------0-0-2----2---2-2-2-2-
G  0--------2---------2-2----2----0----0--------0---0--------0---------
   Oh of all the money that ere I spent, I-I spent it i-n good
```

```
        G           Am                    C     G          C
E  0-----------0--------------------------------------------0---5-------
A  3-----------2----5---3----0----0----0----3---3------5---3-5-3----3-
D  2---5-5----0----0-2----2----2-5----2----2---2------0---0-0-2-
G  ----0-0--------------2---------2-2----2----0---0----0--------0---------
   Company. And of all the harm that ere I've done, a-a-las it
```

```
        Am           C     F    C              F  C
E  3----0-----------3----3----5----3------3----3----5---3---------
A  3----3---3----0----0----3----3----3----3------3---3----3---3-------
D  2----2---2----2----2----2----2----3----2------2---2----3---2-------
G  ----0---2---------2----0--------------0------0---0--------0---------
   Was to none but me. And all I've done, for want of wit,
```

```
        F    Dm     C          G          Am                C
E  0---1----0-----------0--------------0---------------------------
A  3---0----0----5---3-5-3----------2-5-3----0---0------0-3---3---
D  2---3----------3----3-3-2----5-5------0-0-2----2---2---5-2-2---2-
G  ----------2---------0--------5-0----------2------2-5-----0---0---
   To mem'ry now I-I can't recall. S-o fill to me th-e parting
```

```
        G           C              G     Am
E  --------------0-----5---3----0-----------------------
A  5---------3-5-3----3---3----3-5----3---0-------------
D  0---------0-0-2----2---2----2-0------0---2-----------
G  0---------0----0--------0----0---0----0---2-----------
   Glass; go-odnight and joy be with you all!
```

Chord Forms

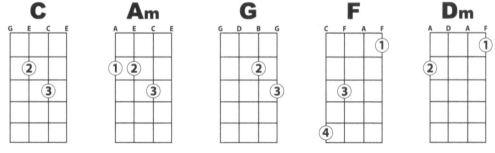

Poor Old Dicey Reilly

Basic Melody
Key of G

This traditional Irish song tells the tale of an old woman completely given over to drunkenness. Each day she visits the "pop" (slang for a pawn shop) and is then off to begin her drinking. Probably the best known version of this song was recorded by The Dubliners.

Words and Music
Traditional

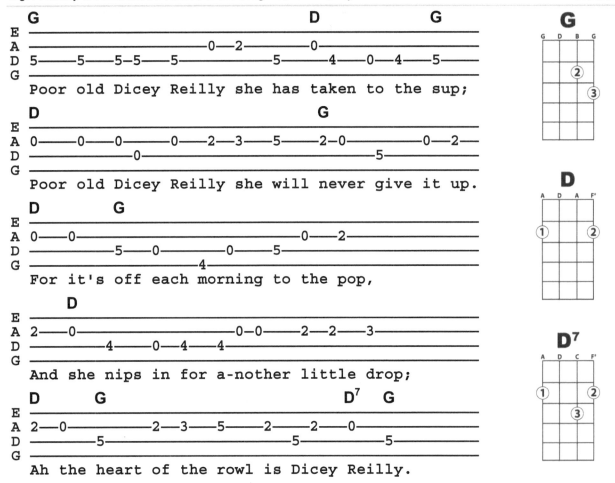

Additional Verses

Oh she walks down Fitzgibbon street with an independent air;
And then it's down by Summerhill and as the people stare...
She says it's nearly half past one, it's time I had another little one...
Oh the heart of the rowl is Dicey Reilly.

She owns a little sweet shop at the corner of the street,
And every evening after school I go to wash her feet;
She leaves me there to mind the shop, while she nips out for another little drop...
Oh the heart of the rowl is Dicey Reilly.

Long years ago when men were men and fancied May Oblong;
Or lovely Becky Cooper or Maggie's Mary Wong...
One woman put them all to shame, only one was worthy of the name...
And the name of that dame was Dicey Reilly.

Oh but time went catching up on her like many pretty whores;
And it's after you along the street before you're out the doors...
The balance weighed and the looks all fade, but out of all that great brigade...
Still the heart of the rowl is Dicey Reilly.

Poor Old Dicey Reilly

Melody & Chords

Key of G

(continued)

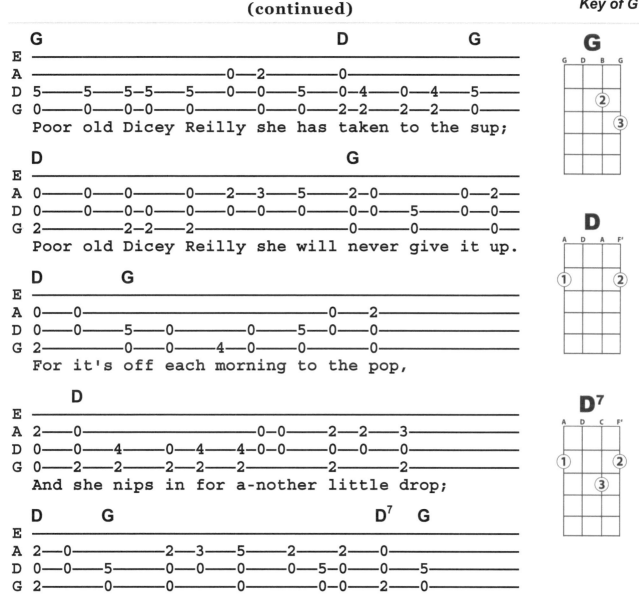

Poor old Dicey Reilly she has taken to the sup;

Poor old Dicey Reilly she will never give it up.

For it's off each morning to the pop,

And she nips in for a-nother little drop;

Ah the heart of the rowl is Dicey Reilly.

Here's to a long life and a merry one...
A quick death and an easy one...
A pretty girl and an honest one...
A cold pint -- and another one!

Irish Toast

Poor Old Dicey Reilly

(continued)

Basic Melody

Key of C

```
        C                               G           C
E ——————————————————————————0———————————————————————————————————
A 3———————3———3-3————3——————5——————————3———5-2————————2————3—————
D ——————————————————————————————————————————————5————————————————
G ——————————————————————————————————————————————————————————————
```

Poor old Dicey Reilly she has taken to the sup;

```
        G                                       C
E ————————————————————————————0——1——3————0————————————————————0——
A 5———————5———5————————5—————————————————————5———3————5——————————
D ————————————————5——————————————————————————————————————————————
G ——————————————————————————————————————————————————————————————
```

Poor old Dicey Reilly she will never give it up.

```
        G       C
E ———————————————————————————————————————————0——————————————————
A 5———5———3——————————————————————————3———5———————————————————————
D ———————————————5————2——5————————————————————————————————————————
G ——————————————————————————————————————————————————————————————
```

For it's off each morning to the pop,

```
              G
E 0——————————————————————————————————0——0——1———————————————————
A ———————5———2————————2——2-5-5————————————————————————————————————
D ———————————————5————————————————————————————————————————————————
G ——————————————————————————————————————————————————————————————
```

And she nips in for a-nother little drop;

```
        G       C                              G7   C
E 0———————————————0——1——3————0——————0———————————————————————————
A ———————5———3————————————————————————————3———5———3——————————————
D ——————————————————————————————————————————————————————————————
G ——————————————————————————————————————————————————————————————
```

Ah the heart of the rowl is Dicey Reilly.

Chord Forms

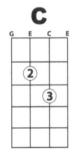

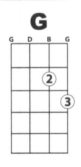

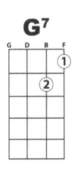

Poor Old Dicey Reilly

Melody & Chords

Key of C

(continued)

```
      C                             G           C
E ———————————————————————0——————————————————————————
A 3——3——3-3——3——5—3——3——5-2————2——3———
D 2——2——2-2——2——2—2——2——0-0——5—0——2———
G 0——————0——————0——————0——————0——0——————0———
  Poor old Dicey Reilly she has taken to the sup;
```

```
      G                                     C
E ——————————————————0—1——3———0——————————0——
A 5——5——5——5—2—2——2——3-5——3——5—3——
D 0——0——0-5——0——————————2-2——2——2—2——
G 0——————0-0——0——————————0——————0——————0——
  Poor old Dicey Reilly she will never give it up.
```

```
      G       C
E ——————————————————————————————0——————
A 5——5——3—————————3—5——3——
D 0——0——2—5——2—5——2—0——2——
G 0——————0——0——0-0——0——————0——
  For it's off each morning to the pop,
```

```
              G
E 0——————————————————————0—0——1——————
A 3——5—2————2——2-5-5——2—2——2——
D 2——0——0——5—0——0-0-0——0——————0——
G ——0——————0-0——————0——————————0——
  And she nips in for a-nother little drop;
```

```
      G       C                         G⁷  C
E 0——————————0—1——3——0———0——————————
A 2—5——3————3—0——3——3—3-3——5——3——
D 0—0——2——2——————2——2-2——3—2——
G ——0——0————————————0——————0—0——
  Ah the heart of the rowl is Dicey Reilly.
```

Chord Forms

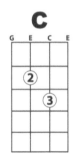 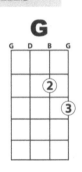 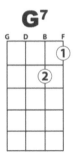

168

Rare Old Mountain Dew

Basic Melody

(page 1)

Key of C (Low)

This is one of the classic Irish drinking songs, which extols the virtues of mountain dew... otherwise known as poteen, red biddy, white lightning, holy water and moonshine whiskey. The chorus is sung as "vocables" - rhyming nonsense words that are often seen in older Irish folk songs. The song was written in 1882.

Words by Edward Harrigan

Music by David Braham

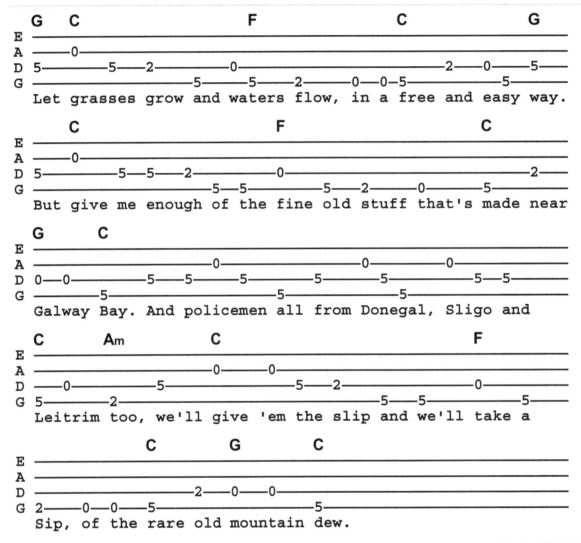

Chord Forms

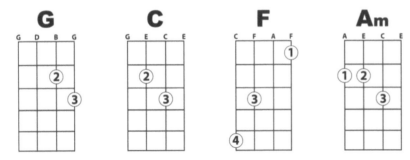

See Chorus and Additional Verses on Next Page

Rare Old Mountain Dew

Basic Melody

(page 2)

Key of C (Low)

CHORUS

C   **F**

```
E ——————————————————————————————————————————————————
A ——————0——0—————————————————————————————————————————
D 5——5———————————5—5——2———————————0——0———————————————
G ————————————————————5——5—————————————5—5——2————————
```
Tye-dee-doodle-ayedee-dum,   Tye-dee doodle-ayedee-dum,

C   **G**   **C**

```
E ——————————————————————————————————————————————————
A ——————————————————————————————0——0—————————————————
D ———————2——0——0—————5—5——5——————————5—5——2———————————
G 5——5———————————————5———————————————————————————————
```
Toodle-aye diddley-aye-ay;   Tye-dee doodle-ayedee-dum,

       F   **C**   **G**   **C**

```
E ——————————————————————————————————————————————————
A ——————————————————————————————————————————————————
D ——————0——0——————————————————————2——0——0————————————
G 5——5———————————5—5——2——0——0—5——5———————————5———
```
Tye-dee diddey-idle dum,   tye-de diddley-aye dool-aye ay.

Additional Verses

At the foot of the hill there's a neat little still,
Where the smoke curls up to the sky;
By the smoke and the smell, you can plainly tell
That the poteen's brewin' nearby.
Well it fills the air with an odor rare,
And betwixt both me and you,
When home you stroll, you can take a bowl...
Or a bucket of the mountain dew.

Now learn'ed men who use the pen
Have wrote her praises high.
That sweet poteen from Ireland green,
Distilled from wheat and rye.
Put away your pills, it will cure all ills,
Be you pagan, or Christian, or Jew.
Take off your coat and grease your throat
With the rare old mountain dew!

Rare Old Mountain Dew

Basic Melody
Key of C (High)

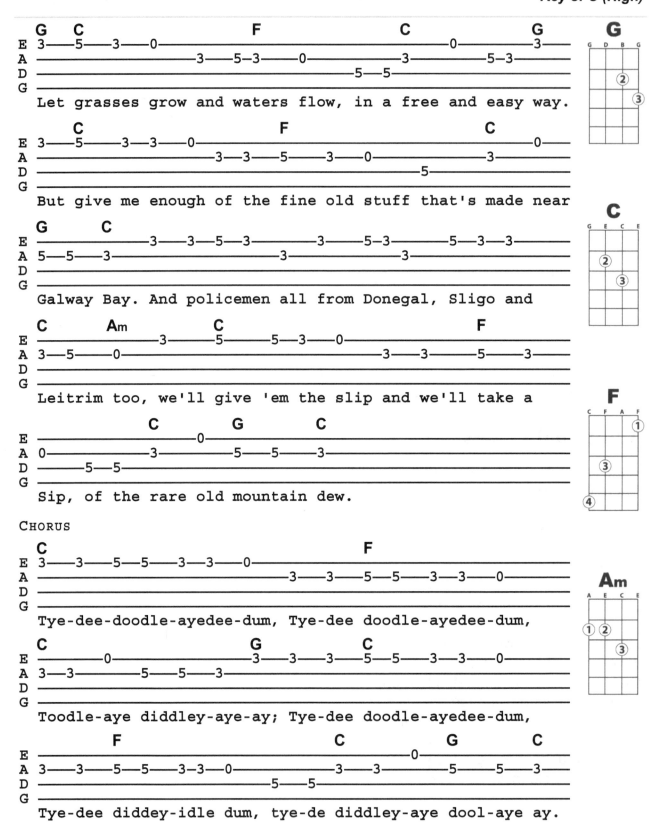

```
   G   C              F              C              G       G
E 3——5——3——0                        0——————————3    [diagram]
A            3——5-3——0————3——————5-3
D                  5——5
G

Let grasses grow and waters flow, in a free and easy way.

       C              F              C
E 3——5——3—3——0                              0——       C
A            3—3——5—3——0              3       [diagram]
D                  5
G

But give me enough of the fine old stuff that's made near

   G      C
E          3——3—5-3——3——5-3——5—3—3
A 5——5——3          3       3
D
G

Galway Bay. And policemen all from Donegal, Sligo and

   C    Am      C              F
E          3——5——5-3——0
A 3——5——0              3——3——5——3         F
D                                          [diagram]
G

Leitrim too, we'll give 'em the slip and we'll take a

            C    G    C
E              0
A 0          3——5—5——3
D     5—5
G

Sip, of the rare old mountain dew.
```

CHORUS

```
   C              F
E 3——3—5—5——3—3——0
A            3——3—5—5——3—3——0
D                                  Am
G                                  [diagram]

Tye-dee-doodle-ayedee-dum, Tye-dee doodle-ayedee-dum,

   C         G    C
E     0         3——3—5—5—3—3——0
A 3—3    5—5—3
D
G

Toodle-aye diddley-aye-ay; Tye-dee doodle-ayedee-dum,

         F              C    G    C
E                          0
A 3—3—5—5—3-3—0          3——3    5—5—3
D                  5——5
G

Tye-dee diddey-idle dum, tye-de diddley-aye dool-aye ay.
```

Rare Old Mountain Dew

Melody & Chords

Key of C (High)

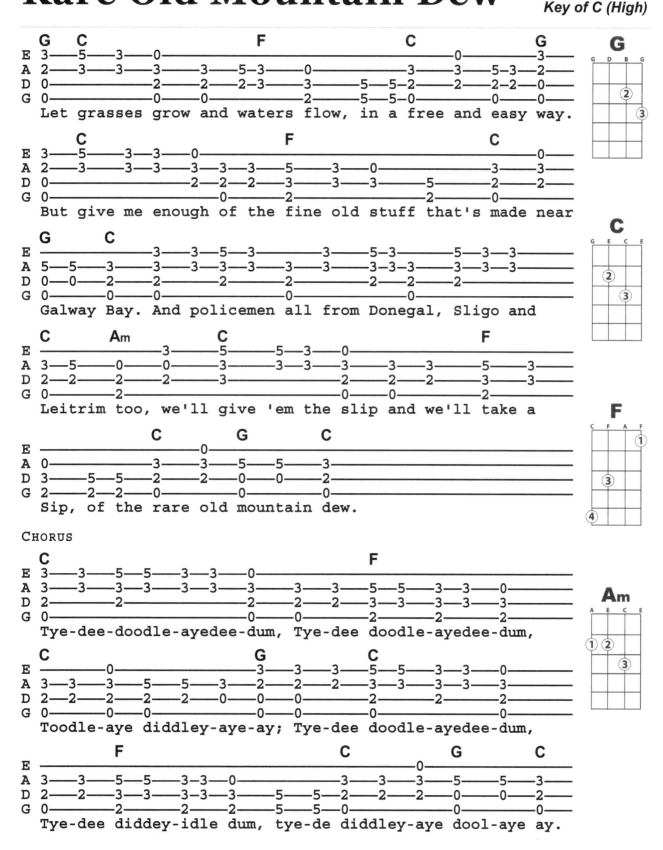

Rare Old Mountain Dew

Basic Melody

Key of G

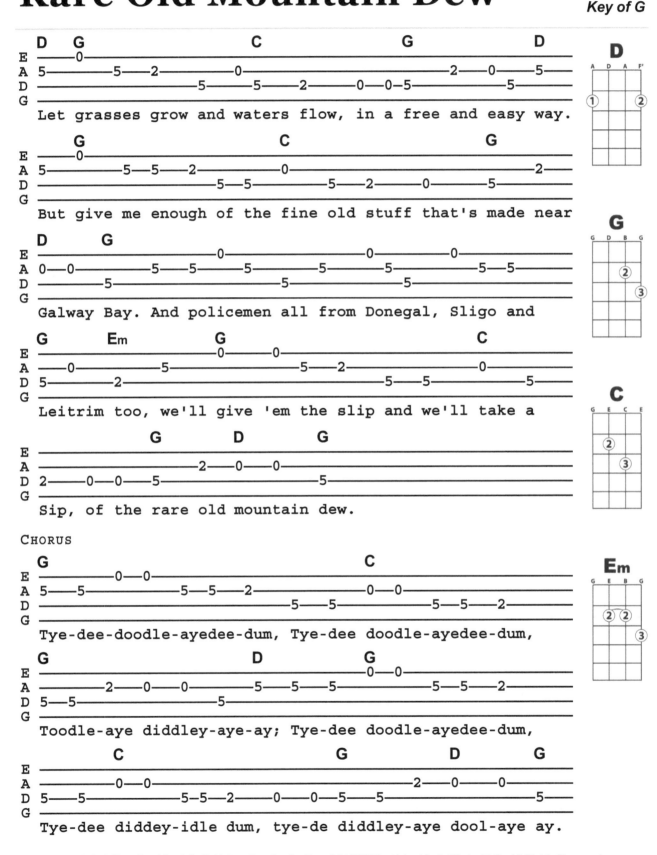

Rare Old Mountain Dew

Melody & Chords

Key of G

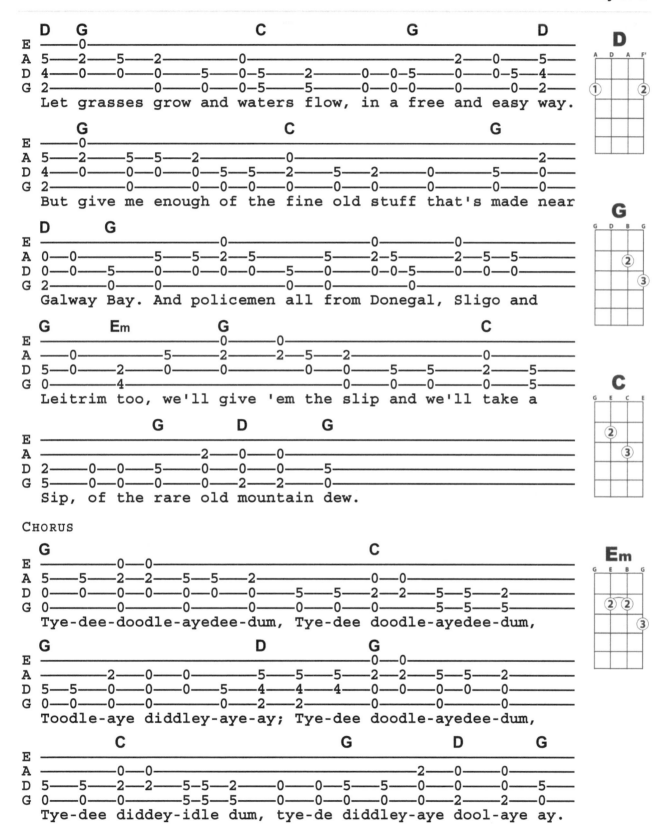

The Rattlin' Bog

Basic Melody

Key of C (Low)

Words and Music

Traditional

This is a classic Irish folk song, sung in an "accumulative" manner, where additional lines are added to the verse each time through. The tradition is to start off a bit slower and gentler and then speed up as the length of each run-through increases. This is a fun one to play and sing, and is popular with kids. Rattlin' means "splendid" in the context of this song.

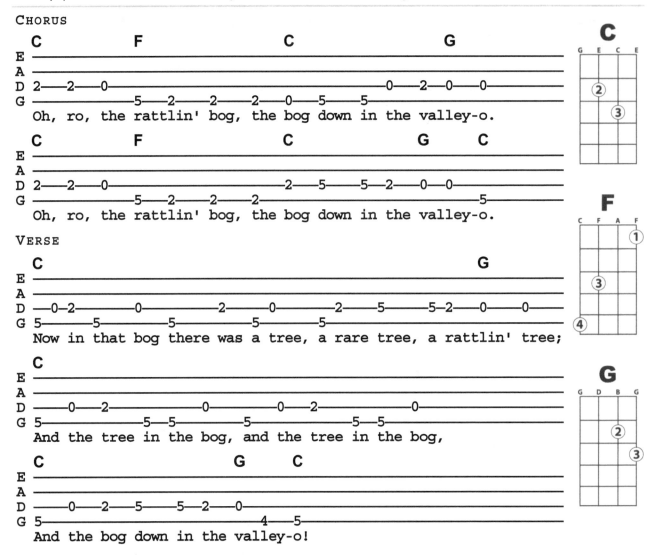

CHORUS

```
     C            F              C              G
E ────────────────────────────────────────────────────────
A ────────────────────────────────────────────────────────
D 2───2───0─────────────────────────────0───2───0───0──────
G ───────────5───2───2───2───0───5───5──────────────────────
  Oh,  ro,  the rattlin' bog,  the bog down in the  valley-o.
```

```
     C            F              C              G   C
E ────────────────────────────────────────────────────────
A ────────────────────────────────────────────────────────
D 2───2───0───────────────2───5───5───2───0───0────────────
G ───────────5───2───2───2──────────────────────────5──────
  Oh,  ro,  the rattlin' bog,  the bog down in the  valley-o.
```

VERSE

```
     C                                                    G
E ────────────────────────────────────────────────────────
A ────────────────────────────────────────────────────────
D ──0─2───────0───────2───0───────2───5───5─2───0───0──────
G 5───────5───────5───────5───────5─────────────────────────
  Now in that bog there was a tree, a rare tree, a rattlin' tree;
```

```
     C
E ────────────────────────────────────────────────────────
A ────────────────────────────────────────────────────────
D ──────0───2─────────0───────0───2─────────0──────────────
G 5───────────5───5───────5─────────5───5──────────────────
  And the tree in the bog, and the tree in the bog,
```

```
     C                    G       C
E ────────────────────────────────────────────────────────
A ────────────────────────────────────────────────────────
D ──────0───2───5───5─2───0─────────────────────────────────
G 5─────────────────────────4───5──────────────────────────
  And the bog down in the valley-o!
```

Additional Verses

Repeat all previous verses each time through as shown in the first example below.

And on that tree there was a limb,
A rare limb, and a rattlin' limb...
The limb on the tree,
And the tree in the bog,
And the bog down in the valley-o.

And on that limb there was a branch,
A rare branch and a rattlin' branch...

And on that branch there was a twig,
A rare twig and a rattlin' twig...

And on that twig there was a nest,

A rare nest and a rattlin' nest...

And in that nest there was an egg,
A rare egg and a rattlin' egg...

And in that egg there was a bird,
A rare bird and a rattlin' bird...

And on that bird there was a feather,
A rare feather and a rattlin' feather...

And on that feather there was a flea,
A rare flea and a rattlin' flea...

The Rattlin' Bog (continued)

Basic Melody
Key of C (High)

CHORUS

```
    C           F           C               G
E 0——0————————————————————————————————0————————————————————————
A ————————5——3——0————0————0————3——3—5————5——5———————————————————
D ——————————————————————————5———————————————————————————————————
G ——————————————————————————————————————————————————————————————
```

Oh, ro, the rattlin' bog, the bog down in the valley-o.

```
    C           F           C           G       C
E 0——0————————————————————0——3————3—0——————————————————————————
A ————————5——3——0————0————0———————————————5—5——3————————————————
D ——————————————————————————————————————————————————————————————
G ——————————————————————————————————————————————————————————————
```

Oh, ro, the rattlin' bog, the bog down in the valley-o.

VERSE

```
    C                                                   G
E ——————0————————————————0————————————0——3————3—0——————————————
A 3—5————3——5——3————————3—5————3——————————————————5——5—————————
D ——————————————————————————————————————————————————————————————
G ——————————————————————————————————————————————————————————————
```

Now in that bog there was a tree, a rare tree, a rattlin' tree;

```
    C
E ——————0————————————————0——————————————————————————————————————
A 3——5————————3—3——5————3——5————————3—3——5——————————————————————
D ——————————————————————————————————————————————————————————————
G ——————————————————————————————————————————————————————————————
```

And the tree in the bog, and the tree in the bog,

```
    C               G       C
E ——————0——3————3—0—————————————————————————————————————————————
A 3——5————————————————5—2——3————————————————————————————————————
D ——————————————————————————————————————————————————————————————
G ——————————————————————————————————————————————————————————————
```

And the bog down in the valley-o!

Chord Forms

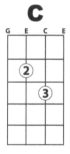

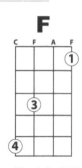

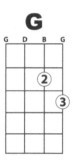

The Rattlin' Bog (continued)

Melody & Chords
Key of C (High)

CHORUS

```
     C              F                 C                 G
E  0----0----------------------------------------------0----------------
A  3----3----5----3----0----0----0----3----3----5----3----5----5--------
D  2----2----2----3----3----3----3----5----2----2----2----2----0----0---
G  0----0---------2---------2----2----5--------------0---------0----0----
```
Oh, ro, the rattlin' bog, the bog down in the valley-o.

```
     C              F                 C                 G         C
E  0----0--------------------------------0----3----3----0-----------------
A  3----3----5----3----0----0----0----3----3----3----3----5----5----3-----
D  2----2----2----3----3----3----3----2---------2---------0----0----2-----
G  0------0--------2---------2---------0---------------0---------0---------
```
Oh, ro, the rattlin' bog, the bog down in the valley-o.

VERSE

```
     C                                                           G
E  ------0----------------------0----------------0----3------3-0--------------
A  3-5-3----3-------5----3-------3----3-5-------3-3-------3----3-3----5------5--
D  2-2-2----2-------2----2-------2----2-2-------2-2-------2-------2----2----0---
G  0------0---------0----------0---------0----------0----0---------0---------0--
```
Now in that bog there was a tree, a rare tree, a rattlin' tree;

```
     C                                       
E  ------0--------------------------0---------------------------
A  3----5----3-------3-3----5-------3----5----3-------3-3----5---
D  2----2----2-------2-2----2-------2----2----2-------2-2----2---
G  0--------0----------------0----------0----------------0------
```
And the tree in the bog, and the tree in the bog,

```
     C                      G         C
E  ------0----3------3-0----------------------
A  3----5----3-------3----3-3----5----2----3--
D  2----2----2----------------2----0----0----2
G  0--------0---------------------0---------0-
```
And the bog down in the valley-o!

Chord Forms

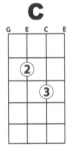

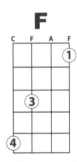

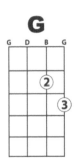

The Rattlin' Bog (continued)

CHORUS

```
          G            C                  G                  D
E ————————————————————————————————————————————————————————————————————————
A 2———2——0——————————————————————————————————————0———2——0———0——————————————
D ——————————5———2————2————2———0———5———5——————————————————————————————————
G ————————————————————————————————————————————————————————————————————————
```
Oh, ro, the rattlin' bog, the bog down in the valley-o.

```
          G            C                  G                  D      G
E ————————————————————————————————————————————————————————————————————————
A 2———2——0————————————————————————2———5———5——2———0———0—————————————————————
D ——————————5———2————2————2————————————————————————————————5——————————————
G ————————————————————————————————————————————————————————————————————————
```
Oh, ro, the rattlin' bog, the bog down in the valley-o.

VERSE

```
          G                                                             D
E ————————————————————————————————————————————————————————————————————————
A ——0—2————————0————————2————0————————2———5————5—2———0———0————————————————
D 5———————5————————5————————5————————5——————————————————————————————————
G ————————————————————————————————————————————————————————————————————————
```
Now in that bog there was a tree, a rare tree, a rattlin' tree;

```
          G
E ————————————————————————————————————————————————————————————————————————
A ——————0———2——————————0————————0———2————————0——————————————————————————
D 5————————————5———5————————5—————————————5———5—————————————————————————
G ————————————————————————————————————————————————————————————————————————
```
And the tree in the bog, and the tree in the bog,

```
          G                      D      G
E ————————————————————————————————————————————————————————————————————————
A ——————0———2———5————5—2———0———————————————————————————————————————————————
D 5—————————————————————————————————4———5————————————————————————————————
G ————————————————————————————————————————————————————————————————————————
```
And the bog down in the valley-o!

Chord Forms

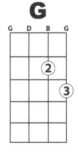 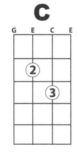 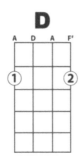

The Rattlin' Bog (continued)

Melody & Chords
Key of G

CHORUS

```
   G            C                  G                  D
E ————————————————————————————————————————————————————————————————————
A 2———2———0——————————————————————————————————0———2———0———0————————————
D 0———0———0———5———2———2———2———0———5———5———0———0———0———0————————————————
G 0———0———————5———5———5———5———0———0———0———————0———————2————————————————
```
Oh, ro, the rattlin' bog, the bog down in the valley-o.

```
   G            C                  G               D        G
E ————————————————————————————————————————————————————————————————————
A 2———2———0———————————————————————2———5———5———2———0———0————————————————
D 0———0———0———5———2———2———2———0———0———0———0———0———0———5————————————————
G 0———0———————5———5———5———5———0———————0———————2———————0————————————————
```
Oh, ro, the rattlin' bog, the bog down in the valley-o.

VERSE

```
   G                                                              D
E ————————————————————————————————————————————————————————————————————
A ——0—2————————0——————2———0——————2———5———5—2———0———0———————————————————
D 5—0—0—5———0———5———0—5—0———5—0———0———0———0—0———0———0——————————————————
G 0———0—0———0——0—————0——0—0———0—0———0———————0———————2—————————————————
```
Now in that bog there was a tree, a rare tree, a rattlin' tree;

```
   G
E ————————————————————————————————————————————————————————————————————
A ——————0———2—————————0————————0———2——————————0———————————————————————
D 5———0———0———5—5———0———5———0———0———5—5———0———————————————————————————
G 0———————0———0——0———0———0———————0———0—0———0—————————————————————————
```
And the tree in the bog, and the tree in the bog,

```
   G                      D       G
E ————————————————————————————————————————————————————————————————————
A ——————0———2———5———5—2———0—————————————————————————————————————————————
D 5———0———0———0———0—0———0—4———5————————————————————————————————————————
G 0———————0———————0———2—2———0—————————————————————————————————————————
```
And the bog down in the valley-o!

Chord Forms

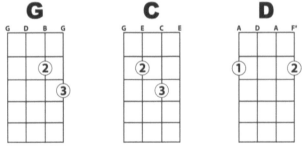

179

Reilly's Daughter

This humorous and fast-paced song presents the dangers there used to be when marrying a girl without her father's consent. In this case though the new husband is able to send his father-in-law packing. It is meant to be performed energetically, often while pantomiming the story being sung (firing pistols into the air, dunking heads in barrels of water, etc.).

Words and Music
Traditional

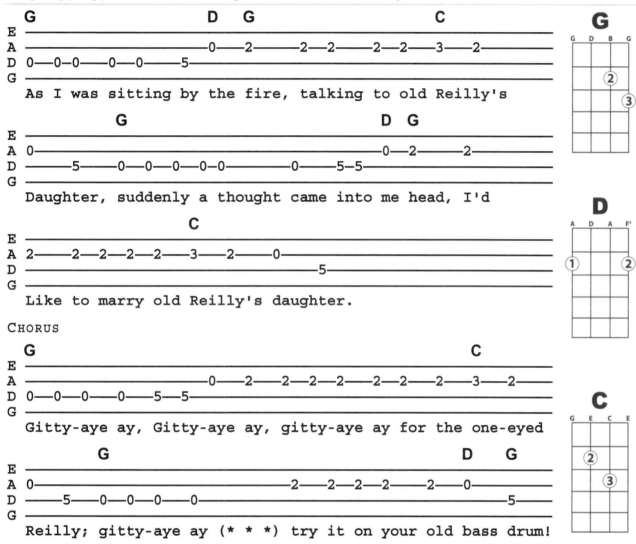

As I was sitting by the fire, talking to old Reilly's

Daughter, suddenly a thought came into me head, I'd

Like to marry old Reilly's daughter.

CHORUS

Gitty-aye ay, Gitty-aye ay, gitty-aye ay for the one-eyed

Reilly; gitty-aye ay (* * *) try it on your old bass drum!

* either clap or rap your instrument body with your knuckles three times.

Additional Verses

Reilly played on the big bass drum,
Reilly had a mind for murder and slaughter;
Reilly had a bright red glitterin' eye,
And he kept that eye on his lovely daughter.

Her hair was black and her eyes were blue,
The colonel & the major & the captain sought her,
The sergeant the private and the drum boy too,
Never had a chance with old Reilly's daughter!

I got me a ring and a parson too,
Got me a scratch in the married quarter;

Settled me down for a peaceful life,
Happy as a king with old Reilly's daughter.

Suddenly a footstep on the stair,
Who could it be but Reilly out for slaughter;
With two pistols in his hands,
Looking for the man that had married his daughter.

Well I caught old Reilly by the hair,
Rammed his head in a pail of water;
Fired his pistols into the air,
A damned sight quicker than I married his daughter!

Reilly's Daughter
(continued)

Melody & Chords

Key of G

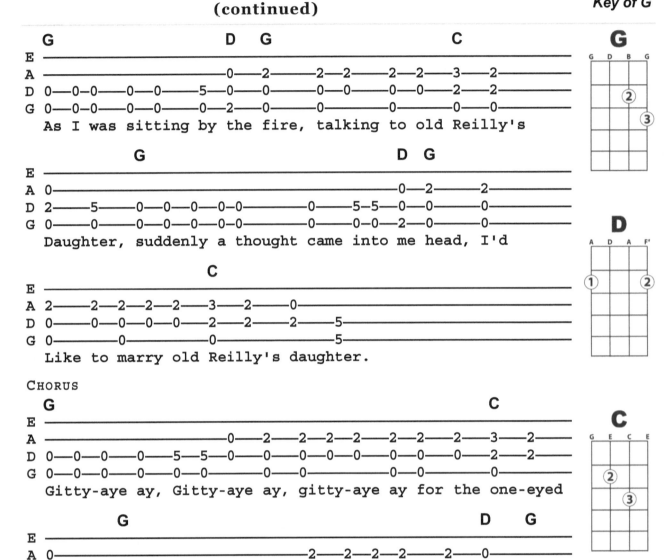

CHORUS

> May you have love that never ends,
> lots of money, and lots of friends.
> Health be yours, whatever you do,
> and may God send many blessings to you!
>
> *Irish Wedding Blessing*

Reilly's Daughter
(continued)

Basic Melody

Key of C (Low)

```
       C                    G    C                    F
E _____
A _____
D _____0___2_____2__2____2__2___3___2_____
G 0__0_0___0__0___5_____
  As  I  was sitting by the  fire, talking to old Reilly's
```

```
                   C                              G   C
E _____
A _____
D 0_____0___2_____2_____
G ____5_____0__0__0__0_0_____0___5_5_____
  Daughter, suddenly a thought came into me  head,  I'd
```

```
                   F
E _____
A _____
D 2___2__2__2__2__3___2_____0_____
G _____5_____
  Like to marry old Reilly's daughter.
```

CHORUS

```
       C                                                   F
E _____
A _____
D _____0___2__2__2__2___2__2__2___3___2_____
G 0__0__0__0___5__5_____
  Gitty-aye ay, Gitty-aye ay, gitty-aye ay for the one-eyed
```

```
              C                                    G      C
E _____
A _____
D 0_____2__2__2__2____2___0_____
G ___5__0__0__0__0_____5_____
  Reilly; gitty-aye ay (* * *) try it on your old bass drum!
```

Chord Forms

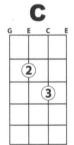

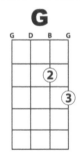

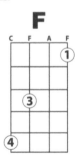

182

Reilly's Daughter
(continued)

Basic Melody

Key of C (High)

```
     C                      G   C                              F
E ────────────────────────0────0──0────0──0────1────0─────────────
A ──────────────────3────5───────────────────────────────────────
D 5──5─5────5──5───────────────────────────────────────────────────
G ────────────────────────────────────────────────────────────────
```
As I was sitting by the fire, talking to old Reilly's

```
              C                               G   C
E ─────────────────────────────────────────0──────0───────────────
A 5─────3─────────────────────────3─3────5─────────────────────────
D ───────────5──5──5─5─5────────5──────────────────────────────────
G ────────────────────────────────────────────────────────────────
```
Daughter, suddenly a thought came into me head, I'd

```
            F
E 0────0──0──0──0────1────0────────────────────────────────────────
A ──────────────────────5─────3────────────────────────────────────
D ──────────────────────────────────────────────────────────────────
G ──────────────────────────────────────────────────────────────────
```
Like to marry old Reilly's daughter.

CHORUS

```
    C                                                         F
E ────────────────────────0────0──0──0────0──0────0────1────0──────
A ──────────────────3──3────5──────────────────────────────────────
D 5──5──5────5──────────────────────────────────────────────────────
G ──────────────────────────────────────────────────────────────────
```
Gitty-aye ay, Gitty-aye ay, gitty-aye ay for the one-eyed

```
            C                                            G    C
E ───────────────────────────────0────0──0──0────0─────────────────
A 5─────3──────────────────────────────────────────5─────3─────────
D ───────────5──5──5────5───────────────────────────────────────────
G ──────────────────────────────────────────────────────────────────
```
Reilly; gitty-aye ay (* * *) try it on your old bass drum!

Chord Forms

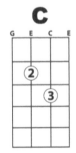

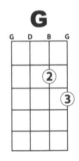

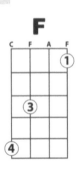

Reilly's Daughter
(continued)

Melody & Chords

Key of C (High)

```
     C                              G   C                             F
E ——————————————————————————————0——————0——0————0——0——1——0———————————————————
A ——————————————————————3——5——3——————3——3——————3——3——0——————0———————————————
D 5——5—5——————5——5——————2——0——2———————————2——————————————3——————3———————————
G 5——5—5——————5——5——————0——0——0———————————0————————————————————————————————
```
As I was sitting by the fire, talking to old Reilly's

```
                   C                                   G   C
E ————————————————————————————————————————————0———————————0———————————————————
A 5——————3—————————————————————————————3——3——5——3——————3———————————————————————
D 3——————3——————5——5——5——5—5——————————5——————2—2——0——2——————2—————————————————
G 2——————2——————5——5——5——5—5——————————5——————0——————0——0————————————————————
```
Daughter, suddenly a thought came into me head, I'd

```
                        F
E 0——————0——0——0——0——1——0————————————————————————————————————————————————————
A 3——————3——3——3——3——0——0——————5——————3———————————————————————————————————————
D 2——————————2————————3——3——————3——————3——————————————————————————————————————
G 0——————————————————————————2——————2—————————————————————————————————————————
```
Like to marry old Reilly's daughter.

CHORUS

```
     C                                                          F
E ——————————————————————————0——0——0——0————0——0——0——1——0————————————————————————
A ——————————————3——3——5——3——3——3——3——3——3——3——0——————0—————————————————————————
D 5—5——5——————5——2—2——2——2——2————————————2—2——————3——————3—————————————————————
G 5—5——5——————5——0—————————0——0—————————————————————————————————————————————————
```
Gitty-aye ay, Gitty-aye ay, gitty-aye ay for the one-eyed

```
                   C                                     G   C
E ————————————————————————————————0——0——0——0————0————————————————————————————
A 5——————3———————————————————————3——3——3——3——————3——5——3——————————————————————
D 3——————3——————5——5——5——————5——2——————2——————2——0——2—————————————————————————
G 2——————2——————5——5——5——————5——0——————————————————0——0———————————————————————
```
Reilly; gitty-aye ay (* * *) try it on your old bass drum!

Chord Forms

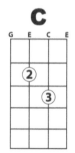

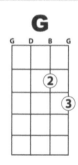

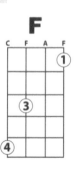

The Rising of the Moon

Basic Melody
Key of C

This classic Irish rebel song tells the story of the ill-fated uprising of 1798, one of the larger of the uprisings against British rule. It is one of the most beautiful and best-known of all the rebel songs and has been recorded by pretty much every Irish musician of note at some point.

Words and Music
Traditional

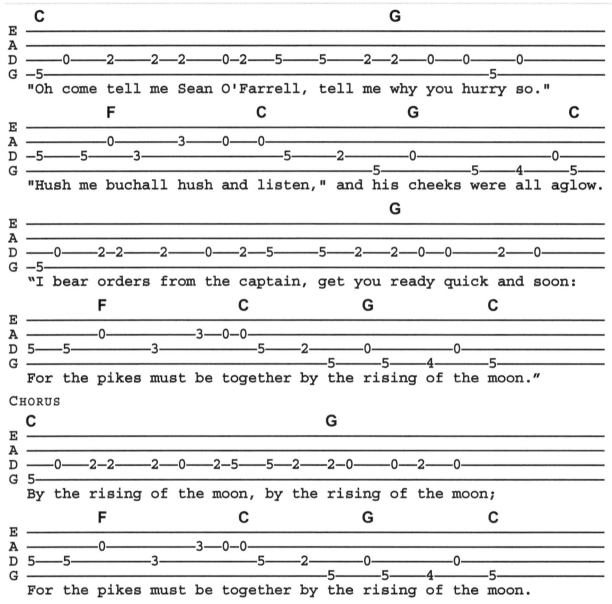

```
         C                                           G
E _____
A _____
D ____0____2____2_2_____0_2___5_____5_____2__2____0___0_____0_____
G _5_____5_____
  "Oh come tell me Sean O'Farrell, tell me why you hurry so."
```

```
              F              C            G              C
E _____
A _____0_____3____0___0_____
D _5_____5____3_____5____2_____0_____0_____
G _____5_____5___4____5_____
  "Hush me buchall hush and listen," and his cheeks were all aglow.
```

```
                                             G
E _____
A _____
D ___0____2_2____2____0_2_5_____5____2__2_0_0_____2___0_____
G _5_____
  "I bear orders from the captain, get you ready quick and soon:
```

```
              F            C            G            C
E _____
A _____0_____3_0_0_____
D _5____5_____3_____5____2_____0_____0_____
G _____5____5____4_____5_____
  For the pikes must be together by the rising of the moon."
```

CHORUS

```
         C                                       G
E _____
A _____
D ____0____2_2_____2__0___2_5___5__2____2_0_____0__2____0_____
G _5_____
  By the rising of the moon, by the rising of the moon;
```

```
              F            C            G            C
E _____
A _____0_____3_0_0_____
D _5____5_____3_____5____2_____0_____0_____
G _____5____5____4_____5_____
  For the pikes must be together by the rising of the moon.
```

Chord Forms

C

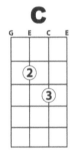

G

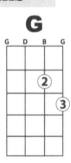

F

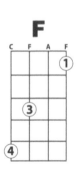

The Rising of the Moon
(continued)

Melody & Chords
Key of C

```
        C                                    G
E ——————————————————————————————————————————————————————————————————————
A ——————————————————————————————————————————————————————————————————————
D ———0———2———2—2———0—2——5———5————2—2——0———0————0—————————————————————————
G —5—5———5———5—5———0—5——5———5———5—0——0———0—5—0——————————————————————————
  "Oh come tell me Sean O'Farrell, tell me why you hurry so."

        F              C              G              C
E ——————————————————————————————————————————————————————————————————————
A ———————0——————————3———0——0—————————————————————————————————————————————
D —5———5—3—3———3———3——2—5———2————————0————0———0——0—5—————————————————————
G —0———0—2—2———2————0—0———0——5——0——————5———4——4—5————————————————————————
  "Hush me buchall hush and listen," and his cheeks were all aglow.

                                             G
E ——————————————————————————————————————————————————————————————————————
A ——————————————————————————————————————————————————————————————————————
D ———0———2—2———2——0——2—5———5——2———2—0—0——————2——0————————————————————————
G —5—5———5—5———5——0——5—5———5——5——0—0—0——————0——0————————————————————————
  "I bear orders from the captain, get you ready quick and soon:

        F              C              G              C
E ——————————————————————————————————————————————————————————————————————
A ———————0——————————3—0—0—————————————————————————————————————————————————
D 5———5—3———————3———3—3—2—5———2——————0—0——0——0——5————————————————————————
G 0———0—2———————2———2—5—5———5—5——0—5——4—4——5————————————————————————————
  For the pikes must be together by the rising of the moon."
```

CHORUS

```
        C                                    G
E ——————————————————————————————————————————————————————————————————————
A ——————————————————————————————————————————————————————————————————————
D ———0——2—2———2—0——2—5———5—2———2—0———0—2———0————————————————————————————
G 5—5———5———5—5—0——5—5———5—5——0—0——0—0——0————————————————————————————————
  By the rising of the moon, by the rising of the moon;

        F              C              G              C
E ——————————————————————————————————————————————————————————————————————
A ———————0——————————3—0—0—————————————————————————————————————————————————
D 5———5—3———————3———3—3—2—5———2——————0—0——0——0——5————————————————————————
G 0———0—2———————2———2—5—5———5—5——0—5——4—4——5————————————————————————————
  For the pikes must be together by the rising of the moon.
```

Chord Forms

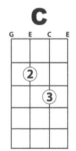 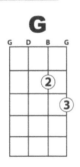 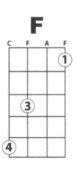

The Battle of Oulart Hill during the Rebellion of 1798.

The Rising of the Moon

Basic Melody

(continued)

Key of G

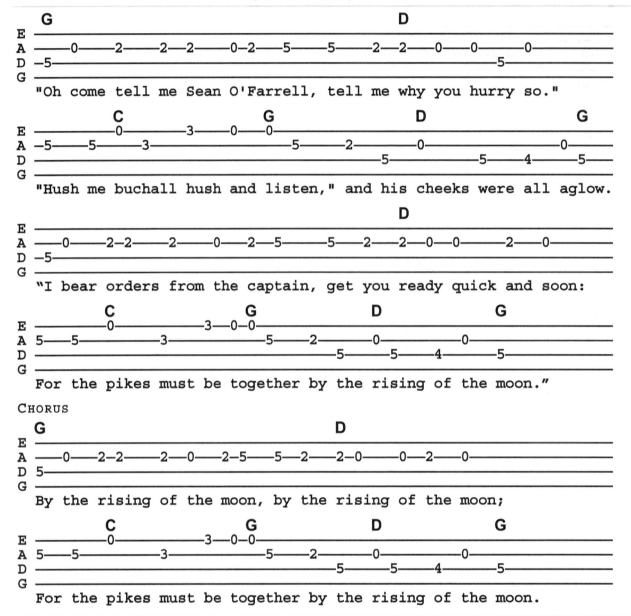

"Oh come tell me Sean O'Farrell, tell me why you hurry so."

"Hush me buchall hush and listen," and his cheeks were all aglow.

"I bear orders from the captain, get you ready quick and soon:

For the pikes must be together by the rising of the moon."

CHORUS

By the rising of the moon, by the rising of the moon;

For the pikes must be together by the rising of the moon.

Chord Forms

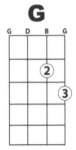
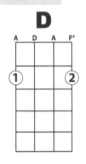
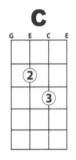

The Battle of Antrim during the Rebellion of 1798.

The Rising of the Moon

Melody & Chords

(continued)

Key of G

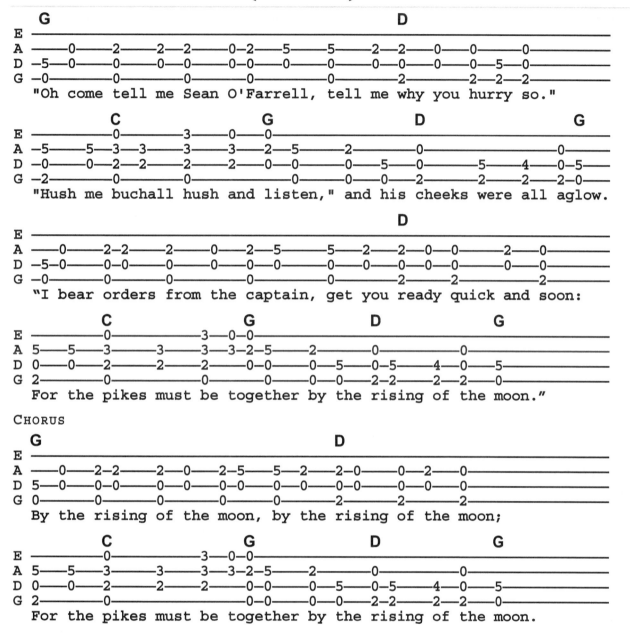

"Oh come tell me Sean O'Farrell, tell me why you hurry so."

"Hush me buchall hush and listen," and his cheeks were all aglow.

"I bear orders from the captain, get you ready quick and soon:

For the pikes must be together by the rising of the moon."

CHORUS

By the rising of the moon, by the rising of the moon;

For the pikes must be together by the rising of the moon.

Chord Forms

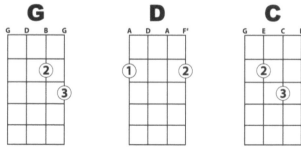

Rocky Road To Dublin
(page 1)

Basic Melody

Key of Am (Low)

This fast-paced old song tells the story of an Irishman's journeys abroad to England and the troubles he meets along the way. The melody is in the old "Dorian" minor-key style, and the rhythm is also non-standard: a 9/8 time slip jig. Watch a YouTube video of The Dubliners performing this one to get an idea of how it's supposed to go.

Words by D. K. Gavan

Music Traditional

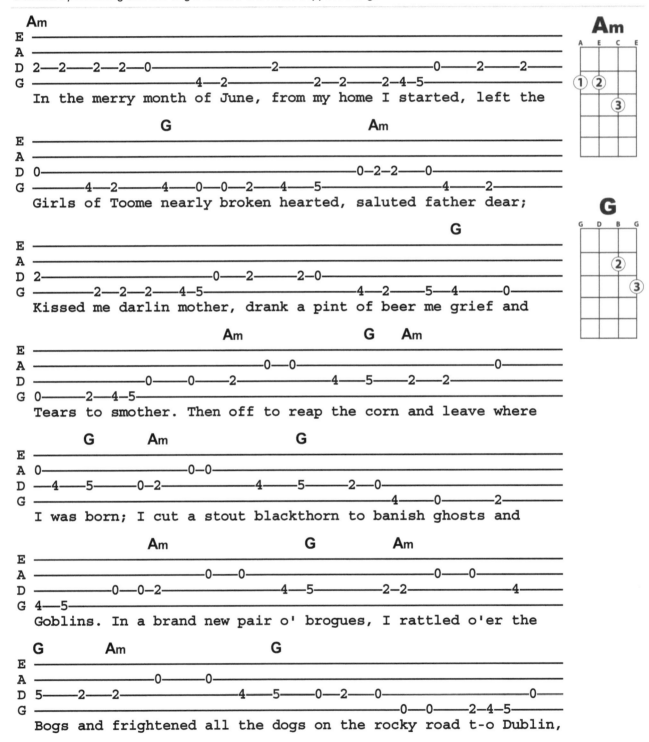

See Chorus and Additional Verses on Next Page

189

Rocky Road To Dublin

Basic Melody
Key of Am (Low)

(page 2)

CHORUS

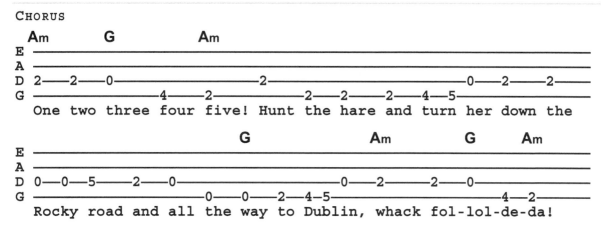

Am	G	Am		

```
E ————————————————————————————————————————————————————
A ————————————————————————————————————————————————————
D 2——2——0————————————————2————————————————0——2——2—————
G ————————————4——2——————————2——2——2——4——5—————————————
```
One two three four five! Hunt the hare and turn her down the

G	Am	G	Am

```
E ————————————————————————————————————————————————————
A ————————————————————————————————————————————————————
D 0——0——5————2——0——————————————0——2————2——0———————————
G ————————————————0——0——2——4——5——————————————4——2—————
```
Rocky road and all the way to Dublin, whack fol-lol-de-da!

Additional Verses

When in Mullingar that night, I rested limbs so weary,
Started by daylight, me spirits bright an airy,
Took a drop o' the pure, to keep me heart from sinking,
That's the paddy's cure, when e're he's on for drinking;
To see the lassies smile, laughing all the while,
At me curious style, would set your heart to bubbling,
Asked me was I hired, wages I required,
Til I was almost tired on the rocky road to Dublin...

When in Dublin next arrived, I thought it was a pity
To be so soon deprived a view of that fine city,
Then I took a stroll, all among the quality,
Me bundle it was stole, in a neat locality;
Something crossed me mind, when I looked behind,
No bundle could I find upon me stick a wobbling;
Enquiring for the rogue, they said me Connacht brogue
Wasn't much in vogue on the rocky road to Dublin...

Well from there I got away, me spirits never failing,
Landed on the quay, just as the ship was sailing,
Captain at me roared - said that no room had he,
When I jumped aboard a cabin found for Paddy,
Down among the pigs, played some hearty rigs,
Danced some hearty jigs, the water round be bubblin'
When off Holyhead, I wished meself was dead,
Or better far instead on the rocky road to Dublin...

Well the boys of Liverpool, when we safely landed,
Called meself a fool, I could no longer stand it -
Blood began to boil! Temper I was losing,
Poor auld Erin's isle, they began abusing...
Hurrah me soul says I, shillelagh I'll apply,
Some Galway boys were by and saw I was a-hobblin'
Then with a loud hurray, they joined into the affray,
Quickly cleared the way for the rocky road to Dublin...

Rocky Road To Dublin
(continued)

Basic Melody
Key of Am (High)

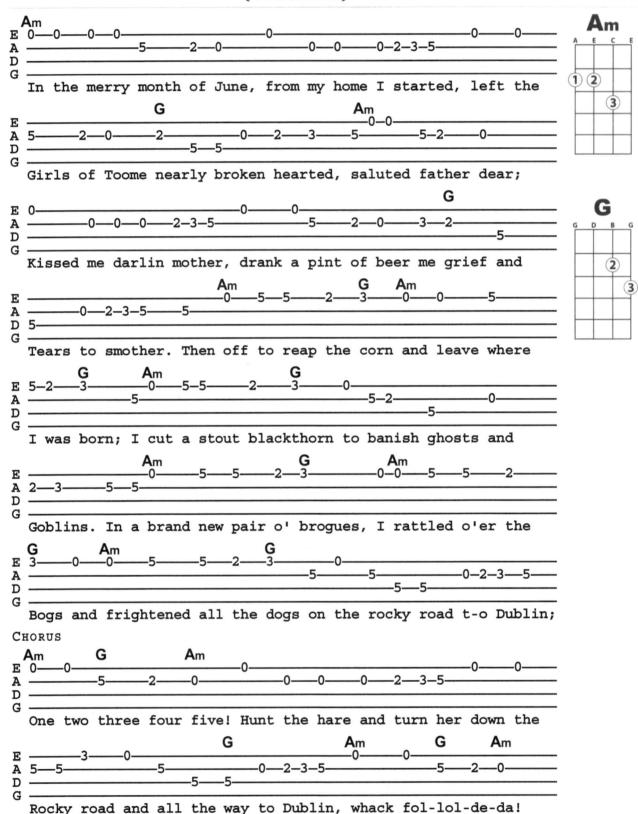

In the merry month of June, from my home I started, left the

Girls of Toome nearly broken hearted, saluted father dear;

Kissed me darlin mother, drank a pint of beer me grief and

Tears to smother. Then off to reap the corn and leave where

I was born; I cut a stout blackthorn to banish ghosts and

Goblins. In a brand new pair o' brogues, I rattled o'er the

Bogs and frightened all the dogs on the rocky road t-o Dublin;

CHORUS

One two three four five! Hunt the hare and turn her down the

Rocky road and all the way to Dublin, whack fol-lol-de-da!

Rocky Road To Dublin
(continued)

Melody & Chords

Key of Am (High)

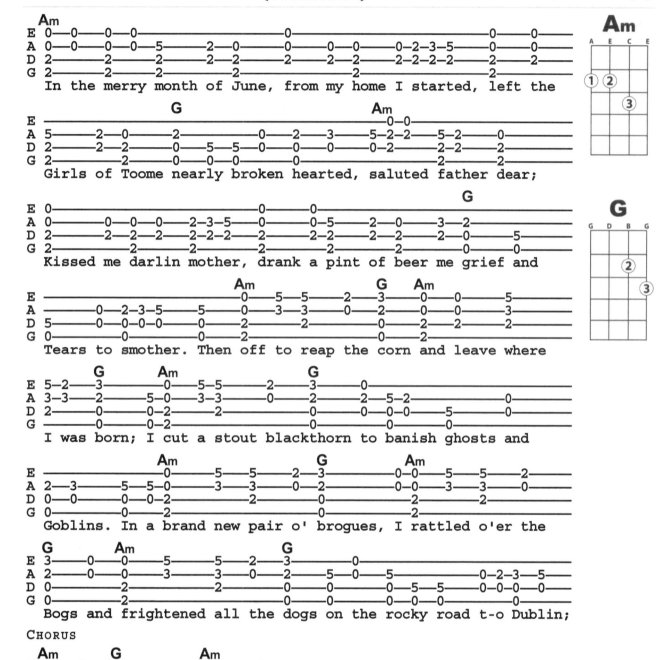

In the merry month of June, from my home I started, left the

Girls of Toome nearly broken hearted, saluted father dear;

Kissed me darlin mother, drank a pint of beer me grief and

Tears to smother. Then off to reap the corn and leave where

I was born; I cut a stout blackthorn to banish ghosts and

Goblins. In a brand new pair o' brogues, I rattled o'er the

Bogs and frightened all the dogs on the rocky road t-o Dublin;

CHORUS

One two three four five! Hunt the hare and turn her down the

Rocky road and all the way to Dublin, whack fol-lol-de-da!

Rocky Road To Dublin

(continued)

Basic Melody
Key of Em

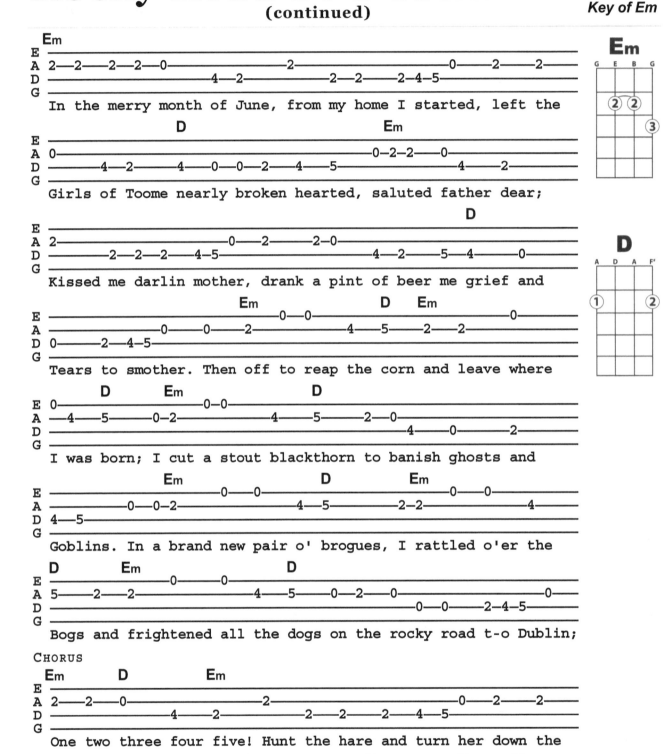

In the merry month of June, from my home I started, left the

Girls of Toome nearly broken hearted, saluted father dear;

Kissed me darlin mother, drank a pint of beer me grief and

Tears to smother. Then off to reap the corn and leave where

I was born; I cut a stout blackthorn to banish ghosts and

Goblins. In a brand new pair o' brogues, I rattled o'er the

Bogs and frightened all the dogs on the rocky road t-o Dublin;

CHORUS

One two three four five! Hunt the hare and turn her down the

Rocky road and all the way to Dublin, whack fol-lol-de-da!

Rocky Road To Dublin
(continued)

Melody & Chords
Key of Em

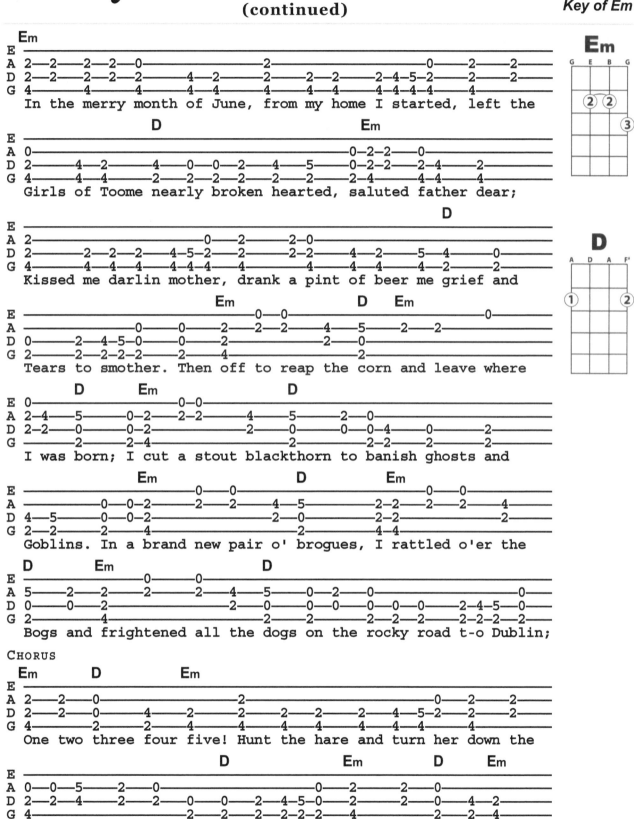

Em

```
E ------------------------------------------------------------------------------------
A 2—2——2—2—0——————————2————————————————————0——2———2————
D 2—2——2—2—2——4—2———2————2—2——2-4-5-2———2———2————
G 4————4————4———4—4———4———4—4——4-4-4-4———4————
```
In the merry month of June, from my home I started, left the

```
            D                              Em
E ------------------------------------------------------------------------------------
A 0——————————————————————————0-2-2——0————————
D 2———4—2———4——0—0—2——4——5———0-2-2——2-4———2———
G 4———4—4———2—2—2—2——2—2——2-4———4-4———4———
```
Girls of Toome nearly broken hearted, saluted father dear;

```
                                            D
E ------------------------------------------------------------------------------------
A 2——————————0—2———2-0—————————————
D 2———2—2—2—4-5-2———2———2-2——4—2——5—4———0——
G 4————4—4—4——4-4-4———4———4——4—4——4-2——2——
```
Kissed me darlin mother, drank a pint of beer me grief and

```
                          Em          D  Em
E ————————————————0—0———————————————0———
A ———————0———0——2—2-2——4—5——2—2————
D 0——2-4-5-0——0——2———2——0————
G 2——2-2-2-2——2——4———————2——
```
Tears to smother. Then off to reap the corn and leave where

```
      D   Em                D
E 0——————————0-0——————————————————
A 2-4——5———0-2——2-2——4——5——2-0———
D 2-2——0———0-2——2———0——0-0-4——0———2——
G ——2——2-4————2———2-2——2——2——
```
I was born; I cut a stout blackthorn to banish ghosts and

```
              Em                D      Em
E ————————0—0————————————0—0——
A ——————0-0-2——2—2——4—5——2-2——2—2——4—
D 4—5———0-0-2——2—0——2-2————2—
G 2-2——2—4————2——4-4———
```
Goblins. In a brand new pair o' brogues, I rattled o'er the

```
  D     Em            D
E ——————0—0————————————————
A 5—2—2——2——2—4-5——0-2—0————————0—
D 0——0-2——2—0——0-0-0—2-4-5—0—
G 2——4————2——2——2-2-2——2-2-2-2—
```
Bogs and frightened all the dogs on the rocky road t-o Dublin;

CHORUS

```
Em        D        Em
E ------------------------------------------------------------------------------------
A 2——2—0——————2—————————0——2———2—
D 2——2—0——4—2——2——2—2——2-4-5-2——2——2—
G 4————2——2—4——4—4——4—4——4-4-4——4—
```
One two three four five! Hunt the hare and turn her down the

```
                        D          Em      D   Em
E ------------------------------------------------------------------------------------
A 0-0-5——2——0——————0—2——2-0——
D 2-2-4——2—2——0—0-2-4-5-0——2——2——0—4-2—
G 4————2—2——2-2-2-2——4——2—2-4—
```
Rocky road and all the way to Dublin, whack fol-lol-de-da!

Roddy McCorley

Basic Melody
Key of G

This song is thought by many to be fully traditional, but other sources list an Irish poet named Ethna Carbery as the composer. It was written in the 1890's and tells the story of an Irish Republican hero Roddy McCorley. He is claimed by the folk lore of both Catholic and Protestant groups.

Words and Music by

Ethna Carbery

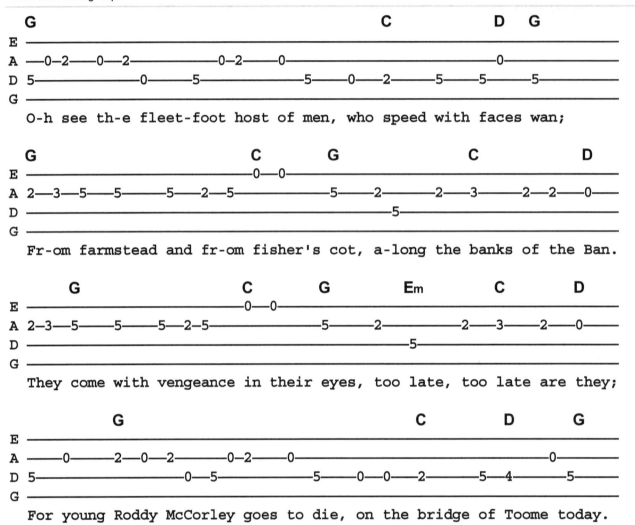

O-h see th-e fleet-foot host of men, who speed with faces wan;

Fr-om farmstead and fr-om fisher's cot, a-long the banks of the Ban.

They come with vengeance in their eyes, too late, too late are they;

For young Roddy McCorley goes to die, on the bridge of Toome today.

Chord Forms

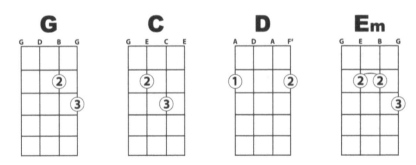

See Additional Verses on Next Page

Roddy McCorley (continued)

Melody & Chords
Key of G

G		C	D	G

```
E -------------------------------------------------------------------
A ---0-2----0-2---------------0-2----0-----------------------0-------
D 5-0-0----0--0-0------5---0-0----0-5----0---2----5----5-0---5-------
G 0-----0----------0------0-----0-----0---0-5----5----5-2---0--------
```
O-h see th-e fleet-foot host of men, who speed with faces wan;

G		C	G	C	D

```
E -------------------------0--0--------------------------------------
A 2--3--5----5------5--2-5--3--3------5----2------2--3-----2--2---0---
D 0--0--0---0------0--0-0--0-2--------0----0-5----0--2-----2--2---0---
G 0------0-------0--------0------------0----0-0------0---------2------
```
Fr-om farmstead and fr-om fisher's cot, a-long the banks of the Ban.

G		C	G	Em	C	D

```
E -------------------------0--0--------------------------------------
A 2-3--5----5------5--2-5--3--3------5----2------2--3----2---0--------
D 0-0--0---0------0--0-0--0-2--------0----0-5----2--2----2---0--------
G 0------0-------0--------0------------0----0-4------0-------2--------
```
They come with vengeance in their eyes, too late, too late are they;

G		C	D	G

```
E -------------------------------------------------------------------
A -----0-----2-0-2-----0-2----0-----------------------------0--------
D 5----0-----0--0-0-0--5-0-0-----0-5----0--0---2-----5--4---0-5------
G 2---------0----0----0-----------0--0-0----5------5--2---2-0--------
```
For young Roddy McCorley goes to die, on the bridge of Toome today.

Additional Verses

Up the narrow streets he steps,
So smiling proud and young.
About the hemp rope on his neck,
The golden ringlets clung;
There was never a tear in his blue eye,
No, sad and bright are they;
For young Roddy McCorley goes to die,
On the bridge of Toome today.

When he last stepped up the street,
His shining pike in hand;
Behind him marched in grim array,
A stalwart, earnest band.

For Antrim town, for Antrim town,
He led them to the fray;
And young Roddy McCorley goes to die,
On the bridge of Toome today.

Oh there was never a one of all your dead
More bravely fell in fray;
Than he who marches to his fate,
On the bridge of Toome today.
True to the last, true to the last!
He treads the upward way.
For young Roddy McCorley goes to die,
On the bridge of Toome today.

Roddy McCorley (continued)

Basic Melody
Key of C (Low)

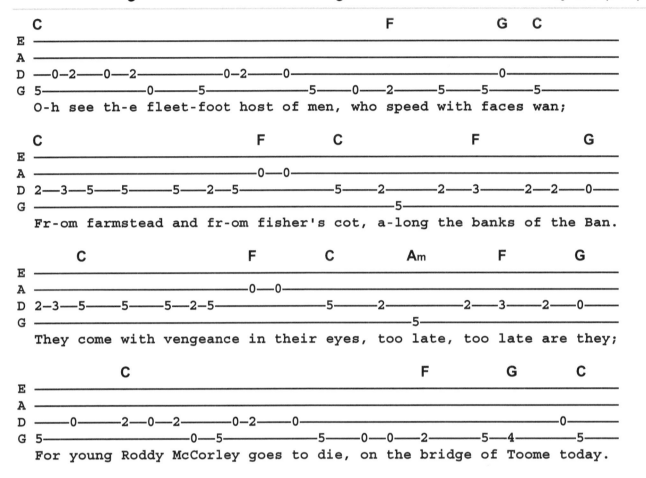

```
        C                                    F         G    C
E  ————————————————————————————————————————————————————————————————
A  ————————————————————————————————————————————————————————————————
D  —0—2———0—2—————————————0—2——————0——————————————————————0—————————
G  5——————————0——————5———————————5———0———2————5————5———————5————————
```
O-h see th-e fleet-foot host of men, who speed with faces wan;

```
        C                      F        C                F         G
E  ————————————————————————————————————————————————————————————————
A  —————————————————————————0——0—————————————————————————————————————
D  2—3—5———5—————5—2—5———————————————5——————2——————2—3————2—2——0—————
G  ————————————————————————————————————5————————————————————————————
```
Fr-om farmstead and fr-om fisher's cot, a-long the banks of the Ban.

```
          C                    F        C       Am      F         G
E  ————————————————————————————————————————————————————————————————
A  —————————————————————————0——0—————————————————————————————————————
D  2-3—5———5—————5—2-5———————————————5——————2——————2—3————2——0———————
G  ————————————————————————————————————5————————————————————————————
```
They come with vengeance in their eyes, too late, too late are they;

```
            C                                    F        G      C
E  ————————————————————————————————————————————————————————————————
A  ————————————————————————————————————————————————————————————————
D  ———0————2—0—2—————————0—2——————0—————————————————————————0———————
G  5——————————————0——5—————————5——————0——0———2————5——4————————5—————
```
For young Roddy McCorley goes to die, on the bridge of Toome today.

Chord Forms

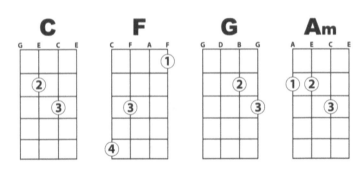

Roddy McCorley

Roddy McCorley (continued)

```
         C                                        F          G     C
E ———————0———————0———————————0———————————————————————————————————————————————
A 3—5———————5———————————3—5———————5—3—————————0———————3———3—5———3———————————
D ———————————5———————————————————————————5———————————————————————————————————
G ——————————————————————————————————————————————————————————————————————————
```
O-h see th-e fleet-foot host of men, who speed with faces wan;

```
  C               F        C                    F           G
E 0—1—3———3———————3———0—3—5—5———————3———————0———————0—1———————0—0———————————
A ——————————————————————————————————————3———————————————————————————5———
D ——————————————————————————————————————————————————————————————————————————
G ——————————————————————————————————————————————————————————————————————————
```
Fr-om farmstead and fr-om fisher's cot, a-long the banks of the Ban.

```
     C               F        C        Am         F           G
E 0—1—3———3———————3———0—3———5—5———————3———————0———————0—1———————0———————————
A ——————————————————————————————————————————3———————————————————————5———
D ——————————————————————————————————————————————————————————————————————————
G ——————————————————————————————————————————————————————————————————————————
```
They come with vengeance in their eyes, too late, too late are they;

```
         C                                F          G          C
E ———————0———————0———————————0——————————————————————————————————————————————
A 3———5———————5———————————3—5———————5—3—————————0———————3—2———5—3———————————
D ———————————————5———————————————————5—5———————————————————————————————————
G ——————————————————————————————————————————————————————————————————————————
```
For young Roddy McCorley goes to die, on the bridge of Toome today.

Chord Forms

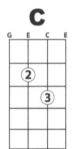
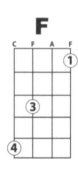
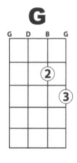
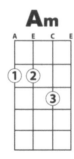

Roddy McCorley (continued)

```
         C                                    F            G    C
E ——————0—————————0———————————————0———————————————————————————————————————————
A 3—5—3————5—3——————————3—5—3————5—3——————————0————3————3—5——3—————————————————
D 2—0—2————0———————5————2—0—2————0—2————5———3———————3————3—0——2—————————————————
G 0—————0————————5——————0————2——————0—5———5———————————5——————0—————————————————
  O-h see th-e fleet-foot host of men, who speed with faces wan;
```

```
  C                          F        C                      F           G
E 0—1—3————3——————3—0—3—5—5——————3————0——————0——1——————0—0———————————————————
A 3—3—3————3——————3—3—3—3—3——————3————3—3————3——3——————3—3——5————————————————
D 2—————2——2——————2——————3———————2————2—2——————0—————————0——0————————————————
G 0————————0——————0————————————0——————0————————————————————0——
  Fr-om farmstead and fr-om fisher's cot, a-long the banks of the Ban.
```

```
    C                          F        C          Am         F           G
E 0—1—3————3——————3—0—3——5—5——————3————0——————————0——1——————0———————————————
A 3—3—3————3——————3—3—3——3—3——————3————3—3—————————0——0——————0——5————————————
D 2—————2——2——————2———————3—3——————2————2—2————————————3——————3——0———————————
G 0————————0——————————————————————0————0——2————————————————————————0——
  They come with vengeance in their eyes, too late, too late are they;
```

```
      C                                  F        G        C
E ——————————0——————0——————————0—————————————————————————————————————————————
A 3————5————3—5—3——————3—5—3————5—3——————0——————3——2————5—3————————————————
D 0————0————2—0——————5—2—0—2——————0—2——5—5———3——————3——0—————————0—2————————
G 0——————————0——————5————0——————————0—5—5———5——————————0————————0—————————
  For young Roddy McCorley goes to die, on the bridge of Toome today.
```

Chord Forms

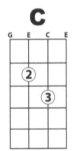
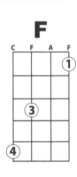
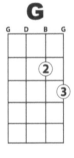
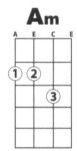

Rosin the Bow

Basic Melody
Key of C

This old drinking ballad comes down from the British Isles (no one is sure whether from Ireland, England or Scotland) and has been sung with various lyrics over the years. It tells the tale of a man, once young and popular with the ladies, now grown old and preparing for death - but in a darkly humorous way.

Words and Music
Traditional

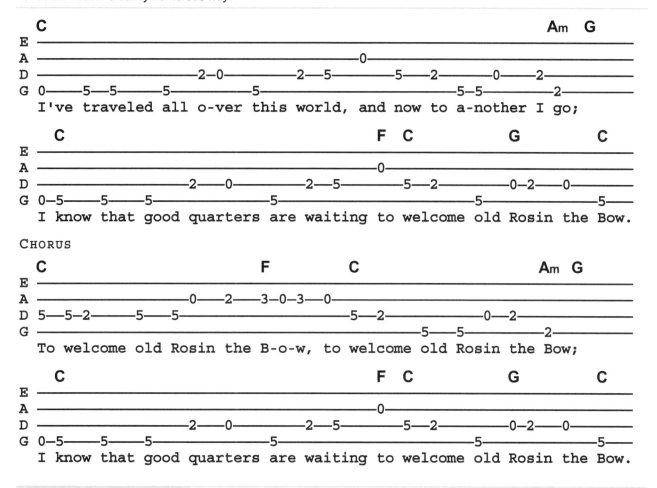

```
      C                                                      Am   G
E ───────────────────────────────────────────────────────────────────────
A ───────────────────────────────────────0───────────────────────────────
D ─────────────2─0─────────2─5────────5───2─────────0───2─────────────────
G 0──────5─5────────5──────────5──────────────5─5────────2────────────────
```
I've traveled all o-ver this world, and now to a-nother I go;

```
      C                                     F  C          G          C
E ───────────────────────────────────────────────────────────────────────
A ─────────────────────────────────────0──────────────────────────────────
D ─────────────2────0─────────2─5─────────5──2──────────0─2────0───────────
G 0─5──────5─────5──────────────5──────────────────5─────────────5─────────
```
I know that good quarters are waiting to welcome old Rosin the Bow.

CHORUS

```
      C                     F            C                    Am   G
E ───────────────────────────────────────────────────────────────────────
A ───────────0────2─────3─0─3───0─────────────────────────────────────────
D 5──5─2────────5──────5─────────────────5──2──────────0──2─────────────────
G ─────────────────────────────────5─────5───────────────2────────────────
```
To welcome old Rosin the B-o-w, to welcome old Rosin the Bow;

```
      C                                     F  C          G          C
E ───────────────────────────────────────────────────────────────────────
A ─────────────────────────────────────0──────────────────────────────────
D ─────────────2────0─────────2─5─────────5──2──────────0─2────0───────────
G 0─5──────5─────5──────────────5──────────────────5─────────────5─────────
```
I know that good quarters are waiting to welcome old Rosin the Bow.

Chord Forms

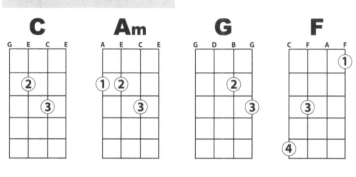

See Additional Verses on Next Page

Rosin the Bow (continued)

Additional Verses

When I'm dead and laid out on the counter,
A voice you will hear from below;
Saying "Send down a hogshead of whiskey,
To drink with old Rosin the Bow!"
To drink with old Rosin the Bow,
To drink with old Rosin the Bow;
Saying "Send down a hogshead of whiskey,
To drink with old Rosin the Bow!"

Then get a half dozen stout fellows,
And line them all up in a row;
Let them drink out of half gallon bottles,
To the memory of Rosin the Bow.
To the memory of Rosin the Bow,
To the memory of Rosin the Bow;
Let them drink out of half gallon bottles,
To the memory of Rosin the Bow.

Then get this half dozen stout fellows,
And let them all stagger and go...
And dig a great hole in the meadow,
And in it put Rosin the Bow.
And in it put Rosin the Bow,
And in it put Rosin the Bow;
And dig a great hole in the meadow,
And in it put Rosin the Bow.

Then get ye a couple of bottles,
Put one at me head and me toe;
With a diamond ring scratch upon them
The name of old Rosin the Bow.
The name of old Rosin the Bow,
The name of old Rosin the Bow;
With a diamond ring scratch upon them
The name of old Rosin the Bow.

I've only this one consolation,
As out of this world I go;
I know that the next generation
Will resemble old Rosin the Bow.
Will resemble old Rosin the Bow,
Will resemble old Rosin the Bow.
I know that the next generation,
Will resemble old Rosin the Bow.

I fear that old tyrant approaching,
That cruel remorseless old foe;
And I lift up me glass in his honor,
Take a drink with old Rosin the Bow!
Take a drink with old Rosin the Bow,
Take a drink with old Rosin the Bow.
And I lift up me glass in his honor,
Take a drink with old Rosin the Bow!

*"Young people don't know what old age is,
and old people forget what youth was. "*

"The older the fiddle the sweeter the tune."

"There's nothing so bad that it couldn't be worse."

*"Lose an hour in the morning and
you'll be looking for it all day."*

Old Irish Proverbs & Sayings

Rosin the Bow (continued)

Basic Melody
Key of G

```
        G                                                          Em   D
E ──────────────────────────────────────────0─────────────────────────────────
A ──────────────────2─0──────────2──5──────────5──2──────────0──2──────────────
D 0─────5──5──────5────────────5──────────────────5─5──────────────2────────────
G ──────────────────────────────────────────────────────────────────────────────
```

I've traveled all o-ver this world, and now to a-nother I go;

```
        G                                      C  G              D            G
E ──────────────────────────────────────────0──────────────────────────────────
A ──────────────────2────0──────────2──5──────5──2──────────0─2────0───────────
D 0─5──────5──────5────────────────5─────────────────────────5──────────────5──
G ──────────────────────────────────────────────────────────────────────────────
```

I know that good quarters are waiting to welcome old Rosin the Bow.

CHORUS

```
        G                      C              G                  Em   D
E ──────────────────0────2────3─0─3──0─────────────────────────────────────────
A 5──5─2──────5──────5──────────────────────5──2──────────0──2──────────────────
D ──────────────────────────────────────────5──────5──────────2──────────────────
G ──────────────────────────────────────────────────────────────────────────────
```

To welcome old Rosin the B-o-w, to welcome old Rosin the Bow;

```
        G                                      C              D            G
E ──────────────────────────────────────────0──────────────────────────────────
A ──────────────────2────0──────────2──5──────5──2──────────0─2────0───────────
D 0─5──────5──────5────────────────5─────────────────────────5──────────────5──
G ──────────────────────────────────────────────────────────────────────────────
```

I know that good quarters are waiting to welcome old Rosin the Bow.

Chord Forms

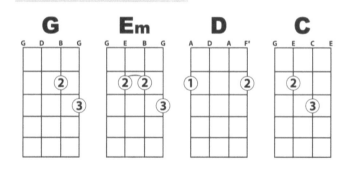

Front-piece from an 1850 publication of sheet music, of the American-ized version of Rosin the Bow.

Rosin the Bow (continued)

Melody & Chords
Key of G

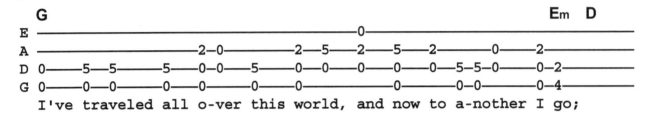

I've traveled all o-ver this world, and now to a-nother I go;

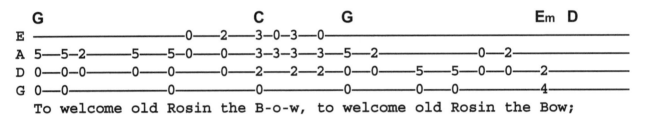

I know that good quarters are waiting to welcome old Rosin the Bow.

CHORUS

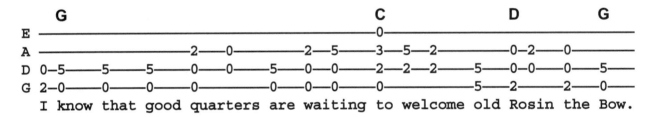

To welcome old Rosin the B-o-w, to welcome old Rosin the Bow;

I know that good quarters are waiting to welcome old Rosin the Bow.

Chord Forms

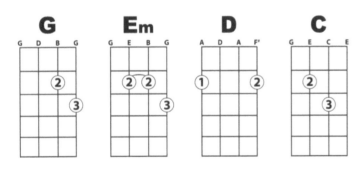

Rothsea-O

Basic Melody
Key of C

Rothesay is a seaside town in Scotland that was popular with tourists in days past. This song, while not specifically about drinking, is a great one for singing out over a couple of pints in a pub. The rolling lyrics and melody are particularly well suited for convivial singing. The version presented here is in the style recorded by the Clancy Brothers & Tommy Makem.

Words and Music
Traditional

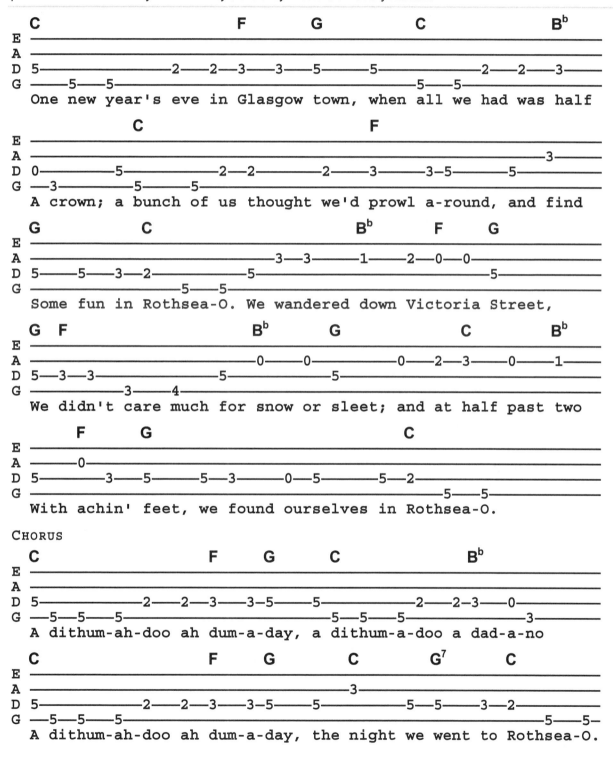

See Chord Forms and Additional Verses on Next Page

Rothsea-O (continued)

Additional Verses

Pat Boyle here, he's a bit of a lout,
Said he'd treat us all to a pint of stout;
So as quick as we could we all set out,
For a public house in Rothsea-O.
Said he "My lads I'd like to sing,"
Says I "You'll do no such a thing."
He said, "Clear the room and we'll make a ring,
And I'll fight ye all in Rothsea-O."

We had to find a place to sleep,
We were all too drunk to even creep;
We found a place that was really cheap,
In a boarding house in Rothsea-O.
We all laid down to take our ease,
When somebody happened for to sneeze;
And he wakened half a million fleas,
In a single room in Rothsea-O!

There were several different kinds of pests,
They ran and they jumped inside our vests;
They got in our hair and they built their nests,
And they cried "Hurrah for Rothsea-O!"
Says I "I think I'll head for home,"
And we swore we never more would roam;
And we're scratching still as we sing this song,
Of the night we went to Rothsea-O.

Chord Forms (Key of C)

C
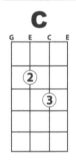

F
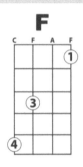

G
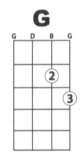

B♭
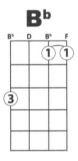

G⁷
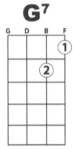

Chord Forms (Key of G)

G
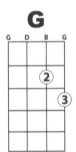

C
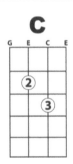

D
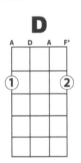

F
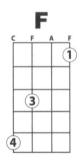

D⁷
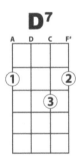

205

Rothsea-O (continued)

Melody & Chords
Key of C

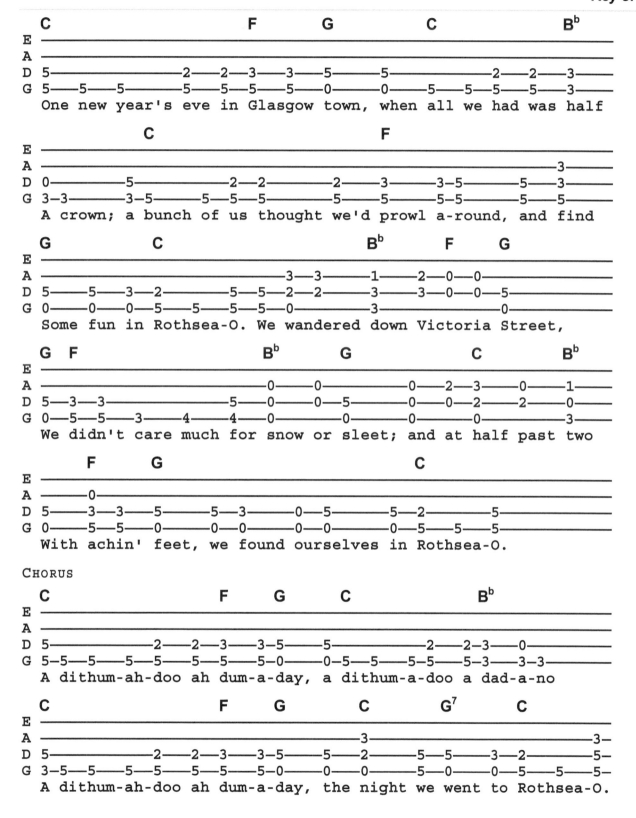

See Chord Forms on Previous Page

Irish Pub Favorites Mandolin Tablature Songbook · Copyright 2020 by Hobo Music Works LLC · All Rights Reserved

Rothsea-O (continued)

Basic Melody
Key of G

```
        G                      C     D        G              F
E _____
A 5_____2___2___3___3___5___5_____2___2___3____
D ____5___5_____5___5_____
G _____
```
One new year's eve in Glasgow town, when all we had was half

```
          G                              C                    3
E _____
A 0_____5_____2__2_____2___3___3-5_____5_____
D _3_____5_____5_____
G _____
```
A crown; a bunch of us thought we'd prowl a-round, and find

```
   D      G                      F       C     D
E _____3__3_____1___2__0__0_____
A 5___5__3__2_____5_____5_____
D _____5__5_____
G _____
```
Some fun in Rothsea-O. We wandered down Victoria Street,

```
     C                    F     D            G         F
E _____0___0_____0__2__3_____0___1_____
A 5__3__3_____5_____5_____
D _____3_____4_____
G _____
```
We didn't care much for snow or sleet; and at half past two

```
     C     D                        G
E _____0_____
A 5_____3__5_____5__3____0__5_____5__2_____
D _____5___5_____
G _____
```
With achin' feet, we found ourselves in Rothsea-O.

CHORUS

```
   G                   C    D   G              F
E _____
A 5_____2___2___3___3-5___5_____2___2-3___0____
D _5__5___5_____5__5___5_____3_
G _____
```
A dithum-ah-doo ah dum-a-day, a dithum-a-doo a dad-a-no

```
   G                   C    D   G         D7      G
E _____3_____
A 5_____2___2___3___3-5___5_____5__5___3__2_____
D _5__5___5_____5___5-____
G _____
```
A dithum-ah-doo ah dum-a-day, the night we went to Rothsea-O.

See Chord Forms Two Pages Previous

Rothsea-O (continued)

Melody & Chords
Key of G

```
     G                       C      D        G              F
E ---------------------------------------------------------------------
A 5-------------------2---2---3---3---5-------5-----------2---2---3------
D 0------5---5----------0---0---2---2---0-------0---5---5---0---0---3----
G 0------0---0----------0---------0---------2-------2---0---0---0-------5
```
One new year's eve in Glasgow town, when all we had was half

```
             G                           C
E ----------------------------------------------------------------3----
A 0-----------5-----------2---2-------2---3-----3-5-------5----3--------
D 3-3---------0-5-------5---0---0---------0-------2-------2-0------0---2-
G ---5--------0-0----------0---0-------------------0-----------0-------0-
```
A crown; a bunch of us thought we'd prowl a-round, and find

```
   D         G                              F      C      D
E --------------------------------3---3------1---2---0---0-------------
A 5----5---3---2----------5---2---2------0-----0---3---3---5-----------
D 0------0---0---0---5---5---0---0------------3------2---2---4---------
G 2----2---2---2------0---0---0---0----------------0-------2----------
```
Some fun in Rothsea-O. We wandered down Victoria Street,

```
     C                       F      D          G      F
E ----------------------------0-----0-----------0---2-3------0---1-----
A 5---3---3--------------5-----0-----0---5-------0---0-2------2------0--
D 0---2---2---3---4---2-----3------4---------0---------0----------3----
G ----0-------5---5---------------------2-----------0---------------
```
We didn't care much for snow or sleet; and at half past two

```
     C      D                            G
E ---------0-----------------------------------------------------------
A 5-----3---3---5------5---3-------0---5-------5---2--------------------
D 0------2---2---4------4---0------0---4-------0---0---5---5------------
G -------0------2--------------2-----------0------0---0---0-----------
```
With achin' feet, we found ourselves in Rothsea-O.

CHORUS

```
     G                       C      D   G              F
E ---------------------------------------------------------------------
A 5-------------------2---2---3---3-5---5---------------2---2-3----0----
D 0-5---5-----5---0-----0---2---2-0-----0---5---5-----5-0------0-3-3-3--
G 0-0---0-------0---0------------0-------2-------0---0---0-0------2----2-
```
A dithum-ah-doo ah dum-a-day, a dithum-a-doo a dad-a-no

```
     G                       C      D   G        D⁷     G
E ------------------------------------------3--------------------------
A 5-------------------2---2---3---3-5---2-------5---5---3-2-------------
D 0-5---5-----5---0-----0---2---2-0-----0-------0---0------0---0---5--5-
G 0-0---0-------0---0------------0-------2-------0---0-2------0---0--0-
```
A dithum-ah-doo ah dum-a-day, the night we went to Rothsea-O.

See Chord Forms Three Pages Previous

Seven Drunken Nights

Basic Melody
Key of C

Words and Music
Traditional

This old humorous song tells the tale of a drunken husband and unfaithful wife whose explanations get harder to believe as the week progresses. Many versions have been done of this song in the two hundred plus years it's been around.

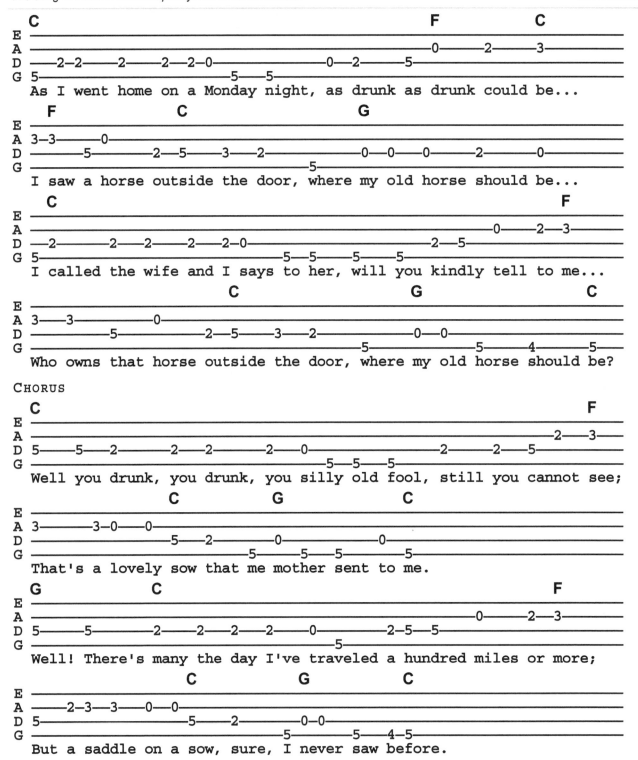

CHORUS

See Chord Forms and Additional Verses on Next Page

Seven Drunken Nights

(continued)

Chords Forms &

Additional Verses

Additional Verses

And as I went home on Tuesday night, as drunk as drunk could be,
I saw a coat behind the door, where my old coat should be.
Well, I called me wife and I said to her,
"Will you kindly tell to me, who owns that coat behind the door,
Where my old coat should be?"

Ay, you're drunk you're drunk you silly old fool, still you cannot see;
That's a woolen blanket that me mother sent to me.
Well, it's many a day I've traveled, a hundred miles or more,
But buttons on a blanket, sure, I never saw before.

And as I went home on Wednesday night, as drunk as drunk could be,
I saw a pipe upon the chair, where my old pipe should be;
Well, I called my wife and I said to her,
"Will you kindly tell to me, who owns that pipe upon the chair,
Where my old pipe should be?"

Ay, you're drunk you're drunk you silly old fool, still you cannot see!
That's a lovely tin-whistle, that me mother sent to me.
Well, it's many a day I've traveled, a hundred miles or more,
But tobacco in a tin-whistle, sure, I never saw before!

And I went home on Thursday night, as drunk as drunk could be,
I saw two boots beneath the bed, where my old boots should be;
Well, I called me wife and I said to her,
"Will you kindly tell to me, who owns them boots beneath the bed,
Where my old boots should be?"

Ay, you're drunk you're drunk you silly old fool, still you cannot see,
They're two lovely geranium pots me mother sent to me.
Well, it's many a day I've traveled, a hundred miles or more,
But laces in geranium pots I never saw before!

And as I came home on Friday night, as drunk as drunk could be,
I saw a head upon the bed where my old head should be;
Well, I called my wife and I said to her,
"Will you kindly tell to me, who owns that head upon the bed,
Where my old head should be?"

Ay, you're drunk you're drunk you silly old fool still you cannot see,
That's a baby boy that me mother sent to me.
Well, it's many a day I've traveled, a hundred miles or more,
But a baby boy with his whiskers on, sure I never saw before!

There are various versions of two additional very bawdy verses that are sometimes sung to this song, though not in polite company. Look them up on Wikipedia if you would like to learn them.

Chord Forms
(Key of C)

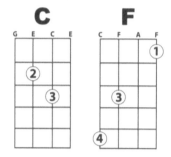

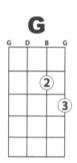

Chord Forms
(Key of G)

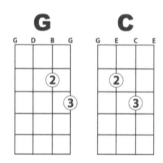

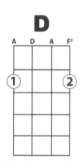

Seven Drunken Nights

Melody & Chords

(continued)

Key of C

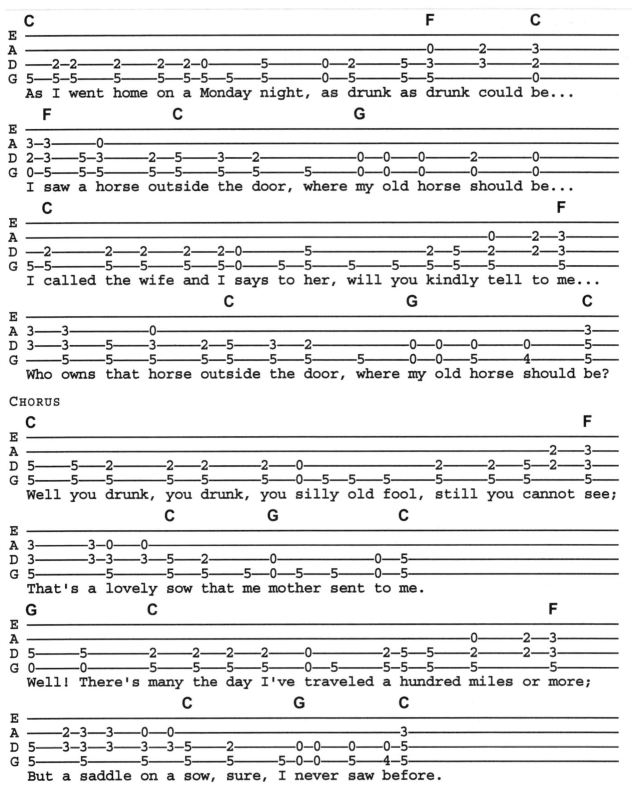

```
     C                                              F          C
E ————————————————————————————————————————————————————————————————————
A ——————————————————————————————————————————0———————2———————3—————————
D ———2-2————2————2—2-0————5————————0—2————5—3————————3———————2—————————
G 5—5-5————5————5—5-5—5————5————0—5————5—5——————————————————————0——————
  As I went home on a Monday night, as drunk as drunk could be...

     F            C                  G
E ———————————————————————————————————————————————————————————————————
A 3—3————————0————————————————————————————————————————————————————————
D 2—3————5—3————2—5————3——2————————————0——0——0—————2————0—————————————
G 0—5————5—5————5—5————5——5————————5———0——0——0—————0————0—————————————
  I saw a horse outside the door, where my old horse should be...

     C                                                              F
E ——————————————————————————————————————————————————————————————————
A ————————————————————————————————————————————0———2—3———————————————
D ——2————2————2————2——2-0————5—————————2—5————2————2—3——————————————
G 5—5————5——5—5——5-5—0————5—5————5———5—5—5————5——————————5—————————
  I called the wife and I says to her, will you kindly tell to me...

                          C                    G               C
E ———————————————————————————————————————————————————————————————————3—
A 3———3————————0—————————————————————————————————————————————————————————
D 3———3————5——3————2—5————3——2————————0——0——0————0————5——————————————
G ————5————5——5————5—5————5——5————5———0——0——5————4————5——————————————
  Who owns that horse outside the door, where my old horse should be?
```

CHORUS

```
     C                                                           F
E ———————————————————————————————————————————————————————————————————
A —————————————————————————————————————————————————————2———3————————
D 5————5——2————2——2————2——0—————————————2————2——5—2———3———————————
G 5————5——5————5——5————5——0—5——5—5————5————5——5——5————5——————————
  Well you drunk, you drunk, you silly old fool, still you cannot see;

                  C            G            C
E ——————————————————————————————————————————————————————————————————
A 3————————3-0——0————————————————————————————————————————————————————
D 3————————3-3——3——5————2———————0——————————0—5———————————————————————
G 5————————5——5—5——5————5—0—5——5————0—5—————————————————————————————
  That's a lovely sow that me mother sent to me.

     G            C                                      F
E ——————————————————————————————————————————————————————————————————
A —————————————————————————————————————————0————2—3———————————————
D 5————5————2——2——2——2————0————2—5—5————2———2—3————————————————
G 0————0————5——5—5——5————0—5——5—5—5————5—————————5—————————————
  Well! There's many the day I've traveled a hundred miles or more;

                  C            G            C
E ——————————————————————————————————————————————————————————————————
A ——2—3—3——0—0——————————————————3————————————————————————————————
D 5—3-3——3—3-3—5————2———————0—0——0——0-5——————————————————————————
G 5————5————5——5————5—0-0——5——4-5——————————————————————————————
  But a saddle on a sow, sure, I never saw before.
```

See Chord Forms on Previous Page

Seven Drunken Nights

Basic Melody

Key of G

(continued)

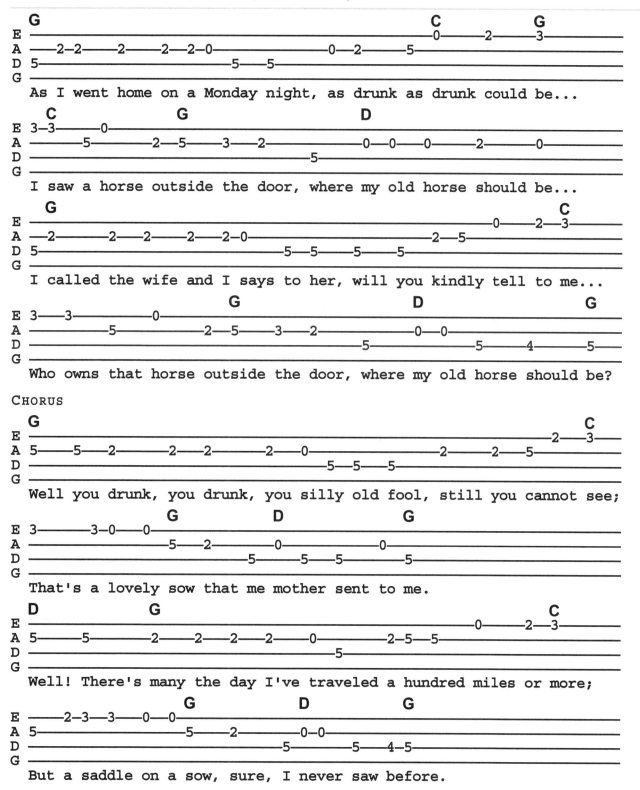

```
     G                                      C        G
E  ───────────────────────────────────0────2────3────────
A  ──2─2────2────2──2─0────────0─2────5────────────────────
D  5──────────────────5──5──────────────────────────────
G  ────────────────────────────────────────────────────
```
As I went home on a Monday night, as drunk as drunk could be...

```
     C          G              D
E  3─3────0────────────────────────────────────────────
A  ────5──────2─5──3──2────0─0─0────2────0──────────────
D  ────────────────────5──────────────────────────────
G  ────────────────────────────────────────────────────
```
I saw a horse outside the door, where my old horse should be...

```
     G                                        C
E  ────────────────────────────────0──2─3──────────────
A  ─2────2──2──2──2─0──────────2─5──────────────────────
D  5──────────────5─5──5──5───────────────────────────
G  ────────────────────────────────────────────────────
```
I called the wife and I says to her, will you kindly tell to me...

```
            G              D            G
E  3────3────0──────────────────────────────────────────
A  ────5────2─5──3──2──────0─0──────────────────────────
D  ──────────────5────────────5──4──5───────────────────
G  ────────────────────────────────────────────────────
```
Who owns that horse outside the door, where my old horse should be?

CHORUS

```
     G                                          C
E  ──────────────────────────────────────2─3──────────
A  5──5──2────2──2────2──0────────2──2─5─────────────────
D  ────────────────5─5──5──────────────────────────────
G  ────────────────────────────────────────────────────
```
Well you drunk, you drunk, you silly old fool, still you cannot see;

```
            G        D        G
E  3────3─0──0──────────────────────────────────────────
A  ──────5──2──────0────────0───────────────────────────
D  ──────────5────5──5────5─────────────────────────────
G  ────────────────────────────────────────────────────
```
That's a lovely sow that me mother sent to me.

```
  D          G                              C
E  ────────────────────────────────0────2─3────────────
A  5────5────2──2──2──2──0────2─5──5────────────────────
D  ──────────────────5─────────────────────────────────
G  ────────────────────────────────────────────────────
```
Well! There's many the day I've traveled a hundred miles or more;

```
            G        D        G
E  ──2─3─3──0──0──────────────────────────────────────────
A  5──────────5──2────0─0──────────────────────────────
D  ──────────────5────────5──4─5────────────────────────
G  ────────────────────────────────────────────────────
```
But a saddle on a sow, sure, I never saw before.

See Chord Forms Two Pages Previous

Seven Drunken Nights

(continued)

Melody & Chords

Key of G

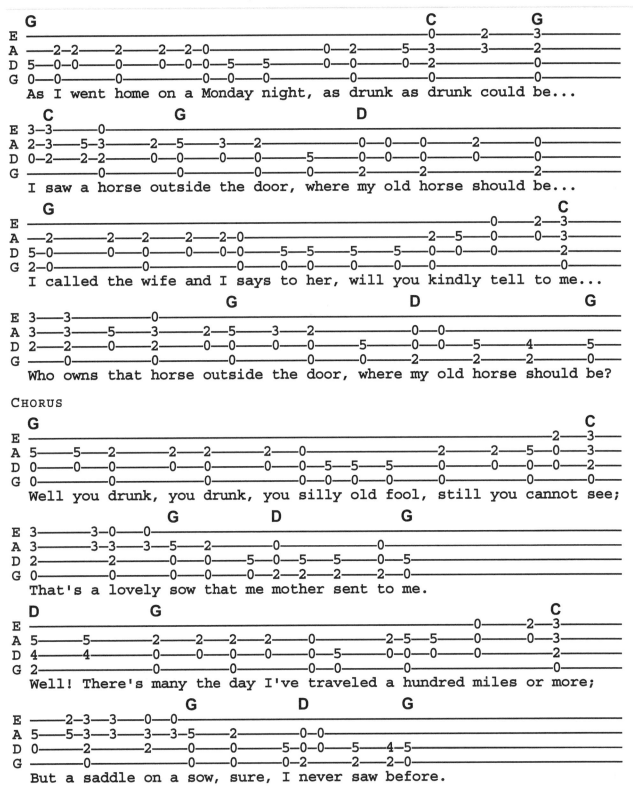

See Chord Forms Three Pages Previous

South Australia

Basic Melody

Key of C

Words and Music

Traditional

Part seafaring song and part drinking song, this great old traditional tune is perfect for belting out over a few pints in your favorite pub. Patrick Boyle has been performing this one for many years at sessions and Irish parties in and around Dover, New Hampshire.

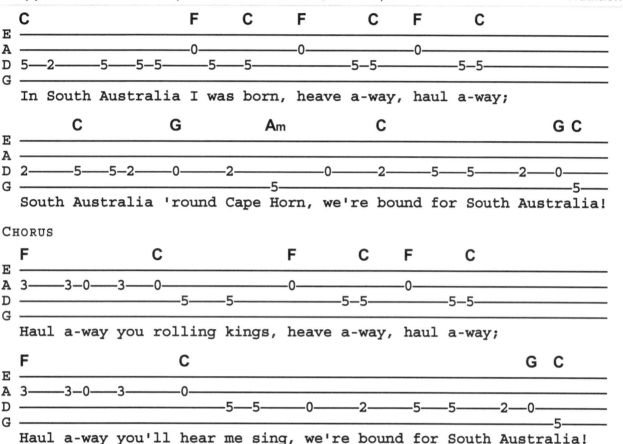

In South Australia I was born, heave a-way, haul a-way;

South Australia 'round Cape Horn, we're bound for South Australia!

CHORUS

Haul a-way you rolling kings, heave a-way, haul a-way;

Haul a-way you'll hear me sing, we're bound for South Australia!

Additional Verses

As I walked out one morning fair,
Heave away, haul away;
It's there I met Miss Nancy Blair,
We're bound for South Australia.

I shook her up, I shook her down,
Heave away, haul away;
I shook her 'round and 'round the town,
We're bound for South Australia.

There is just one thing grieves me mind,
Heave away, haul away;
To leave Miss Nancy Blair behind,
We're bound for South Australia.

And as we wallop around Cape Horn,
Heave away, haul away;
You'll wish to Christ you'd never been born,
We're bound for South Australia.

Chord Forms

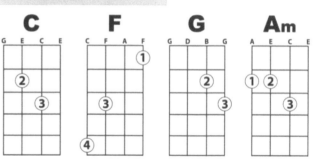

214

South Australia (continued)

```
    C                F    C    F     C    F     C
E ——————————————————————————————————————————————————————————
A ——————————————————0—————————0—————————0———————————————————
D 5—2———————5————5—5———3—5———5———3———5—5———3———5—5———————————
G 5—0———————0————0—0——2—0———5———2———0—0———2———0—5———————————
```
In South Australia I was born, heave a-way, haul a-way;

```
                G          Am           C                G C
E ——————————————————————————————————————————————————————————
A ——————————————————————————————————————————————————————————
D 2———————5———5—2———0———2———————0———2———5———5———2———0———————
G 5———————5———5—5———0———0———5———0———5———5———5———5———0—5———————
```
South Australia 'round Cape Horn, we're bound for South Australia!

CHORUS

```
    F          C           F     C    F     C
E ——————————————————————————————————————————————————————————
A 3———————3—0———3———0———————————0———————————0———————————————
D 3———————3—3———3———2—5———5———3———5—5———3———5—5———————————
G 5———————5———————5—5———5———5———5—5———5———5—5———————————————
```
Haul a-way you rolling kings, heave a-way, haul a-way;

```
    F              C                        G   C
E ——————————————————————————————————————————————————————————
A 3———————3—0———3———0———————————————————————————————————————
D 3———————3—3———3———2—5—5———0———2———5—5———2—0—5———————————
G 5———————5———————5—5—5———0———0———0—0———0—0—5———————————————
```
Haul a-way you'll hear me sing, we're bound for South Australia!

Victorian era British sailors.

South Australia (continued)

```
        G                   C     G     C       G     C       G
E ————————————————————————————————————————————————————————————————————
A ————————————————————————————————————————————————————————————————————
D 0———————————0———0—0——————2—0———0———————2——————0—0———————2————0—0—————
G ———4—————————————————————————————————————————————————————————————————
  In South Australia I was born, heave a-way, haul a-way;
```

```
                          D       Em          G                   D G
E ————————————————————————————————————————————————————————————————————
A ————————————————————————————————————————————————————————————————————
D ————————————0———0—————————————————————————————0———0——————————————————
G 4———————————————4———————2———————4———0———————2———4——————————————4——2—0——
  South Australia 'round Cape Horn, we're bound for South Australia!
```

CHORUS

```
  C               G               C       G     C       G
E ————————————————————————————————————————————————————————————————————
A ————————————————————————————————————————————————————————————————————
D 5———————5—2————5———2———0————0—————————2————0—0————2————0—0————————————
G ————————————————————————————————————————————————————————————————————
  Haul a-way you rolling kings, heave a-way, haul a-way;
```

```
  C               G                                       D G
E ————————————————————————————————————————————————————————————————————
A ————————————————————————————————————————————————————————————————————
D 5———————5—2————5———————2———0—0—————————————0———0—————————————————————
G ——————————————————————————————————————2————4——————————4——2—0————————
  Haul a-way you'll hear me sing, we're bound for South Australia!
```

Chord Forms

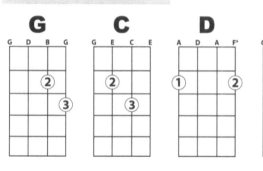

Patrick and Charlie Boyle at the Greenhouse,
St. Patrick's Day 2017.

South Australia (continued)

```
       G                  C    G    C      G    C       G
E ——————————————————0———————0————————————0————————————————
A 5—2———————5——5–5———5———5——————————5–5———————5–5————————
D ——————————————————————————————————————————————————————
G ——————————————————————————————————————————————————————
```

In South Australia I was born, heave a-way, haul a-way;

```
                  D         Em          G                D G
E ————————————————————————————————————————————————————————————
A 2———5——5–2———0———2————————0———2———5——5———2——0————————
D ————————————————————5——————————————————————————5———
G ————————————————————————————————————————————————————————
```

South Australia 'round Cape Horn, we're bound for South Australia!

CHORUS

```
    C          G          C      G    C      G
E 3———3–0———3———0————————0—————————0——————————————————
A ————————————5———5——————————5–5————————5–5——————————
D ——————————————————————————————————————————————————
G ——————————————————————————————————————————————————
```

Haul a-way you rolling kings, heave a-way, haul a-way;

```
    C          G                              D  G
E 3———3–0———3————0————————————————————————————————————
A ————————————5——5———0———2———5——5———2——0——————————
D ——————————————————————————————————————————5———
G ——————————————————————————————————————————————————
```

Haul a-way you'll hear me sing, we're bound for South Australia!

Chord Forms

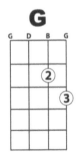
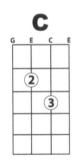
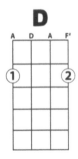
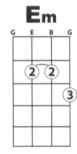

South Australia (continued)

Melody & Chords
Key of G (High)

```
          G                    C      G    C      G    C      G
E ——————————————————0—————————0————————————0——————————————————
A 5—2——————5——5-5——3-5——5——————3——————5-5——————3——————5-5——————
D 0—0——————0——0-0——2-0——0——————2——————0-0——————2——————0-0——————
G 0—0——————0————————0——————————0——————0—————————0——————0———————
```
In South Australia I was born, heave a-way, haul a-way;

```
                        D        Em              G                    D G
E ————————————————————————————————————————————————————————————————————————
A 2——————5——5-2——0——————2——————————0——————2——————5——5——————2——0———————
D 0——————0——0-0——0——————0——————5——2——————0——————0——0——————0——0-5——————
G 0——————————0——2——————0——————0——————0——————————0——————————2-0——————
```
South Australia 'round Cape Horn, we're bound for South Australia!

Chorus

```
      C                G                C      G    C      G
E 3——————3-0——3——————0——————————————————0——————————0———————————————
A 3——————3-3——3——————2——5——————5——————3——————5-5——————3——————5-5——————
D 2——————2——————————0——0——————0——————2——————0-0——————2——————0-0——————
G 0——————0——————————————————0——————0——————————0——————0——————0———————
```
Haul a-way you rolling kings, heave a-way, haul a-way;

```
      C                G                              D  G
E 3——————3-0——3——————0———————————————————————————————————————————————
A 3——————3-3——3——————2——5——5——————0——————2——————5——5——————2——0————————
D 2——————2——————————0——0-0——————0——————0——————0——0——————0——0-5———————
G 0——————————————————————0——————————0——————————0——————————2-0———————
```
Haul a-way you'll hear me sing, we're bound for South Australia!

Chord Forms

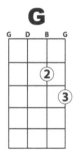
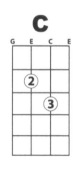
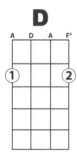
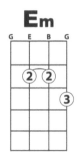

Star of the County Down

Basic Melody
Key of Em

A tale of beauty, determination and fierce love at first sight, this energetic song is a quintessential Irish favorite. It tells the story of a County Down farmer who falls for a local beauty and sets himself to win her hand in marriage. This song is usually performed in a lively and forceful style.

Words and Music

Traditional

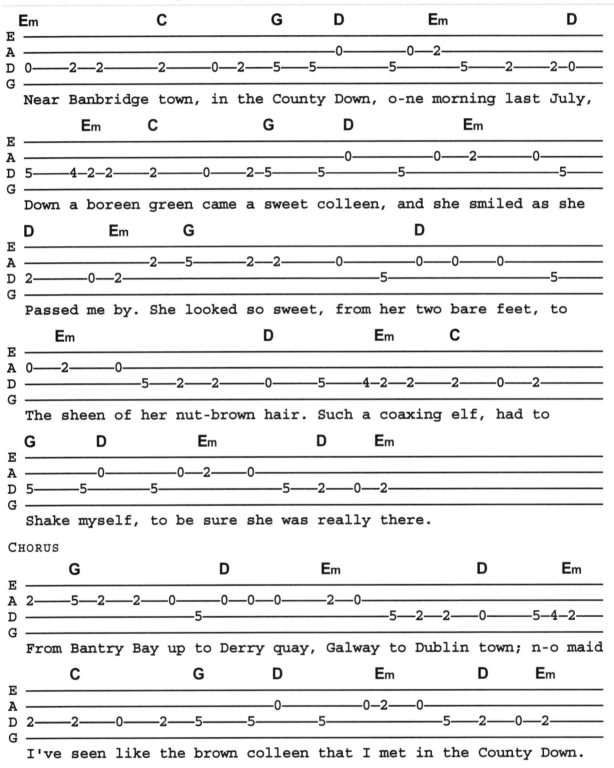

See Chord Forms and Additional Verses on Next Page

Star of the County Down
(continued)

Additional Verses

As she onward sped I shook my head,
And I gazed with a feeling queer.
And I said, says I, to a passerby,
"Who's the maid with the nut-brown hair?"
Oh he smiled at me, and he said, said he,
"That's the gem of old Ireland's crown:
Young Rosie McCann from the banks of the Ban
She's the star of the County Down."

She'd a soft brown eye and a look so sly,
And a smile like the rose in June.
And you'd crave each note from her lily-white throat,
As she lilted an Irish tune;
At the pattern dance you'd be in trance,
As she skipped through a jig or reel.
When her eyes she'd roll, she'd lift your soul,
And your heart she would plainly steal.

At the harvest fair she'll be surely there,
And I'll dress my Sunday clothes.
With my hat cocked right and my shoes shone bright,
For a smile from the nut-brown Rose.
No horse I'll yoke, no pipe I smoke,
Let the plow with the rust turn brown;
Til a smiling bride by my own fireside,
Sits the star of the County Down.

Chord Forms (Key of Em)

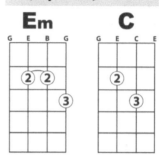

Chord Forms (Key of Am)

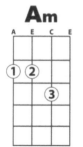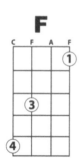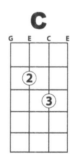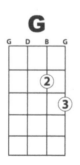

220

Star of the County Down
(continued)

Melody & Chords

Key of Em

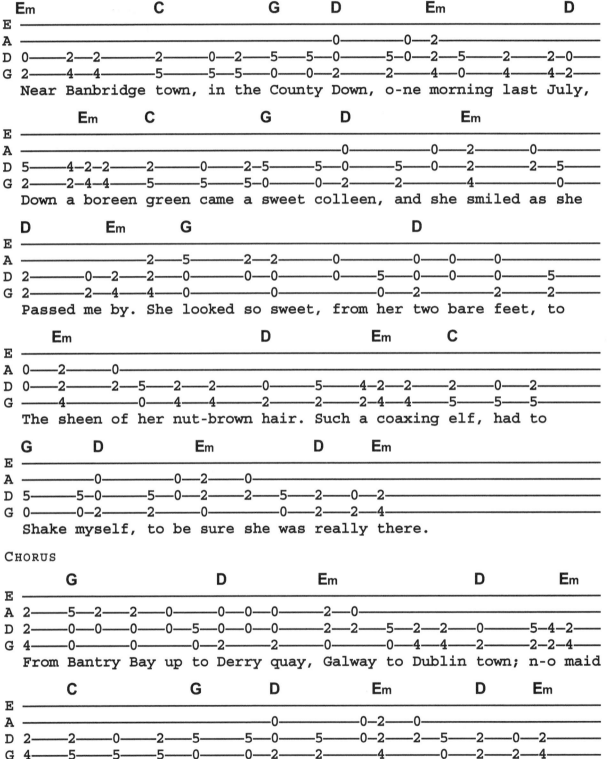

See Chord Forms on Previous Page

Star of the County Down
(continued)

Basic Melody

Key of Am (Low)

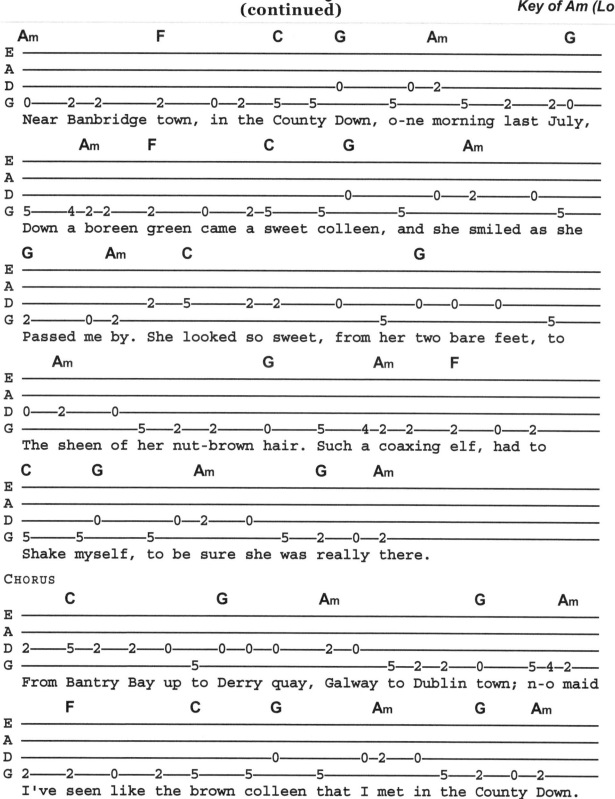

```
          Am            F           C       G       Am              G
E ─────────────────────────────────────────────────────────────────────────
A ─────────────────────────────────────────────────────────────────────────
D ──────────────────────────────────────────0───────0──2────────────────────
G 0─────2──2────────2──────0──2────5────5────────5────────5────2────2─0──────
  Near Banbridge town, in the County Down, o-ne morning last July,

          Am      F           C           G           Am
E ─────────────────────────────────────────────────────────────────────────
A ─────────────────────────────────────────────────────────────────────────
D ────────────────────────────────────0───────0──2──────────0───────────────
G 5─────4─2─2──────2────0──2─5────5──────────5──────────────────────5────────
  Down a boreen green came a sweet colleen, and she smiled as she

  G       Am      C                       G
E ─────────────────────────────────────────────────────────────────────────
A ─────────────────────────────────────────────────────────────────────────
D ──────────────2────5──────2──2──────0────────0──0──────0───────────────────
G 2────────0──2────────────────────────5──────────────────5─────────────────
  Passed me by. She looked so sweet, from her two bare feet, to

          Am                  G           Am      F
E ─────────────────────────────────────────────────────────────────────────
A ─────────────────────────────────────────────────────────────────────────
D 0─────2────────0───────────────────────────────────────────────────────────
G ──────────────5──2──2──────0────5────4─2─2──────2──0──2─────────────────────
  The sheen of her nut-brown hair. Such a coaxing elf, had to

  C       G           Am          G       Am
E ─────────────────────────────────────────────────────────────────────────
A ─────────────────────────────────────────────────────────────────────────
D ────────0──────0──2────0───────────────────────────────────────────────────
G 5────5────────5──────────────5────2──0──2──────────────────────────────────
  Shake myself, to be sure she was really there.
```

CHORUS

```
          C               G           Am              G       Am
E ─────────────────────────────────────────────────────────────────────────
A ─────────────────────────────────────────────────────────────────────────
D 2─────5──2────2────0────────0──0──0────────2──0─────────────────────────────
G ──────────────────5──────────────────────5──2──2────0──────5─4─2────────────
  From Bantry Bay up to Derry quay, Galway to Dublin town; n-o maid

          F           C       G           Am          G       Am
E ─────────────────────────────────────────────────────────────────────────
A ─────────────────────────────────────────────────────────────────────────
D ────────────────────────────0───────0─2──0─────────────────────────────────
G 2────2────0──2────5────5────────5──────────────────5────2──0──2────────────
  I've seen like the brown colleen that I met in the County Down.
```

See Chord Forms Two Pages Previous

Star of the County Down
(continued)

Basic Melody

Key of Am (High)

```
         Am              F              C         G         Am              G
E ─────────────────────────────────────────────────────0──────────────────────────
A ──────0──0──────────0──────────0──3───3──5──────3─5──────3──────0──0──────────────
D 5──────────────────────5───────────────────────────────────────────────────5─────
G ─────────────────────────────────────────────────────────────────────────────────
```
Near Banbridge town, in the County Down, o-ne morning last July,

```
          Am      F              C         G            Am
E ─────────────────────────────────────────────────0───────────────────────────────
A 3──────2─0──0──────0──────────0─3───3──5──────3──5──────────5──3───────────────────
D ──────────────────────5────────────────────────────────────────────────────────────
G ─────────────────────────────────────────────────────────────────────────────────
```
Down a boreen green came a sweet colleen, and she smiled as she

```
  G      Am       C                         G
E ───────────────0──3───────0──0────────────────────────────────────────────────────
A 0──────────0──────────────────────────5───3──5──5──────5───3──────────────────────
D ──────5────────────────────────────────────────────────────────────────────────────
G ─────────────────────────────────────────────────────────────────────────────────
```
Passed me by. She looked so sweet, from her two bare feet, to

```
          Am                         G         Am      F
E ────────0─────────────────────────────────────────────────────────────────────────
A 5──────────────5──3──0──0──────────3──2─0──0──────0──────────0─────────────────────
D ──────────────────────────5────────────────────────────5──────────────────────────
G ─────────────────────────────────────────────────────────────────────────────────
```
The sheen of her nut-brown hair. Such a coaxing elf, had to

```
  C      G          Am       G      Am
E ───────────────0───────────────────────────────────────────────────────────────────
A 3──────3─5──────3─5──────5───3──0──────0───────────────────────────────────────────
D ────────────────────────────────5─────────────────────────────────────────────────
G ─────────────────────────────────────────────────────────────────────────────────
```
Shake myself, to be sure she was really there.

CHORUS
```
     C                  G         Am              G      Am
E 0──3──0──0───────────────────────0─────────────────────────────────────────────────
A ───────────5─3──5──5──5──────5──3──0──0──────────3─2─0─────────────────────────────
D ───────────────────────────────────────────5──────────────────────────────────────
G ─────────────────────────────────────────────────────────────────────────────────
```
From Bantry Bay up to Derry quay, Galway to Dublin town; n-o maid

```
     F              C         G         Am      G      Am
E ─────────────────────────────────0────────────────────────────────────────────────
A 0──────0──────────0─3───3──5──3──5──────5─3──0──────0──────────────────────────────
D ──────────5────────────────────────────────────────5──────────────────────────────
G ─────────────────────────────────────────────────────────────────────────────────
```
I've seen like the brown colleen that I met in the County Down.

See Chord Forms Three Pages Previous

Star of the County Down
(continued)

Melody & Chords

Key of Am (High)

Near Banbridge town, in the County Down, o-ne morning last July,

Down a boreen green came a sweet colleen, and she smiled as she

Passed me by. She looked so sweet, from her two bare feet, to

The sheen of her nut-brown hair. Such a coaxing elf, had to

Shake myself, to be sure she was really there.

CHORUS

From Bantry Bay up to Derry quay, Galway to Dublin town; n-o maid

I've seen like the brown colleen that I met in the County Down.

See Chord Forms Four Pages Previous

What Do We Do With A Drunken Sailor

Basic Melody

Key of Am (Low)

Words and Music

Traditional

This is one of the quintessential sailing songs, or sea shanties, known throughout the English-speaking world. It asks the question of what the crew is to do with one of their inebriated fellows, and proposes some more or less humorous courses of action. Quite a few other verses have been penned over the years, some of them quite bawdy.

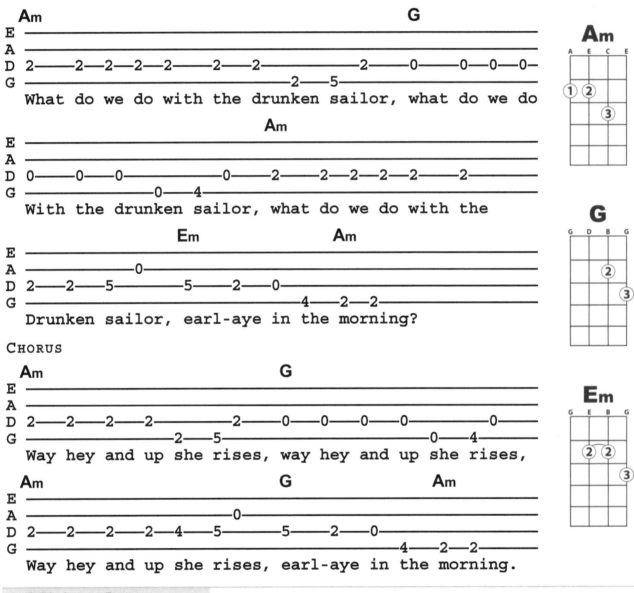

CHORUS

Additional Verses

Put him in a longboat, throw the tarp over... (3x)
Earl-aye in the morning!

Put him in the guardroom till he's sober... (3x)
Earl-aye in the morning!

Shave his belly with a rusty razor... (3x)
Earl-aye in the morning!

Put him in the scuppers with a hosepipe on him...(3x)
Earl-aye in the morning!

Pull out the plug and wet him all over… (3x)
Earl-aye in the morning!

Give 'im a hair of the dog that bit him… (3x)
Earl-aye in the morning!

What Do We Do With A Drunken Sailor (continued)

Basic Melody

Key of Am (High)

```
     Am                                                    G
E  0———0——0——0——0————0——0————————————0—————————————————————
A  ——————————————————————————————0———3————————5——5—5—5—
D  ———————————————————————————————————————————————————————
G  ———————————————————————————————————————————————————————
```
What do we do with the drunken sailor, what do we do

```
                                    Am
E  —————————————————————————0———0——0——0—0————0—————————
A  5———5——5————————2—5————————————————————————————————
D  ————————————5———————————————————————————————————————
G  ———————————————————————————————————————————————————————
```
With the drunken sailor, what do we do with the

```
                     Em              Am
E  0——0——3—5————3————0————————————————————————————————
A  ——————————————————————5—2——0——0——————————————————
D  ———————————————————————————————————————————————————————
G  ———————————————————————————————————————————————————————
```
Drunken sailor, earl-aye in the morning?

CHORUS

```
     Am                     G
E  0——0——0——0————————0——————————————————————————————
A  ——————————————0———3———5——5——5——5————————2—5————
D  —————————————————————————————————————5———————————
G  ———————————————————————————————————————————————————————
```
Way hey and up she rises, way hey and up she rises,

```
     Am                          G            Am
E  0——0——0——0—2——3—5———3————0—————————————————
A  ————————————————————————————5—2——0——0——————————
D  ———————————————————————————————————————————————————————
G  ———————————————————————————————————————————————————————
```
Way hey and up she rises, earl-aye in the morning.

Chord Forms

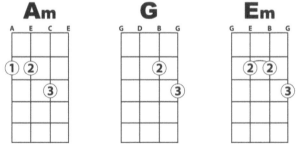

What Do We Do With A Drunken Sailor (continued)

Melody & Chords

Key of Am (High)

```
   Am                                                    G
E  0——0—0—0—0——0——0——————————0
A  0——0—0—0—0——0——0——0——3—0——5————5—5—5—
D  2————2————————2——2——2—2——0————0—0—0—
G  2————2————————2——2—2——0————————0—
   What do we do with the drunken sailor, what do we do
```

```
   Am
E  ————————————————0————0—0—0—0——0————
A  5——5—5——————2—5——0——0—0—0—0——0————
D  0——0—0——5——0—0——2————2————————
G  0————0—0——0—0——2————2————————
   With the drunken sailor, what do we do with the
```

```
              Em              Am
E  0——0—3—5——3——0————————————————
A  0——0—0—3——2——2——5—2——0—0————————
D  2————2——2——2——0—0——2—2————————
G  2————————0————————2—2————————
   Drunken sailor, earl-aye in the morning?
```

CHORUS

```
   Am                        G
E  0——0——0——0————0————————————
A  0——0——0——0—0——3—3——5——5——5——5————2—5—
D  2—2————2—2——2—2——0——0——0——0—5——0—0——
G  2—2————————2—2——0——0————————0—0————0—
   Way hey and up she rises, way hey and up she rises,
```

```
   Am                        G           Am
E  0——0——0——0—2——3—5——3——0————————————
A  0——0——0——0—0——3—3——2——2——5—2——0—0——
D  2—2————2————2——0——0——0—0——2—2————
G  2—2————————————0————0————2—2————
   Way hey and up she rises, earl-aye in the morning.
```

Chord Forms

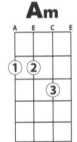 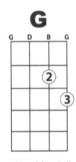 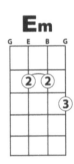

What Do We Do With A Drunken Sailor (continued)

Basic Melody

Key of Em

```
      Em                                          D
E ─────────────────────────────────────────────────────────────
A 2────2──2──2──2──────2──────2──────────────2──────0────0──0──0─
D ─────────────────────────────────2──────5─────────────────────
G ─────────────────────────────────────────────────────────────
```
What do we do with the drunken sailor, what do we do

```
                                      Em
E ─────────────────────────────────────────────────────────────
A 0──────0──────0──────────────0──────2──────2──2──2──2──────2───
D ─────────────────0──────4──────────────────────────────────────
G ─────────────────────────────────────────────────────────────
```
With the drunken sailor, what do we do with the

```
                      Bm                  Em
E ─────────────────0────────────────────────────────────────────
A 2────2──5────────────5──────2──────0──────────────────────────
D ─────────────────────────────────────4──────2──2──────────────
G ─────────────────────────────────────────────────────────────
```
Drunken sailor, earl-aye in the morning?

CHORUS

```
      Em                                          D
E ─────────────────────────────────────────────────────────────
A 2────2──2──2──────────2──────0──────0──────0──────0──────────0─
D ─────────────2──────5────────────────────────────0──────4──────
G ─────────────────────────────────────────────────────────────
```
Way hey and up she rises, way hey and up she rises,

```
      Em                              D              Em
E ─────────────────────0───────────────────────────────────────
A 2────2──2──2──4──────5────────────5──────2──────0──────────────
D ─────────────────────────────────────────4──────2──2──────────
G ─────────────────────────────────────────────────────────────
```
Way hey and up she rises, earl-aye in the morning.

Chord Forms

Em

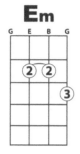

D

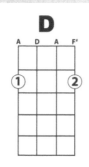

Bm

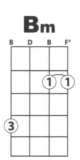

What Do We Do With A Drunken Sailor (continued)

Melody & Chords

Key of Em

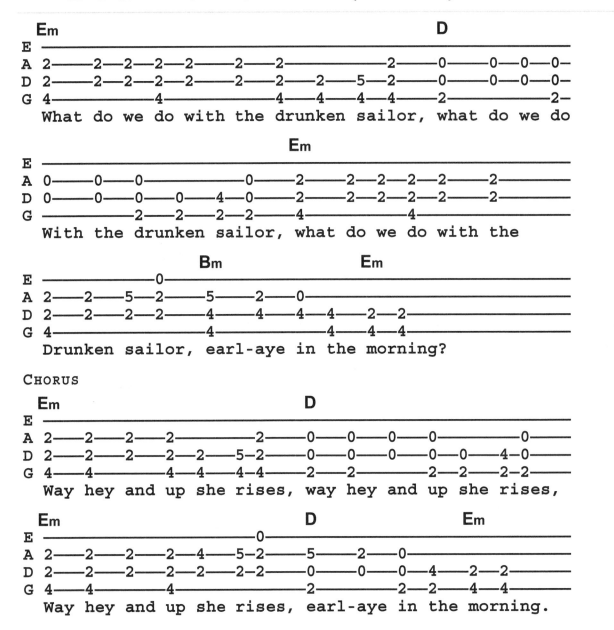

Em   D

```
E ————————————————————————————————————————————————————————————————
A 2———2—2—2—2———2———2——————————2———0———0—0—0—
D 2———2—2—2—2———2———2——2—5—2———0———0—0—0—
G 4———————4———————4—4—4—4———2—————————2—
```
What do we do with the drunken sailor, what do we do

                                            Em

```
E ————————————————————————————————————————————————————————————————
A 0———0——0————————0———2———2—2—2—2———2———————
D 0———0——0——0——4—0———2———2—2—2—2———2———————
G ————————2—2—2—2———4—————————4———————
```
With the drunken sailor, what do we do with the

                  Bm   Em

```
E ——————————0—————————————————————————————————
A 2—2—5—2———5——2——0—————————————————————
D 2—2—2—2———4——4—4—4——2—2—————————
G 4—————————4—————————4—4—4————————
```
Drunken sailor, earl-aye in the morning?

CHORUS

Em   D

```
E ————————————————————————————————————————————————————————————————
A 2——2——2——2————————2———0———0—0—0————————0—
D 2——2——2——2—2—5—2———0———0—0—0—0—4—0———
G 4——4—————4—4—4—4———2——2———————2—2——2—2————
```
Way hey and up she rises, way hey and up she rises,

Em   D   Em

```
E ——————————————————0—————————————————————————
A 2——2——2——2—4—5—2———5——2——0—————————————
D 2——2——2——2—2—2—2———0———0—0—4———2—2————
G 4——4—————4—————————2——————2—2——4—4————
```
Way hey and up she rises, earl-aye in the morning.

Chord Forms

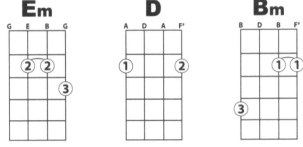

Whiskey In the Jar

Basic Melody

Key of C

This well-known Irish song is set in the mountains of Ireland and tells the story of a highwayman who runs afoul of the law. It has been recorded by a wide range of performers over the years, from Burl Ives to Thin Lizzy, The Grateful Dead to Metallica. There are a number of variations on the lyrics and verses, but the tune seems to have remained unchanged over the years.

Words and Music

Traditional

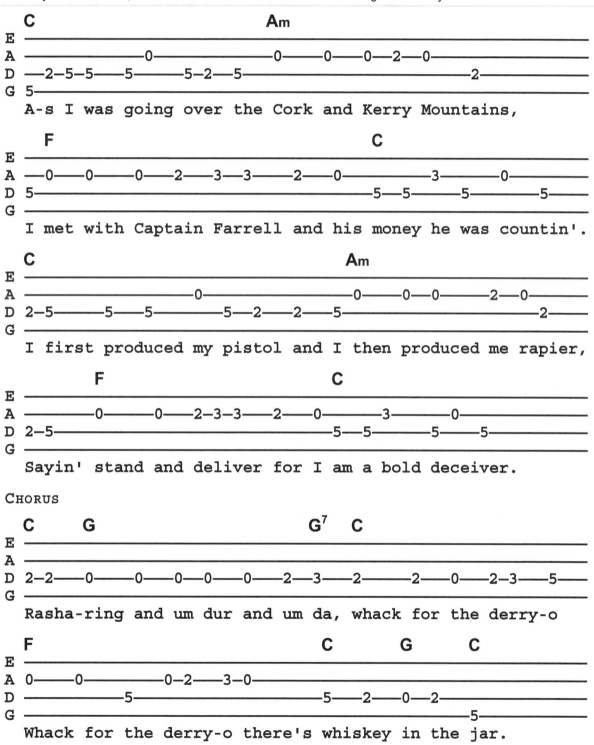

A-s I was going over the Cork and Kerry Mountains,

I met with Captain Farrell and his money he was countin'.

I first produced my pistol and I then produced me rapier,

Sayin' stand and deliver for I am a bold deceiver.

CHORUS

Rasha-ring and um dur and um da, whack for the derry-o

Whack for the derry-o there's whiskey in the jar.

See Chord Forms and Additional Verses on Next Page

Whiskey In the Jar
(continued)

Chord Forms

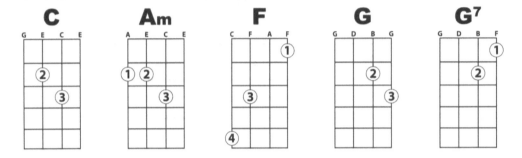

Additional Verses

I counted out his money and it made a pretty penny,
I put it in me pockets and I took it home to Jenny.
She sighed and she swore that she never would betray me;
But the Devil take the women for they never can be easy.

I went unto me chamber, all for to take a slumber.
I dreamt of gold and jewels, and sure it was no wonder.
But Jenny took me charges and she filled them up with water,
And sent for Captain Farrell to be ready for the slaughter.

It was early in the morning just before I rose to travel,
Up stepped a band of footmen, and likewise Captain Farrell.
I first produced me pistols for she'd stolen away me rapier,
But I couldn't shoot the water so a pris'ner I was taken.

If anyone can aid me, 'tis me brother in the army,
If I can find his station, in Cork or in Killarney.
And if he'll go with me, we'll go rollin' in Kilkenny;
And I'm sure he'll treat me better than me old miss sportin' Jenny.

Now there's some take delight in the carriages a-rollin',
And others take delight in the hurlin' and the bowlin'.
But I take delight in the juice of the barley,
And courtin' pretty fair maids in the morning' bright and early!

Whiskey In the Jar
(continued)

Melody & Chords

Key of C

C   Am
```
E ----------------------------------------------------------------------------
A ------------------0-------------------0-----0---0---2---0--------------------
D ---2-5-5------5-2-----5-2---5-----2-------2-----2---2---2-------2------------
G 5-5-5-5------5--------5-5---5-----5----------5--------5--------5------------
```
A-s I was going over the Cork and Kerry Mountains,

F   C
```
E ----------------------------------------------------------------------------
A ---0------0------0----2----3--3-----2---0-----------3---------0-------------
D 5-3------3------3----3----3--3-----3---3----5--5-2--5----2----5------------
G 5-5------5------5------------5--------------5--5-5------5----5-------------
```
I met with Captain Farrell and his money he was countin'.

C   Am
```
E ----------------------------------------------------------------------------
A ------------------0---------------------0-----0---0------2---0--------------
D 2-5------5----5----2-5-2----2---5-2----2---2------2---2-2---2--------------
G 5-5------5----5---------5---5---5-5-----------5------------------5--------
```
I first produced my pistol and I then produced me rapier,

F   C
```
E ----------------------------------------------------------------------------
A ----------0-----0----2-3-3-----2---0----------3----------0----------------
D 2-5------3------3----3-3-3-----3---3-5--5-2---5-2----5--------------------
G 5-5------5----------------5-----------5-5-5----5----5--------------------
```
Sayin' stand and deliver for I am a bold deceiver.

CHORUS

C   G   G⁷ C
```
E ----------------------------------------------------------------------------
A ----------------------------------------------------------------------------
D 2-2------0------0----0-0----0---2---3---2------2---0---2-3---5-------------
G 5-5------0------0----0-0----4---4---4---5------5---0---5-5---5-------------
```
Rasha-ring and um dur and um da, whack for the derry-o

F   C   G   C
```
E ----------------------------------------------------------------------------
A 0------0----------0-2----3-0--------------------------3------------------
D 3------3----5----3-3----3-3--------5---2---0---2---2--------------------
G 5------5----5----5------5-5--------5---5---0---0---5-------------------
```
Whack for the derry-o there's whiskey in the jar.

See Chord Forms and Additional Verses on Previous Page

Whiskey In the Jar
(continued)

Basic Melody

Key of G (Low)

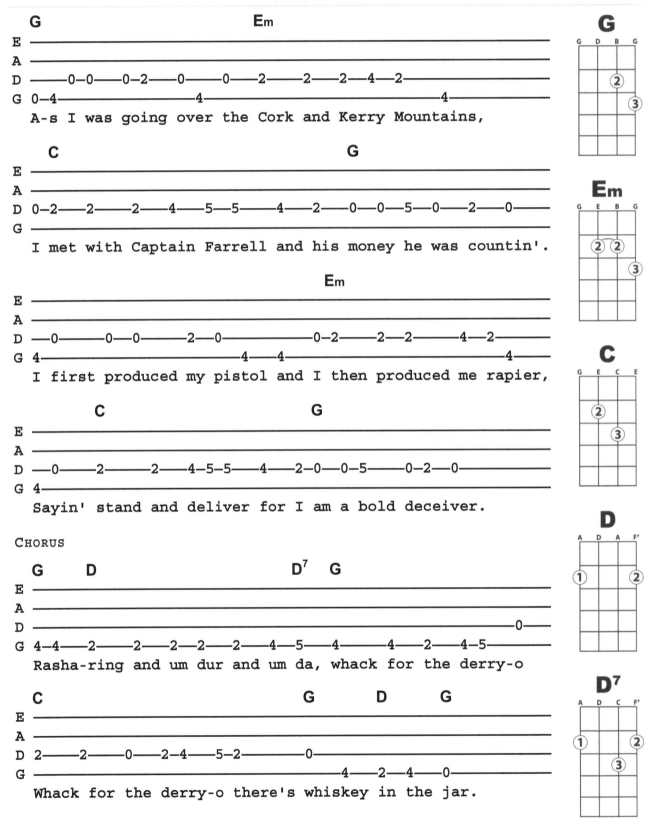

G   Em

A-s I was going over the Cork and Kerry Mountains,

C   G

I met with Captain Farrell and his money he was countin'.

Em

I first produced my pistol and I then produced me rapier,

C   G

Sayin' stand and deliver for I am a bold deceiver.

CHORUS

G   D   D⁷ G

Rasha-ring and um dur and um da, whack for the derry-o

C   G   D   G

Whack for the derry-o there's whiskey in the jar.

Whiskey In the Jar

(continued)

Basic Melody

Key of G (High)

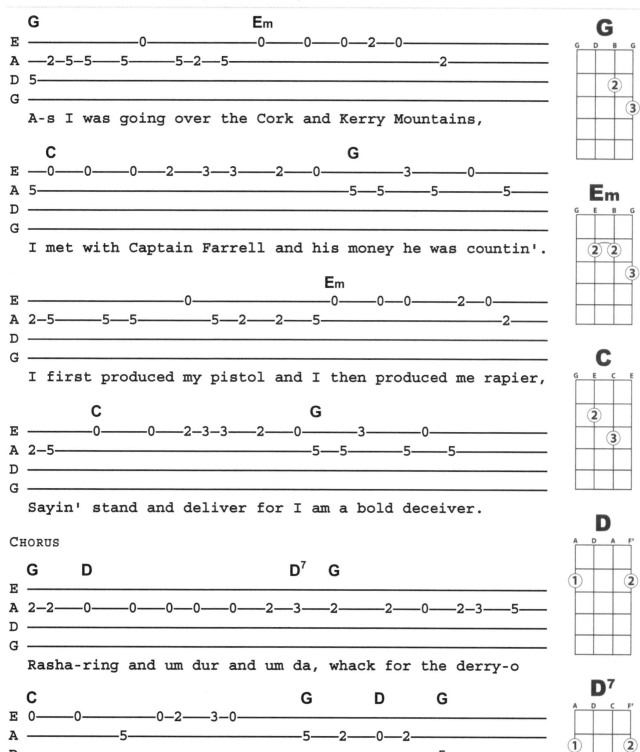

A-s I was going over the Cork and Kerry Mountains,

I met with Captain Farrell and his money he was countin'.

I first produced my pistol and I then produced me rapier,

Sayin' stand and deliver for I am a bold deceiver.

CHORUS

Rasha-ring and um dur and um da, whack for the derry-o

Whack for the derry-o there's whiskey in the jar.

Whiskey In the Jar

(continued)

Melody & Chords

Key of G (High)

G
```
         G                        Em
E ——————————————0————————————0——0——0—2—0————————————
A —2—5—5——5—2——5—2——5——2————2——2——2—2——2————————————
D 5—0—0—0——0————0—0——0——5————5————5——2——————————————
G 0——0————0——0—0—0————————————————————4——————————————
```
A-s I was going over the Cork and Kerry Mountains,

```
       C                        G
E ——0————0————0—2——3—3————2——0——————3————————0——————
A 5—3————3————3——0——3—3————2——0——5—5—2—5——2—5————————
D 5—2——————2————2—2————————————0—0—0—0——0—0——————————
G ——0————————————————————————0——————————————0——————
```
I met with Captain Farrell and his money he was countin'.

```
                          Em                0——0——0—2——0————
E ————————————0————————————————0——0——0—2——0——————————
A 2—5————5—5————2—5—2——2——5—2——2——2——2—2—2——————————
D 0—0————0—0————0—0——0——0—5————5————————2——————————
G 0—0————0————0————0————0————————————————4————————
```
I first produced my pistol and I then produced me rapier,

```
        C                        G
E ————————0————0—2—3—3————2——0————————3————————0——————
A 2—5————3————3——0—3—3————2——0—5—5—2——5—2—5————————
D 2—5——————2————2————2——————————0—0—0——0—0—0————————
G 4————0————————————————————————0————————0————0——0——
```
Sayin' stand and deliver for I am a bold deceiver.

CHORUS

```
  G      D                    D⁷  G
E ——————————————————————————————————————————————————
A 2—2——0————0———0—0——0——2—3——2————2——0——2—3——5——————
D 0—0——0————0———0—0——0——0—0——0————0——0——0—0——0——————
G 0————2——————2————————2——0————0——————0——0————
```
Rasha-ring and um dur and um da, whack for the derry-o

```
  C                        G      D      G
E 0————0————0—2——3—0——————————————————————————————
A 3————3——5—3—0——3—3————5——2——0—2——————————————————
D 2————2—5—2——2—2——————0——0——0—0——5————————————————
G 0————————0————0————0————2————0————————————————————
```
Whack for the derry-o there's whiskey in the jar.

G

Em

C

D

D⁷

Whiskey Is the Life Of Man

Basic Melody
Key of C

This was another favorite shanty to be sung while on a sailing voyage. It is said that the sailors would especially sing this one when working within earshot of the captain's quarters, in the hopes of softening his heart into ordering up an extra round of grog for the men.

Words and Music
Traditional

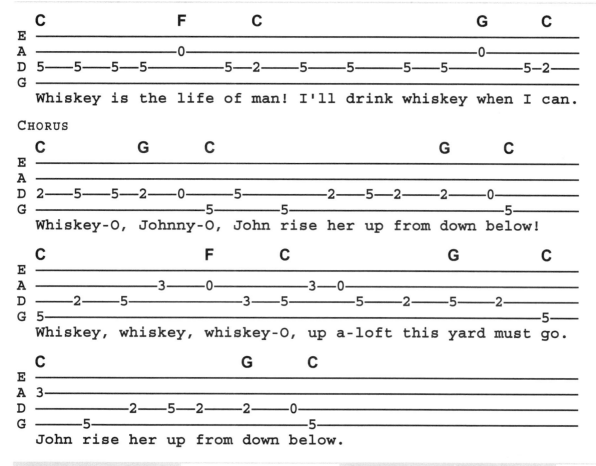

```
        C                    F        C                        G        C
E ─────────────────────────────────────────────────────────────────────────────
A ───────────────────0─────────────────────────────────────────0───────────────
D 5───5───5───5─────────────5──2────5───5───────5───5───5───5─────────5─2────────
G ───────────────────────────────────────────────────────────────────────────────
  Whiskey is the life of man! I'll drink whiskey when I can.
```

CHORUS

```
        C       G       C                        G        C
E ─────────────────────────────────────────────────────────────────
A ─────────────────────────────────────────────────────────────────
D 2───5───5───2───0───────5───────────2───5───2───2───0─────────────
G ───────────────────5───────5───────────────────────────5─────────
  Whiskey-O, Johnny-O, John rise her up from down below!
```

```
        C                    F        C                G        C
E ─────────────────────────────────────────────────────────────────────────
A ───────────────3───0───────────3──0───────────────────────────────────────
D ───2───5───────────3───5───────────5───2───5───2──────────────────────────
G 5──────────────────────────────────────────────────────────────────5──────
  Whiskey, whiskey, whiskey-O, up a-loft this yard must go.
```

```
        C                        G        C
E ───────────────────────────────────────────────
A 3───────────────────────────────────────────────
D ───────────2───5───2───2───0─────────────────────
G ───────5───────────────────────5─────────────────
  John rise her up from down below.
```

Chord Forms

C   **F**   **G**

Additional Verses

Now whiskey made me pawn me clothes,
And whiskey gave me a broken nose.

Now whiskey is the life of man,
Whiskey from an old tin can.

I thought I heard the first mate say:
I treats me crew in a decent way.

I treat me crew in a decent way,
Give them whiskey twice a day.

O whiskey killed my poor old dad,
And whiskey drove my mother mad.

O whiskey hot and whiskey cold,
O whiskey new and whiskey old.

Whiskey Is the Life Of Man (continued)

```
     C                F         C                          G        C
E ──────────────────────────────────────────────────────────────────────
A ──────────────────0──────────────────────────────────────0──────────────
D 5───5──5──5────3────5──2────5──────5────5───5────0────5─2──
G 0───0──0──0────2────5──5────0──────0────0───0────0────0─5──
  Whiskey is the life of man! I'll drink whiskey when I can.
```

CHORUS

```
     C        G    C                          G        C
E ──────────────────────────────────────────────────────────────────
A ──────────────────────────────────────────────────────────────────
D 2───5──5──2────0────5──────2──5──2────2────0──────────
G 5───5──5──0────0─5──0────5────0──5─5────0────0─5────────
  Whiskey-O, Johnny-O, John rise her up from down below!
```

```
     C                F         C                 G              C
E ──────────────────────────────────────────────────────────────────────
A ──────────3────0──────────3──0────────────────────────────
D ────2────5──2────3──3────5──2──2─5────2────5────2────────
G 5───5──5──5────5──5────5──0──────5────5────0────0────5──
  Whiskey, whiskey, whiskey-O, up a-loft this yard must go.
```

```
     C                        G    C
E ──────────────────────────────────────────────────────
A 3──────────────────────────3──────────────────────────
D 2──────────2──5──2────2──────0─2──────────────────────
G 0───5──5──5──5────0────0─5────────────────────────────
  John rise her up from down below.
```

Whiskey Is the Life Of Man (continued)

Basic Melody

Key of G (Low)

```
     G              C      G              D     G
E -----------------------------------------------------
A -----------------------------------------------------
D 0----0---0---0---2---0------0-------0------0---0--2----0---
G -----------------------4-------------------------------4---
```
Whiskey is the life of man! I'll drink whiskey when I can.

CHORUS

```
     G        D     G                 D     G
E -----------------------------------------------------
A -----------------------------------------------------
D ---0---0---------0----------0-------------------------
G 4--------4--2-0------0---4------4---4--2-0-------------
```
Whiskey-O, Johnny-O, John rise her up from down below!

```
     G                C      G              D       G
E -----------------------------------------------------
A -----------------------------------------------------
D -------0--5---2---0--5--2-0--------0------------------
G 0--4-----------5-----------4--------4--0-------------
```
Whiskey, whiskey, whiskey-O, up a-loft this yard must go.

```
     G                    D    G
E -----------------------------------------------------
A -----------------------------------------------------
D 5--------------0-------------------------------------
G ---0--4----4---4--2-0--------------------------------
```
John rise her up from down below.

Chord Forms

G
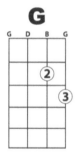

C
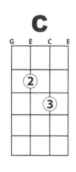

D
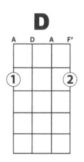

Whiskey Is the Life Of Man (continued)

Basic Melody

Key of G (High)

```
       G              C       G                    D       G
E ————————————————————0————————————————————————————————————————————————
A 5——5——5——5————————5—2——5——————5————5——5————————————5—2———
D ———————————————————————————————————————————————————————————————————
G ———————————————————————————————————————————————————————————————————
```
Whiskey is the life of man! I'll drink whiskey when I can.

CHORUS

```
       G          D       G                    D       G
E ———————————————————————————————————————————————————————————————————
A 2——5——5——2——0————————5——————2——5——2——2————0—————————
D ——————————————————5————————5————————————————————5————
G ———————————————————————————————————————————————————————————————————
```
Whiskey-O, Johnny-O, John rise her up from down below!

```
       G                  C       G                D       G
E ——————————————3————0——————3—0—————————————————————————
A ————2————5——————————3—5————5——2————5——2——————————
D 5————————————————————————————————————————————————————5——
G ———————————————————————————————————————————————————————————————————
```
Whiskey, whiskey, whiskey-O, up a-loft this yard must go.

```
       G                      D       G
E 3————————————————————————————————————————————————————————————————
A ————————————2——5——2————2——0——————————————————————————
D ————5————————————————————5————————————————————————————————
G ———————————————————————————————————————————————————————————————————
```
John rise her up from down below.

Chord Forms

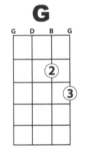

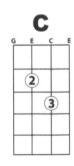

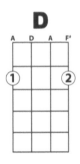

239

Whiskey Is the Life Of Man (continued)

Melody & Chords

Key of G (High)

```
        G                   C         G                           D         G
E ─────────────────0───────────────────────────────────────────────0──────────────
A 5────5────5──5────3────5──2────5────5────────5──5────0────5─2──────
D 0────0────0──0────2────0──0────0────0────────0──0────0────0─0──────
G 0────────0────────0────0──0────0────0────────0────2────2─0────────
```
Whiskey is the life of man! I'll drink whiskey when I can.

CHORUS

```
        G              D      G                           D      G
E ──────────────────────────────────────────────────────────────────────────────
A 2────5────5──2────0────5──────────2──5──2────2────0──────
D 0────0────0──0────0─5──0────────5────0──0──0────0────0─5──────
G 0────────0──2────────0──0────0────────0────2────────0──────
```
Whiskey-O, Johnny-O, John rise her up from down below!

```
        G                       C        G                   D         G
E ────────────3──────0──────────3──0──────────────────────────────────────
A ────2────5──2────3──3────5──2──2─5────2────5────2──────────
D 5────0────0──0────2──2────0──0────0────0────0────0────5────
G 0────────0──────────0──0────0────────0────2────────0──────
```
Whiskey, whiskey, whiskey-O, up a-loft this yard must go.

```
        G                         D      G
E 3──────────────────────────────────────────────────────────────
A 2────────────2──5──2────2────0──────────────────────────
D 0────5────0──0──0────0────0─5──────────────────────────
G 0────0──────────0──0────2────2─0──────────────────────
```
John rise her up from down below.

Chord Forms

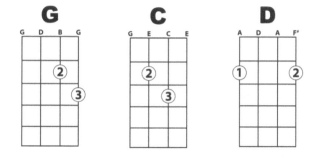

Whiskey You're the Devil
(page 1)

Basic Melody

Key of G (Low)

Words and Music

Traditional

This is another great old drinking song that The Clancy Brothers and Tommy Makem set the standard for. It is meant to be performed at a brisk pace and quite energetically. Search YouTube for the recording on the "Come Fill Your Glass With Us" album.

CHORUS

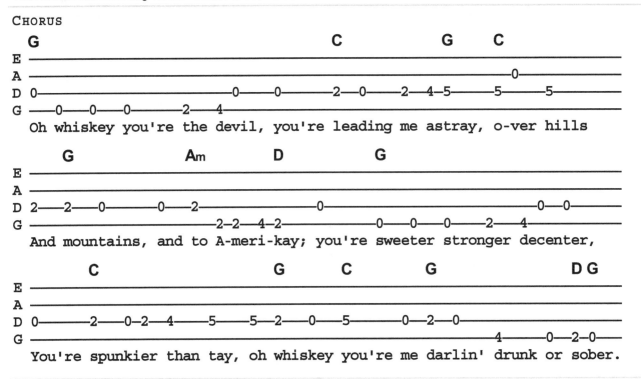

Oh whiskey you're the devil, you're leading me astray, o-ver hills

And mountains, and to A-meri-kay; you're sweeter stronger decenter,

You're spunkier than tay, oh whiskey you're me darlin' drunk or sober.

Chord Forms (Key of G)

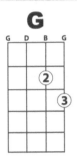
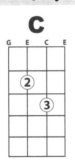
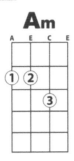
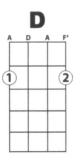
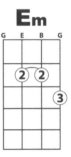

Chord Forms (Key of C)

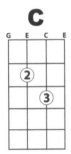
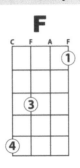
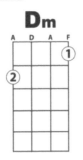
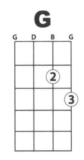
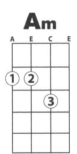

See Verses on Next Page

Whiskey You're the Devil

Basic Melody

(page 2)

Key of G

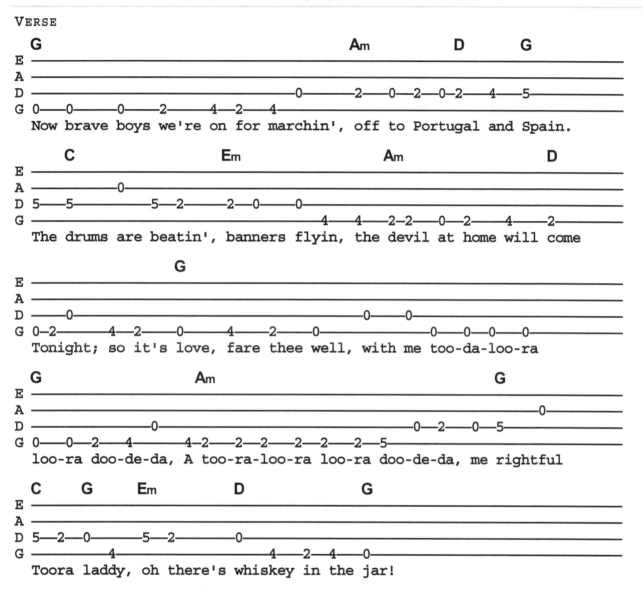

VERSE

```
      G                                   Am        D      G
E ———————————————————————————————————————————————————————————————————
A ———————————————————————————————————————————————————————————————————
D ——————————————————————————————0——————2—0—2—0-2——4——5————————————————
G 0——0——————0——————2——————4—2——4——————————————————————————————————————
```
Now brave boys we're on for marchin', off to Portugal and Spain.

```
      C                 Em              Am                    D
E ———————————————————————————————————————————————————————————————————
A ————————————0————————————————————————————————————————————————————————
D 5——5————————————5—2——————2—0——————0——————————————————————————————————
G ———————————————————————————4——4——2-2——0—2——————4——————2———————————————
```
The drums are beatin', banners flyin, the devil at home will come

```
                          G
E ———————————————————————————————————————————————————————————————————
A ———————————————————————————————————————————————————————————————————
D ——————0——————————————————————————————0——————0————————————————————————
G 0—2——————4—2——————0——————4——————2——————0——————0——0——0——0——0————————————
```
Tonight; so it's love, fare thee well, with me too-da-loo-ra

```
      G                 Am                              G
E ———————————————————————————————————————————————————————————————————
A ——————————————————————————————————————————————————————0——————————————
D ——————————————————0——————————————————0——2——0——5——————————————————————
G 0——0—2——4——————4-2——2—2——2—2——2—5——————————————————————————————————————
```
loo-ra doo-de-da, A too-ra-loo-ra loo-ra doo-de-da, me rightful

```
      C    G    Em        D            G
E ———————————————————————————————————————————————————————————————————
A ———————————————————————————————————————————————————————————————————
D 5——2——0————————5—2——————0————————————————————————————————————————————
G ——————————4——————————————4——2——4——0—————————————————————————————————
```
Toora laddy, oh there's whiskey in the jar!

Additional Verses

The French are fighting boldly, men are dying hot and coldly,
Give every man his flask of powder, his firelock on his shoulder;
And its love, fare thee well with me too da loo ra loo ra doo de da,
A too ra loo ra loo ra doo de, me rightful toora laddie-o,
There's whiskey in the jar!

Says the old one do not wrong me, don't take me daughter from me,
For if you do I will torment you, and when I'm dead my ghost will haunt you;
So its love, fare thee well with me too da loo ra loo ra doo de da,
A too ra loo ra loo ra doo de, me rightful toora laddie-o,
There's whiskey in the jar!

Whiskey You're the Devil

(continued)

Basic Melody

Key of G (High)

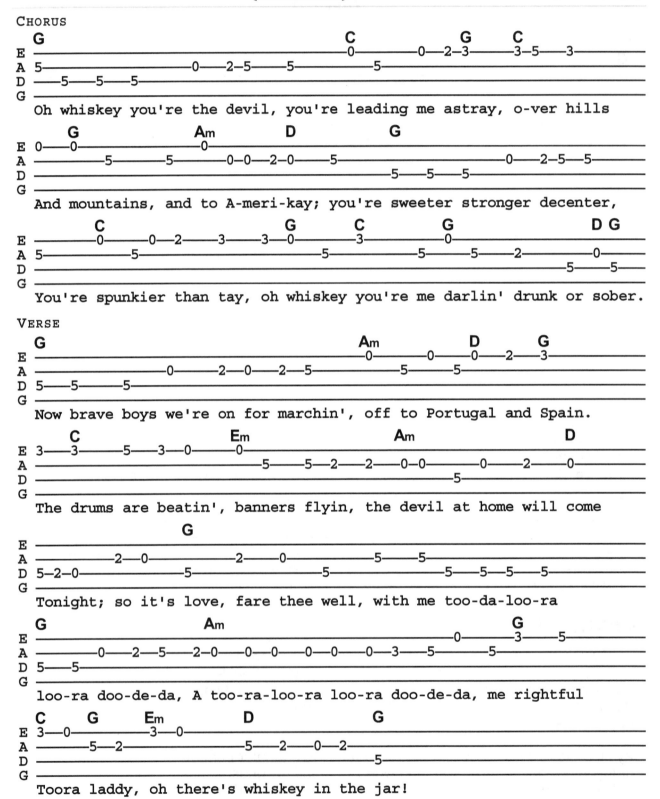

CHORUS

Oh whiskey you're the devil, you're leading me astray, o-ver hills

And mountains, and to A-meri-kay; you're sweeter stronger decenter,

You're spunkier than tay, oh whiskey you're me darlin' drunk or sober.

VERSE

Now brave boys we're on for marchin', off to Portugal and Spain.

The drums are beatin', banners flyin, the devil at home will come

Tonight; so it's love, fare thee well, with me too-da-loo-ra

loo-ra doo-de-da, A too-ra-loo-ra loo-ra doo-de-da, me rightful

Toora laddy, oh there's whiskey in the jar!

See Chord Forms Two Pages Previous

Whiskey You're the Devil
(continued)

Melody & Chords

Key of G (High)

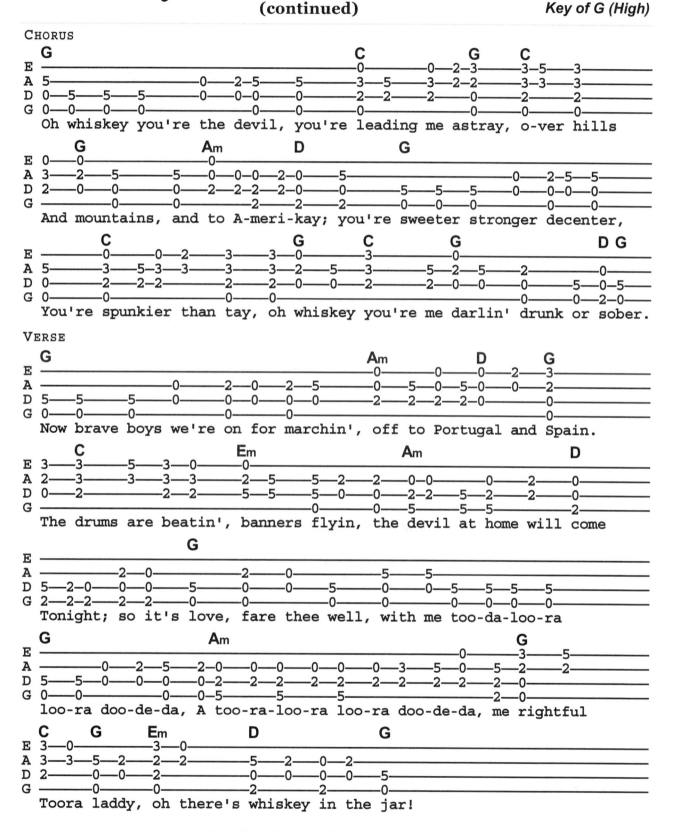

See Chord Forms Three Pages Previous

Whiskey You're the Devil

(continued)

Basic Melody

Key of C

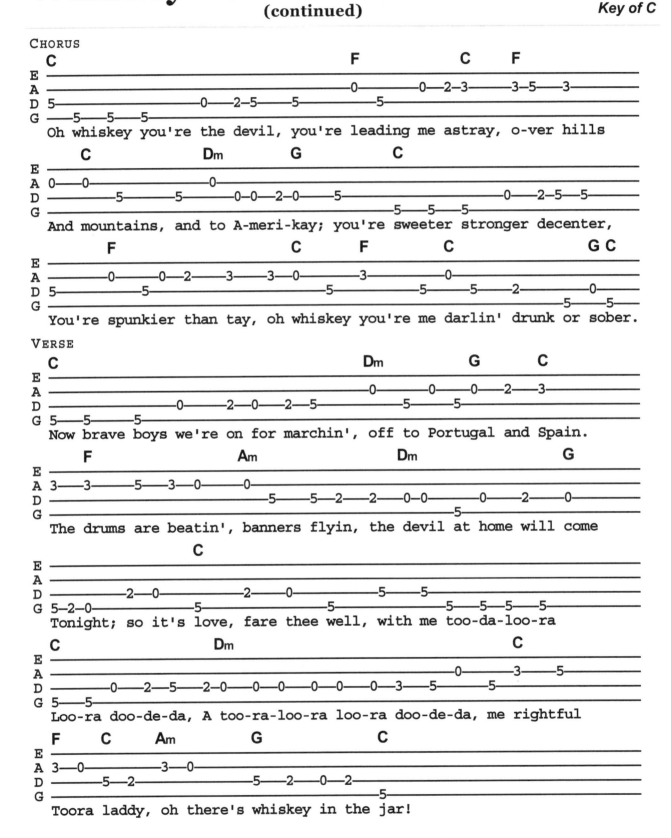

See Chord Forms Four Pages Previous

Whiskey You're the Devil

(continued)

Melody & Chords

Key of C

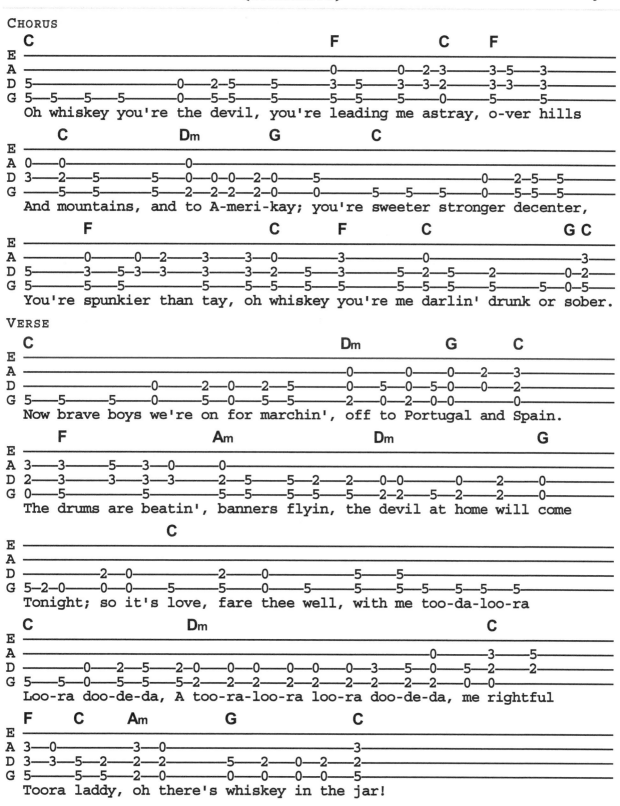

See Chord Forms Five Pages Previous

The Wild Colonial Boy

Basic Melody
Key of C

This old Irish song tells the story of Jack Duggan, who left Ireland to travel to Australia where he became a Robin Hood-style highwayman. He eventually met his fate at the hands of some British soldiers. Traditionally this was sung in a slower, more mournful manner, but the Clancy Brothers and Tommy Makem sped it up to make it a rousing song, and that is the way it is usually performed today.

Words and Music

Traditional

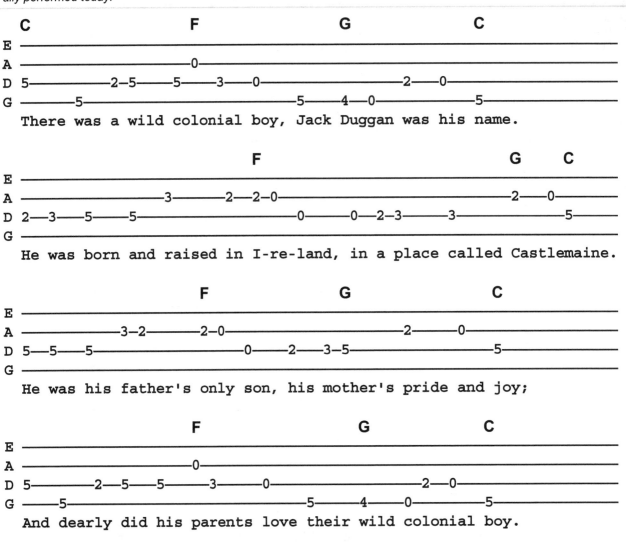

There was a wild colonial boy, Jack Duggan was his name.

He was born and raised in I-re-land, in a place called Castlemaine.

He was his father's only son, his mother's pride and joy;

And dearly did his parents love their wild colonial boy.

Chord Forms

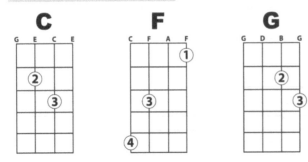

See Additional Verses on Next Page

The Wild Colonial Boy

(continued)

Melody & Chords

Key of C

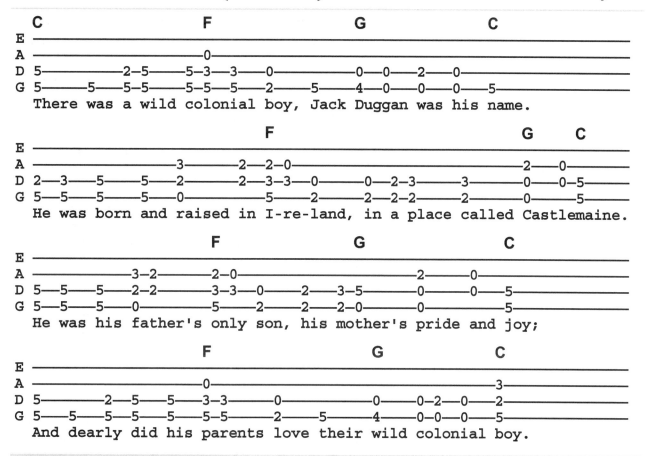

There was a wild colonial boy, Jack Duggan was his name.

He was born and raised in I-re-land, in a place called Castlemaine.

He was his father's only son, his mother's pride and joy;

And dearly did his parents love their wild colonial boy.

Additional Verses

At the early age of sixteen years, he left his native home;
And to Australia's sunny shore he was inclined to roam.
He robbed the rich, he helped the poor, he shot James McAvoy;
A terror to Australia was the wild colonial boy.

One morning on the prairie as Jack he rode along,
A-listening to the mockingbird a singing a cheerful song;
Out stepped a band of troopers, Kelly, Davis and Fitzroy;
They'd all set out to capture him, the wild colonial boy.

"Surrender now Jack Duggan for you see we're three to one.
Surrender in the Queen's high name for you are a plundering son"
Jack drew two pistols from his belt and proudly waved them high;
"I'll fight, but not surrender!" said the wild colonial boy.

He fired a shot at Kelly, which brought him to the ground;
And turning 'round to Davis, he received a fatal wound.
A bullet pierced his proud young heart from the pistol of Fitzroy,
And that was how they captured him, the wild colonial boy.

See Chord Forms on Previous Page

The Wild Colonial Boy

(continued)

Basic Melody

Key of G

```
      G                      C              D              G
E ————————————————————0—————————————————————————————————————————————————
A 5——————————2—5————5————3————0——————————————2————0——————————————————————
D ——————5———————————————————————5————4——0——————————5——————————————————————
G —————————————————————————————————————————————————————————————————————————
```
There was a wild colonial boy, Jack Duggan was his name.

```
                          C                          D    G
E ———————————————3—————————2—2—0————————————————————2————0——————————————
A 2—3————5————5—————————————————————0————0—2—3————3——————————5——————————
D —————————————————————————————————————————————————————————————————————————
G —————————————————————————————————————————————————————————————————————————
```
He was born and raised in I-re-land, in a place called Castlemaine.

```
                      C              D              G
E ————————————3—2———————2—0—————————————————2————0——————————————————
A 5—5————5——————————————————0————2——3—5—————————————5——————————————
D —————————————————————————————————————————————————————————————————————
G —————————————————————————————————————————————————————————————————————
```
He was his father's only son, his mother's pride and joy;

```
                      C              D              G
E ————————————————0—————————————————————————————————————————————————
A 5————————2—5————5————3————0————————————————2————0——————————————————
D ——————5———————————————————————5————4——0——————————5——————————————————
G —————————————————————————————————————————————————————————————————————
```
And dearly did his parents love their wild colonial boy.

Chord Forms

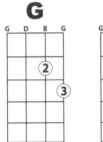
G

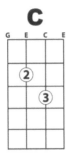
C

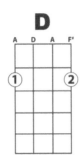
D

249

The Wild Colonial Boy
(continued)

Melody & Chords

Key of G

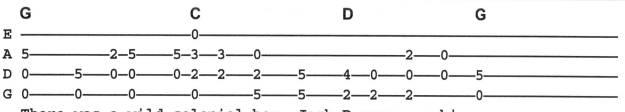

There was a wild colonial boy, Jack Duggan was his name.

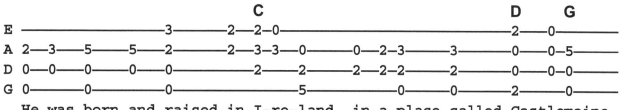

He was born and raised in I-re-land, in a place called Castlemaine.

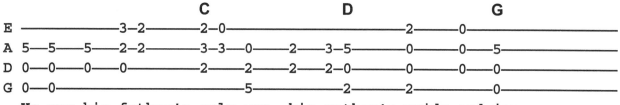

He was his father's only son, his mother's pride and joy;

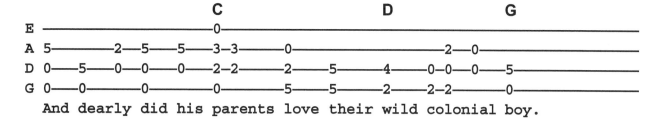

And dearly did his parents love their wild colonial boy.

Chord Forms

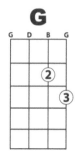

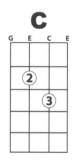

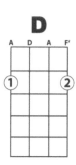

Wild Mountain Thyme

Basic Melody
Key of G

Words and Music

Traditional

This beautiful old song comes down from the mists of history in the British Isles, probably originally from Scotland. There have been many arrangements and adaptations of it over the years, and some have claimed copyright on it, but it is now believed to be wholly traditional. The Clancy Brothers with Tommy Makem helped to popularize it with their recordings and performances.

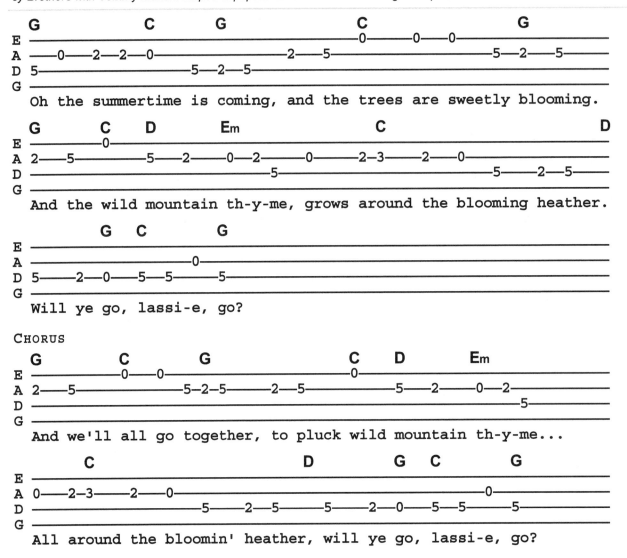

Oh the summertime is coming, and the trees are sweetly blooming.

And the wild mountain th-y-me, grows around the blooming heather.

Will ye go, lassi-e, go?

CHORUS

And we'll all go together, to pluck wild mountain th-y-me...

All around the bloomin' heather, will ye go, lassi-e, go?

Additional Verses

I will build my love a bower,
Beside cool crystal fountain;
And on it I will pile,
All the flowers of the mountain...
Will ye go, lassie, go?

If my true love she were gone,
I would surely find another,
To pluck wild mountain thyme,
All around the blooming heather...
Will ye go, lassie, go?

Chord Forms

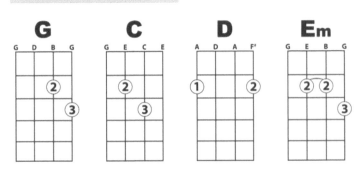

Wild Mountain Thyme
(continued)

Melody & Chords

Key of G

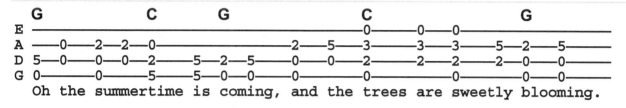

```
      G           C       G                   C               G
E ──────────────────────────────────────0────0──0────────────────────
A ────0───2──2──0───────────2──5───3────3──3────5──2──5──
D 5───0────0──0──2────5──2──5──────0──0────2────2──2────2──0──0──
G 0─────────0─────5────5──0──0──────0────────0──────────0──0──0──
```
Oh the summertime is coming, and the trees are sweetly blooming.

```
      G      C     D       Em                  C                   D
E ────────0──────────────────────────────────────────────────────
A 2───5───3───5──2────0─2──────0───────2─3─────2──0──────────────
D 0──0────2───0──0────2─2─5──2────────2─2────2──2──5─────2──5──
G 0─────────0─────2──────4────4──4──────0────────5──5─────5──5──
```
And the wild mountain th-y-me, grows around the blooming heather.

```
               G  C      G
E ──────────────────────────────────────
A ───────────────0────────────────────
D 5─────2──0──5──5──2──5──────────────
G 5─────5──0──5──5──5──0──────────────
```
Will ye go, lassi-e, go?

CHORUS

```
      G         C        G                   C     D    Em
E ───────────0────0───────────────────0──────────────────
A 2───5──────3──3──5─2─5──────2──5──────3────5──2────0─2──
D 0──0───────2──2──2─0─0───────0──0──────2────0──0────2─2─5──
G 0───────────0──0───0─0──────0──────────0────2──2────4──4──
```
And we'll all go together, to pluck wild mountain th-y-me...

```
          C                       D       G  C      G
E ─────────────────────────────────────────────────────────
A 0───2─3────2──0──────────────────────────────0──────────
D 2──2─2────2──2──5───2──5──────5───2──0──5──5──0──5──
G 4────0─────0──0──5──5──────5───5──0──5──5──2──0──
```
All around the bloomin' heather, will ye go, lassi-e, go?

Chord Forms

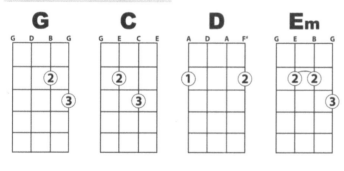

Wild Mountain Thyme
(continued)

Basic Melody

Key of C (Low)

```
      C           F     C             F                 C
E ——————————————————————————————————————————————————————————————————
A ————————————————————————————————0———————0———0—————————————————————
D ———0———2———2———0———————————————2———5—————————————————5———2———5—————
G 5———————————————————————5———2———5——————————————————————————————————
  Oh the summertime is coming, and the trees are sweetly blooming.
```

```
      C       F   G       Am                 F                     G
E ——————————————————————————————————————————————————————————————————
A —————————0————————————————————————————————————————————————————————
D 2———5————————————5———2———0———2————————0———2—3———2———0——————————————
G ———————————————————————————5——————————————————————————5———2———5————
  And the wild mountain th-y-me, grows around the blooming heather.
```

```
          C   F       C
E ——————————————————————————————————————————————————————————————————
A ——————————————————————————————————————————————————————————————————
D —————————————————0—————————————————————————————————————————————————
G 5———2———0———5———5———————5———————————————————————————————————————————
  Will ye go, lassi-e, go?
```

CHORUS

```
      C           F     C                 F   G       Am
E ——————————————————————————————————————————————————————————————————
A —————————0———0———————————————————————0————————————————————————————
D 2———5———————————5—2—5———2———5—————————5———2———0———2————————————————
G ——————————————————————————————————————————————————————5————————————
  And we'll all go together, to pluck wild mountain th-y-me...
```

```
      F                         G       C   F       C
E ——————————————————————————————————————————————————————————————————
A ——————————————————————————————————————————————————————————————————
D 0———2—3———2———0———————————————————————————————————0————————————————
G —————————————————5———2———5———5———2———0———5———5———5—————————————————
  All around the bloomin' heather,  will ye go, lassi-e, go?
```

Chord Forms

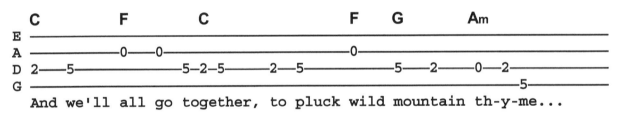

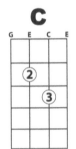 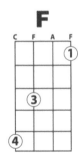 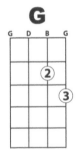 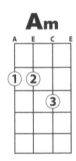

Wild Mountain Thyme
(continued)

Basic Melody

Key of C (High)

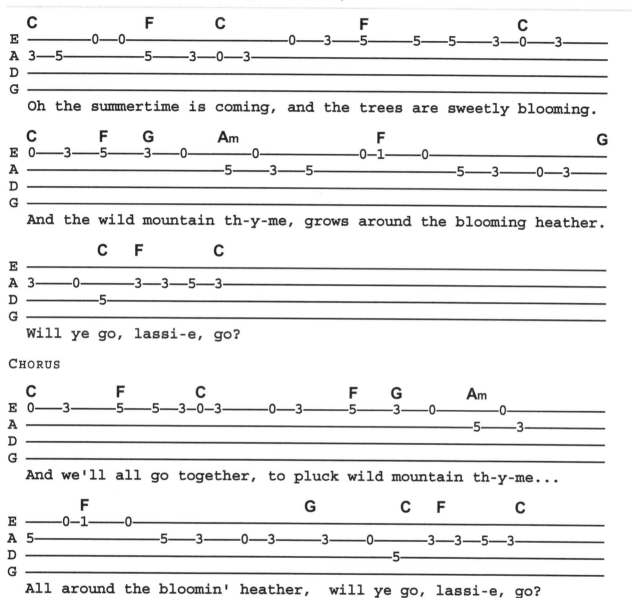

```
    C            F       C               F            C
E ---------0---0---------------0---3---5---5---5---3---0---3------
A 3---5---------5---3---0---3-------------------------------------
D ---------------------------------------------------------------
G ---------------------------------------------------------------
```
Oh the summertime is coming, and the trees are sweetly blooming.

```
    C   F   G       Am              F                       G
E 0---3---5---3---0-------0-----------0-1-----0------------------
A --------------------5---3---5-------------5---3-----0---3------
D ---------------------------------------------------------------
G ---------------------------------------------------------------
```
And the wild mountain th-y-me, grows around the blooming heather.

```
        C   F       C
E ---------------------------------------------------------------
A 3-----0-------3---3---5---3------------------------------------
D --------5------------------------------------------------------
G ---------------------------------------------------------------
```
Will ye go, lassi-e, go?

Chorus

```
    C       F       C           F   G       Am
E 0---3-----5---5---3-0-3-----0---3---5---3---0-------0----------
A -------------------------------------------------5---3--------
D ---------------------------------------------------------------
G ---------------------------------------------------------------
```
And we'll all go together, to pluck wild mountain th-y-me...

```
    F                       G       C   F       C
E -----0-1-----0-------------------------------------------------
A 5-----------5---3---0---3-------3---0-----3---3---5---3---------
D ------------------------------------5--------------------------
G ---------------------------------------------------------------
```
All around the bloomin' heather, will ye go, lassi-e, go?

Chord Forms

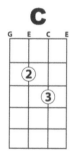
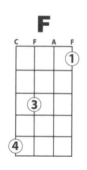
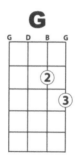
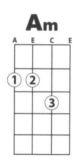

254

Wild Mountain Thyme
(continued)

Melody & Chords

Key of C (High)

```
     C              F      C                      F              C
E ——————————0——0——————————————————————0——3——5————5——5——3——0——3—————————
A 3——5——3——3——5——————3——0——3——————3——3——3————3——3——3——3——3—————————
D 2——2——2——2——3——————3——2——2——————2——2——3————3——3——————2——2——————————
G 0——————————0——————2——————5——0——————0——————5——————5——————0———————————
```
Oh the summertime is coming, and the trees are sweetly blooming.

```
     C      F  G      Am                      F                      G
E 0——3——5——3——0——————0————————————0—1——0——————————————————————————————
A 3——3——3——2——2——5——2—3——5————0—0——3——5——3——0——3——
D 2——2——3——0——0——2——2——2——————3——————3——3——3—3——
G 0——————5——0——————2——2————————————————————————2—2——
```
And the wild mountain th-y-me, grows around the blooming heather.

```
          C   F      C
E ———————————————————————————
A 3——————0——————3——3——5——3——
D 3——————3——5——3——3——3——2——
G 2——————5——5——————0————————
```
Will ye go, lassi-e, go?

CHORUS

```
     C      F      C                      F  G      Am
E 0——3——5——5——3—0—3——————0——3——5————3——0——————0————————
A 3——3——3——3—3-3—3——————3——3——3————2——2——5——0—3——————
D 2——2——3——3—3-2—2——————2——2——3————0——0——2——2——
G 0——————5——5————————0————————————0——————2——2——
```
And we'll all go together, to pluck wild mountain th-y-me...

```
     F                      G      C   F      C
E ——0—1——0——————————————————————————————————————
A 5——0-0——0——5——3——0——3——3——0————3——3——5——3——
D 3——2-3——————3——3——3—3——0——0—5——3——3——3——2——
G 2——————2——————5————0——5——5——————0——————
```
All around the bloomin' heather, will ye go, lassi-e, go?

Chord Forms

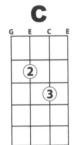
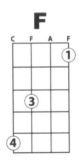
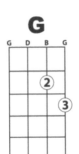
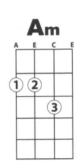

255

The Wild Rover

Basic Melody
Key of G

This is one of the best-known of the Irish pub/drinking songs, and is definitely a Saint Patrick's Day favorite. It is said to date back to the 1500's. The chorus is often accompanied by audience participation via clapping: four claps after the first "no nay never', two claps after "no nay never no more", and then a single clap after the final "no never, no more."

Words and Music
Traditional

```
     G                                  C
E ----------------------------------------------------------
A ------------0------------------2----2-0--2-3--------------
D 5-----5----------5----2-0---------------------------------
G ----------------------------------------------------------
```
I've been a wild rover for many a year,

```
         G           D7                      G
E --------------------------------------------------------
A 2---3----5-----2---5--3-0-------------2----0------------
D ------------------------------4---0----------5---------
G --------------------------------------------------------
```
And I've spent all me money on whiskey and beer.

```
                                                 C
E --------------------------------------------------------
A ----------0------------------2-----2----0-2------3------
D 5----5----------5-2---0----------------------------------
G --------------------------------------------------------
```
But now I've returned with gold in great store,

```
       G           D7                      G
E --------------------------------------------------------
A 2---3-5-2----5-----3-----0-----------2---0-------------
D --------------------------------4-----0------5---------
G --------------------------------------------------------
```
And I never will play the wild rover no more!

CHORUS

```
         D            G              C
E --------------------------------------------------------
A ---------0----0----------2--2----2-0----2-3------------
D 4---5--------------4--0----------------------------------
G --------------------------------------------------------
```
And it's no, nay, never! No nay never, no more...

```
       G           C        G       D  G
E --------------------------------------------------------
A 2---3-5------------------------------2----0------------
D ----------5----5----4-2----2--0----------5------------
G --------------------------------------------------------
```
Will I play the wild rover, no never, no more!

See Additional Verses on Next Page

The Wild Rover (continued)

Melody & Chords
Key of G

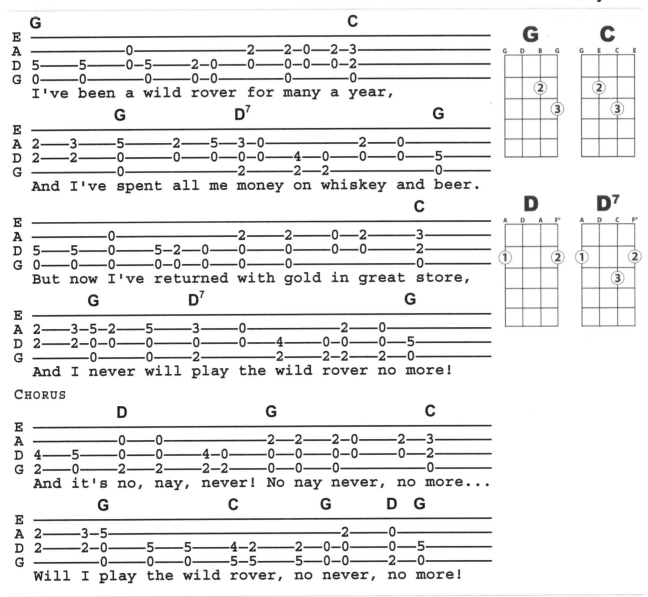

```
        G                                    C
E ─────────────────────────────────────────────────────────
A ─────────────0───────────────2───2─0──2─3─────────────────
D 5─────5──────0─5───────2─0────0───0─0──0─2─────────────────
G 0─────────0──────0───0─0──────────0──────0────────────────
  I've been a wild rover for many a year,
             G              D⁷                    G
E ─────────────────────────────────────────────────────────
A 2─────3─────5───────2───5─3─0───────────2─────0───────────
D 2─────2─────0───────0───0─0─0──────4─0────0───0──────5─────
G ───────────0────────────2───2─2──────────────────────0────
  And I've spent all me money on whiskey and beer.
                                             C
E ─────────────────────────────────────────────────────────
A ─────────────0───────────────2───2────0──2────3───────────
D 5─────5──────0──────5─2──0────0───0────0──0────2───────────
G 0─────0────0───0─0──0─────0───0───────────────0───────────
  But now I've returned with gold in great store,
             G              D⁷                    G
E ─────────────────────────────────────────────────────────
A 2─────3─5─2────5───────3───────0──────────2─────0──────────
D 2─────2─0─0────0───────0───────0────4──────0─0───0──5──────
G ──────────0─────────0──────2──────2───2─2──────2──0────────
  And I never will play the wild rover no more!
```

CHORUS

```
             D                 G                 C
E ─────────────────────────────────────────────────────────
A ──────────────0─────0────────────2─2────2─0──────2─3──────
D 4─────5───────0─────0──────4─0────0─0────0─0──────0─2──────
G 2─────0───────2─────2──────2─2────0─0────0────────0────────
  And it's no, nay, never! No nay never, no more...
             G                 C         G       D   G
E ─────────────────────────────────────────────────────────
A 2─────3─5───────────────────────────────2─────0──────────
D 2─────2─0───────5───5──────4─2────2─0─0────0───5──────────
G ──────────0─────0───0──────5─5────5─0─0────2───0──────────
  Will I play the wild rover, no never, no more!
```

Additional Verses

I went into an alehouse I used to frequent,
And I told the landlady me money was spent.
I asked her for credit, she answered me nay...
Such a custom as yours I can have any day.

Then out of me pockets I took sovereigns bright,
And the landlady's eyes opened wide with delight.
She said I have whiskey, and wines of the best...
And the words that I spoke you were only in jest.

I'll go back to my parents, confess what I've done.
And I'll ask them to pardon their prodigal son.
And if they caress me as oft times before,
Then I never will play the wild rover no more!

The Wild Rover (continued)

Basic Melody
Key of C (Low)

```
     C                                    F
E ----------------------------------------------------------
A ----------------------------------------------------------
D ----------------0--------------2----2-0--2-3-------------
G 5------5--------5------2-0-------------------------------
```
I've been a wild rover for many a year,

```
         C          G7                       C
E ----------------------------------------------------------
A ----------------------------------------------------------
D 2----3------5------2----5--3-0-----------2------0---------
G -----------------------------4---0--------------5---------
```
And I've spent all me money on whiskey and beer.

```
                                             F
E ----------------------------------------------------------
A ----------------------------------------------------------
D -----------0----------------2----2------0--2------3-------
G 5----5-----------5-2--0-----------------------------------
```
But now I've returned with gold in great store,

```
         C          G7                       C
E ----------------------------------------------------------
A ----------------------------------------------------------
D 2----3-5-2----5------3-------0-----------2----0-----------
G ---------------------------4-----0-------------5----------
```
And I never will play the wild rover no more!

CHORUS

```
         G          C            F
E ----------------------------------------------------------
A ----------------------------------------------------------
D -----------0----0----------2--2----2-0-----2--3----------
G 4----5--------------4-0-----------------------------------
```
And it's no, nay, never! No nay never, no more...

```
         C          F          C      G  C
E ----------------------------------------------------------
A ----------------------------------------------------------
D 2----3-5--------------------------2------0---------------
G -----------5----5-----4-2----2--0--------5---------------
```
Will I play the wild rover, no never, no more!

C
F
G7
G

258

The Wild Rover (continued)

Basic Melody
Key of C (High)

C

```
E ———————————————————————0——0———0-1——
A 3———3———5-3———0———————————5—————————
D ———————————5————————————————————————
G ————————————————————————————————————
```
I've been a wild rover for many a year,

C   **G⁷**   **C**
$$C \quad G^7 \quad C$$

```
E 0——1———3———0——3-1———————————0—————
A ———————————————5——2————————5—3————
D ——————————————————5———————————————
G ——————————————————————————————————
```
And I've spent all me money on whiskey and beer.

F

```
E ————————————————0——0——————0——1——
A 3—3———5———3-0————————5———————————
D —————————5———————————————————————
G —————————————————————————————————
```
But now I've returned with gold in great store,

C   **G⁷**   **C**

```
E 0——1-3-0——3———1——————————0————————
A ———————————————5——2—————5—3———————
D ——————————————————5———————————————
G ——————————————————————————————————
```
And I never will play the wild rover no more!

CHORUS

G   **C**   **F**

```
E ——————————————0—0——0———0-1——
A 2——3———5——5——2————————5—————
D —————————5——————————————————
G ————————————————————————————
```
And it's no, nay, never! No nay never, no more...

C   **F**   **C** **G C**

```
E 0——1-3—————————————————0————————
A ————————3——3——2-0———0———5-3——————
D ——————————————————————5——————————
G —————————————————————————————————
```
Will I play the wild rover, no never, no more!

The Wild Rover (continued)

Melody & Chords
Key of C (High)

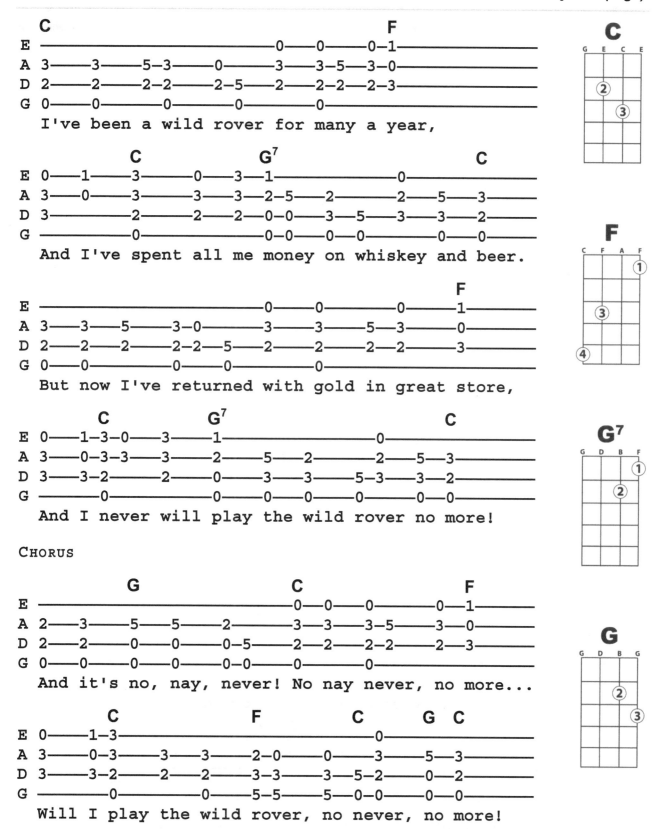

The Work Of the Weavers

Basic Melody
Key of G

This old song extols the virtues of those who weave wool into cloth, and tells how badly off the world would be without them. This is a favorite song of the descendants of Irish immigrants who came over to work in the woolen mills around northern New England.

Words and Music
Traditional

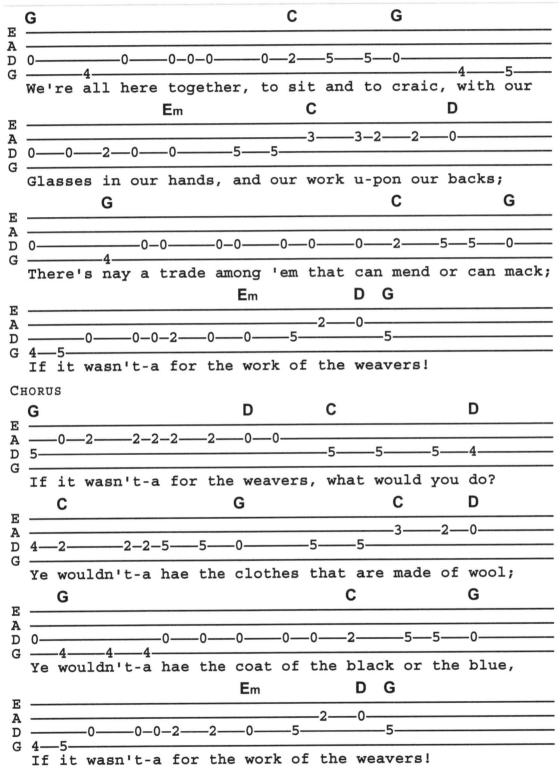

CHORUS

See Chord Forms and Additional Verses on Next Page

The Work of the Weavers

(continued)

Chord Forms and

Additional Verses

Additional Verses

There's soldiers and there's sailors and glaziers and all;
There's doctors and there's ministers and them that live the law.
And our friends in South America, though them we never saw,
But we hear they wear the work of the weavers.

Now weavin' is a trade that never can fail,
As long as we need clothes for to keep another hale;
So let us all be merry and drinkers of good ale,
And we'll drink to the health of the weavers!

Chord Forms

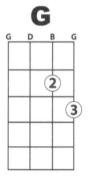
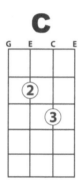
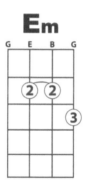
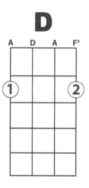

A photo from the 1890's of weaving room workers at the woolen mill in Gonic,
New Hampshire, which now is the home of C. B. Gitty Crafter Supply.

The Work of the Weavers
(continued)

Melody & Chords
Key of G

```
        G                              C          G
E ------------------------------------------------------------------
A ------------------------------------------------------------------
D 0----------0----0-0-0-------0--2----5----5--0--------0------0------
G 0------4---0----0-0-0-------4--5----5----5--0--------4------5------
  We're all here together, to sit and to craic, with our
```

```
            Em                    C              D
E ------------------------------------------------------------------
A -----------------------------------3------3-2----2----0------------
D 0----0---2--0----0--------5--5----2------2-2----2----0-------------
G 0----0---0--0----4--------4--4----0------0-----------2-------------
  Glasses in our hands, and our work u-pon our backs;
```

```
            G                              C          G
E ------------------------------------------------------------------
A ------------------------------------------------------------------
D 0----------0----0-0-------0-0------0--0------0--2----5--5----0------
G 0------4---0-0-----0-0-----0-0-----0--4------4--5----5--5----0------
  There's nay a trade among 'em that can mend or can mack;
```

```
                          Em          D  G
E ------------------------------------------------------------------
A -------------------------------2----0-----------------------------
D 0--0--0-------0-0-2----0----0--5----2--0--5-----------------------
G 4--5--0-------0-0-0----0----4--4----2--0--------------------------
  If it wasn't-a for the work of the weavers!
```

CHORUS

```
      G                    D          C              D
E ------------------------------------------------------------------
A ----0--2------2-2-2----2----0--0----------------------------------
D 5--0--0-------0-0-0----0----0--0----5------5------5----4----------
G 0--------0-------------0----0--2-2--5------5------5----2----------
  If it wasn't-a for the weavers, what would you do?
```

```
      C                    G              C          D
E ------------------------------------------------------------------
A -------------------------------------------3------2--0------------
D 4--2---------2-2-5----5----0--------5------5------2--2----0--------
G 2--5---------5-5-5----5----0--------0------0------0--0----2--------
  Ye wouldn't-a hae the clothes that are made of wool;
```

```
      G                              C          G
E ------------------------------------------------------------------
A ------------------------------------------------------------------
D 0----------0----0-0------0------0--0------2----5--5----0-----------
G 2--4-------4----4-0------0--0---4--4------5----5--5----0-----------
  Ye wouldn't-a hae the coat of the black or the blue,
```

```
                          Em          D  G
E ------------------------------------------------------------------
A -------------------------------2----0-----------------------------
D 0--0--0-------0-0-2----2----0--5----2--0--5-----------------------
G 4--5--0-------0-0-0----0----4--4--4--2--0------------------------
  If it wasn't-a for the work of the weavers!
```

The Work of the Weavers

(continued)

Basic Melody

Key of C

```
    C                        F      C
E ----------------------------------------------------------
A ----------------------------0---3---3----------------------
D 5------2---5---5-5-5--------5----------5------2----3--------
G ----------------------------------------------------------
```
We're all here together, to sit and to craic, with our

```
         Am             F           G
E --------------------1---1-0---0----------------------------
A --------0-----------3---3-----------5----------------------
D 5---5-------5---5------------------------------------------
G ----------------------------------------------------------
```
Glasses in our hands, and our work u-pon our backs;

```
         C                          F      C
E ----------------------------------------------------------
A ----------------------------0---3---3----------------------
D 5------2---5-5----5-5----5-5----5--------------5------------
G ----------------------------------------------------------
```
There's nay a trade among 'em that can mend or can mack;

```
                   Am        G C
E ---------------------0------------------------------------
A --------------0-----------3---5-3-------------------------
D 2---3---5----5-5----5---5----------------------------------
G ----------------------------------------------------------
```
If it wasn't-a for the work of the weavers!

CHORUS

```
    C                    G      F           G
E ------0----0-0-0----0--------------------------------------
A 3---5-------------------5-5----3---3-----3---2--------------
D ----------------------------------------------------------
G ----------------------------------------------------------
```
If it wasn't-a for the weavers, what would you do?

```
    F              C            F   G
E ----------------------------1---0--------------------------
A 2---0-------0-0-3---3------3---3-----5----------------------
D -----------------5---------------------------------------
G ----------------------------------------------------------
```
Ye wouldn't-a hae the clothes that are made of wool;

```
    C                        F      C
E ----------------------------------------------------------
A ----------------------------0---3---3----------------------
D 5---2----2---2-5---5---5---5-5----------5-------------------
G ----------------------------------------------------------
```
Ye wouldn't-a hae the coat of the black or the blue,

```
                   Am        G C
E ---------------------0------------------------------------
A --------------0---0-------3---5-3--------------------------
D 2---3---5----5-5--------5----------------------------------
G ----------------------------------------------------------
```
If it wasn't-a for the work of the weavers!

The Work of the Weavers

Melody & Chords

(continued)

Key of C

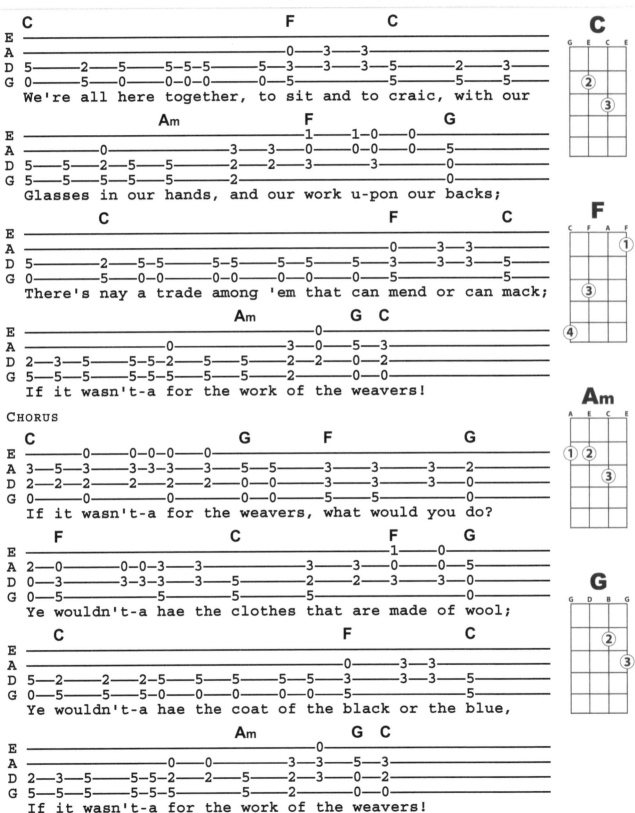

EDUCATIONAL OUTREACH

We have worked with many teachers all around the United States and internationally to help them get instrument building projects added to their school's curriculum. Building handmade instruments fits nicely into most STEAM (Science, Technology, Engineering, Arts & Math) programs!

We have created a number of kits and packages specifically for teachers, from basic one-string canjos (tin can banjos) through more advanced electric guitars. Teachers from grades 3 through 12 have used our kits and parts to teach everything from art and basic music theory and performance through advanced placement high school science courses studying the physics of electrical waves and sound.

If you know of a school or teacher that might be interested in this idea, let them know about us! We also work with summer camps, church groups, Boy Scout troops, community centers, senior centers, and folks wanting to host a local workshop.

E-mail us at **support@cbgitty.com** to get the ball rolling!

ABOUT THE AUTHOR

Ben "Gitty" Baker founded C. B. Gitty Crafter Supply in the basement of his New Hampshire home in 2009, with a mission of providing affordable parts to homemade instrument builders.

Over time the company and product line has grown, now occupying 15,000 square feet of space in an old New Hampshire woolen mill. C. B. Gitty employs fifteen people, producing many unique parts, kits and instruments in-house as well as supplying hundreds of quality parts. They ship thousands of orders each month, all around the world, while also maintaining active helpdesk and community support, educational outreach, event and musician sponsorship and much more.

But most importantly, over the years the core mission has expanded: to spread the word that ANYONE, ANYWHERE can build their own instrument and make music on it.

To support this mission, Ben has devoted his company to creating a wealth of how-to materials, with a goal of teaching others both how to build instruments, as well as how to play them. He has spearheaded the establishment of an online knowledgebase on www.CigarBoxGuitar.com to make as much information as possible freely available to folks all around the world.

Ben has also devoted uncounted hours of his own time to creating songbooks like the one you now hold, arranging hundreds of beloved traditional songs especially for three and four-string cigar box guitars and other handmade instruments.

Ben writes: "My motto is: Build What You Play, and Play What You Love. And also: If You're Having Fun, You're Doing It Right. In this amazing hobby, the only rules are the ones you set for yourself. Find an old cigar box, wine box, cookie tin, whatever... or build your own box out of scrap wood. Find a hardwood stick for the neck. Use old eye bolts from your granddad's odds and ends drawer for tuners, and a couple of rusty bolts for a nut and a bridge. Maybe wrap some salvaged copper wire around the neck for frets, and twist it tight with pliers.

Get some old guitar strings, or baling twine, or screen door wire, or weed whacker line... and put it on there as strings. Twist them up into some semblance of a tuning, and give them a strum. Maybe it will sound horrible at first. That's OK. Tweak and tinker until it makes YOUR sound, the sound only something you built with your own hands can make.

My mission is to spread the message that when it comes to making music, you don't need some shiny factory-made guitar straight off the rack of some chain store. You can make your own, and it will mean far more to you than whatever soulless cookie-cutter guitar you might find out in the retail world.

Trust me. You can build your own. You can build what you play, and learn to play what you love. It is worth the effort!"

Made in United States
Troutdale, OR
12/22/2024

27201039R00153